PROFILES
IN
FOLLY

PROFILES
IN
FOLLY

HISTORY'S WORST DECISIONS
AND WHY THEY WENT WRONG

Alan Axelrod

STERLING

New York / London
www.sterlingpublishing.com

STERLING and the distinctive Sterling logo are registered trademarks of
Sterling Publishing Co., Inc.

Library of Congress Cataloging-in-Publication Data

Axelrod, Alan, 1952-
  Profiles in folly : history's worst decisions and why they went wrong / Alan Axelrod.
    p. cm.
  Includes bibliographical references and index.
  ISBN-13: 978-1-4027-4768-7
  ISBN-10: 1-4027-4768-3
  1. World history—Miscellanea. I. Title.

D21.3.A84 2008

909—dc22

2007041140

2 4 6 8 10 9 7 5 3 1

Published by Sterling Publishing Co., Inc.
387 Park Avenue South, New York, NY 10016
© 2008 by Alan Axelrod
Distributed in Canada by Sterling Publishing
ᶜ/o Canadian Manda Group, 165 Dufferin Street,
Toronto, Ontario, Canada M6K 3H6
Distributed in the United Kingdom by GMC Distribution Services
Castle Place, 166 High Street, Lewes, East Sussex, England BN7 1XU
Distributed in Australia by Capricorn Link (Australia) Pty. Ltd.
P.O. Box 704, Windsor, NSW 2756, Australia

Sterling ISBN-13: 978-1-4027-4768-7
ISBN-10: 1-4027-4768-3

For information about custom editions, special sales, premium and
corporate purchases, please contact Sterling Special Sales
Department at 800-805-5489 or specialsales@sterlingpublishing.com.

Contents

PART SIX

The Decision to Drift

Author's Note

"Lord, what fools these mortals be!"
—Puck, in Shakespeare's *A Midsummer Night's Dream*

A WORD BEFORE WE BEGIN

The unflinchingly unsentimental Katherine Anne Porter called her one full-length novel *Ship of Fools* (1962), after an allegorical figure that was frequently rendered in European woodcuts, paintings, and literature of the Middle Ages. These works depicted humanity as so many distracted passengers packed into a boat, all ignorant of and indifferent to the course on which they sail.

I'm not quite so pessimistic. After all, I managed to collect a number of instances of extraordinary leadership, courage, and wisdom in my 2006 *Profiles in Audacity*. But my belief is this: All people are fools some of the time, and some people are fools all of the time, but all people are not fools all of the time. Still, history offers more than enough to fill this boat, and so I have chosen only those passengers whose actions illuminate the dark flipside of the subtitle of *Profiles in Audacity*: "Great Decisions and How They Were Made." Here are tales of "History's Worst Decisions and Why They Went Wrong."

Profiles in Folly serves up some dumb decisions by stupid people and some evil decisions by evil people, but most of what you'll find here are decisions by good, smart, savvy people that nevertheless went miserably, abominably, and often irreversibly wrong.

Why pick at history's scabs?

The easy answer is another question: Inching along the freeway, who can turn away from a flaming car crash?

The more meaningful answer is that probing our vulnerability is a project poignant and compelling precisely for what it reveals about the ways in which high-stakes decisions—decisions that *must* be made and that *cannot* be evaded—may produce disastrous results. There but for the grace—the grace of what, precisely?—lie us, in flames.

If the narrative vignettes of *Profiles in Folly* are intended to pique interest, satisfy curiosity, and, not least of all, deliver the occasional jolt of gee whiz, they are also meant to teach. Here are snapshots of decision-making processes—some doubtless familiar to many of us, some simply bizarre—together with postmortems undertaken to explain what went wrong and why. Here are cautionary tales, albeit each with an exquisite twist ranging from acerbic to horrific.

One last word. Those who seek objective history are doomed to be disappointed by *Profiles in Folly*. For that matter, those who seek objective history from any writer are doomed to perpetual disappointment. No history is objective, save perhaps a set of old phone books—and even these limit their scope to people with sufficient means to buy a phone. Nevertheless, those who insist on reading both sides of a story will not always find what they want in *Profiles in Folly* for the simple reason that I make no claim to objectivity. When I see two sides to a story, I try to tell them both. But the truth, as I see it, is this: Not every story has two equally valid sides. Sometimes there is right, there is wrong; there is wisdom, and there is folly. And as the ump always says, *I calls 'em like I sees 'em*. So what if I wear glasses?

PART ONE

The Decision to Gamble and Hope

The Trojans and the Trojan Horse (CA. 1250 BC)

THE DECISION TO LET DANGER IN

These days, uttering the phrase *Trojan horse* is likely to elicit a response such as, "Did you lose any data?" We think of a "Trojan horse" as a malicious software program that gets into computers by pretending to be something you want or need. You download a program that promises to rid your computer of viruses, for instance, and end up admitting into the inner sanctum of your virtual fortress a program that unleashes viruses.

As a label for malicious software, "Trojan horse" is derived from the Trojan War, an epic battle between Troy, which was located in what is now Turkey, and Sparta, a Greek city-state. Sparta won the battle after the Trojans were foolish enough to admit into their formidably fortified city a giant wooden horse they believed was a token of peace and submission from the Greeks. It was, to use another computer term, a "fatal error."

The story of the Trojan War has come down to us through a mixture of history and mythology. In *The Iliad*, the Greek poet Homer tells us that the war was rooted in the marriage of Peleus to the sea goddess Thetis. The happy couple had neglected to invite Eris, the goddess of discord, to their wedding ceremony. Outraged, Eris crashed the wedding banquet and tossed onto the feast table a golden apple, announcing that it rightfully belonged to whoever was the fairest. That was sufficient to send Hera, Athena, and Aphrodite diving for the golden fruit, whereupon Zeus, chief among the gods, nominated a judge to award the apple and thereby determine who was the most beautiful. Since the prince of Troy, Paris, was universally deemed the handsomest man alive, Zeus reasoned that he was the most qualified to decide who among the three contenders deserved the apple.

Hermes, messenger of the gods, delivered Zeus's nomination, and Paris agreed. The three contenders did their best to move his decision in their favor, Hera promising him power, Athena wealth, and Aphrodite assuring him that he would enjoy the most beautiful woman in the world.

That turned out to be just the ticket.

Paris chose Aphrodite, who responded by promising that Helen, wife of Menelaus, king of Sparta, would become Paris's wife. Accordingly, Paris prepared to travel to Sparta for the purpose of taking Helen. His sister and brother, the prophetic twins Cassandra and Helenus, did their best to dissuade him, and in this they were joined by their mother, Hecuba; but heedless Paris was determined to collect the wife Aphrodite had promised him.

Menelaus, unsuspecting, greeted Prince Paris as a royal guest and treated him accordingly. But when the old king left Sparta to attend a funeral, Paris made his move. In some versions of the story, he snatched Helen away against her will. In others, moved by the young prince's beauty and tired of life with the old king, Helen left with him willingly. In either case, the two were married in Troy about 1200 BC.

For his part, Menelaus did not go off quietly into the night. Enraged upon his return to Sparta to find both Paris and Helen gone, he called upon all of his wife's former suitors to honor the pledges they had made to him years earlier. Each had sworn an oath to aid Helen's husband in the defense of her honor.

All now backpedaled, and one particularly famous former suitor, Odysseus, feigned madness in an effort to avoid going to war for another man's wife. His dodge, however, was exposed. Others also tried to wiggle out, including Cinyras, king of Paphos, a city-state on Cyprus. Not wishing to go to war, he nevertheless promised Agamemnon, brother of Menelaus, to contribute fifty ships to the Greek fleet. In fact, he did send the vessels, with the lead ship commanded by none other than his own son. The other forty-nine ships, however, were clay toys crewed by tiny clay sailors.

It fell to Agamemnon to assemble an invasion force from among the reluctant former suitors. He also successfully prevailed upon Achilles to join the expedition. Although Achilles was not among the legion of Helen's former suitors, the seer Calchas had foretold that Troy would never be taken without Achilles's participation in the fight. At length, the Greek fleet was assembled in Aulis—only to be delayed by yet another problem. Agamemnon, it seems, had offended the goddess Diana either by killing one of her sacred stags or by making a careless boast. Whatever the particular offense, an outraged Diana calmed the seas and stayed the wind so that the fleet could not get under way.

Once again, the Greeks turned to the seer Calchas. He prescribed the sacrifice of Iphigenia, Agamemnon's daughter, to appease Diana. Agamemnon agreed, the poor girl was sacrificed, and the Greek fleet finally sailed—in search of Troy.

For no one quite knew where Troy was.

They landed first in Mysia, home of the Teuthranians (Teucrians). In some versions of the story, the Greeks were simply lost, but as the historian Herodotus (in the fifth century BC) tells the tale, they were under the misapprehension that the Teuthranians were holding Helen. This the Teuthranians denied, but the Greeks laid siege to Mysia anyway, ultimately taking the city, albeit at a heavy cost. And, of course, they emerged from the victory without Helen.

This instance of fighting the wrong battle in the wrong place nearly brought the Trojan War to a close before it had even begun. The Greek fleet turned back and headed for home; however, Telephus, king of Mysia, having been grievously wounded by Achilles in the siege of his city, sailed to Greece as well, in the hope of finding a cure for his wound. An oracle had told him that only the person who had wounded him—namely, Achilles—could cure him. Telephus thus sought out the warrior, who agreed to administer the cure. In return, Telephus told the Greeks how to get to Troy.

At this point came a rare interval of sanity. Instead of simply sailing off to war again, Odysseus, celebrated for his eloquence, embarked with Menelaus on an embassy to Priam, king of Troy. The pair demanded that

Helen be returned. It was only when Priam stated his absolute refusal that the war was on.

Like many wars begun over relatively trivial matters, the Trojan War was much longer and much more costly than any of the combatants had imagined possible. For nine years there was fighting in Troy and neighboring regions—since the Greeks understood that Troy was being supplied by nearby kingdoms. Throughout, Troy took the worst of it. Its economy suffered, even as the Greeks enjoyed a steady stream of war's spoils. Yet although the Greeks prevailed in battle after battle—and succeeded in killing the Trojan hero Hector—they were unable to penetrate the walled city of Troy itself. In the ongoing struggle for the city, Patroclus, friend—perhaps lover—of Achilles was slain, and then Achilles himself, greatest of the Greek heroes, was felled by none other than Paris.

In the meantime, Odysseus captured Helenus, son of King Priam. A prophet, Helenus revealed to the Greeks that the city of Troy would never fall unless four conditions were met: First, Pyrrhus, son of Achilles, must join the battle; second, the Greeks must employ the bow and arrows of Hercules against the Trojans; third, the remains of Pelops, a famous hero, must be brought to Troy; and, fourth, a statue of Athena, known as the Palladium, must be stolen from Troy. In accordance with the prophecy, Pyrrhus was persuaded to fight; Philoctetes, who had the bow and arrows of Hercules, was likewise persuaded to join the Greeks; the remains of Pelops were collected; and Odysseus managed to infiltrate the Trojan lines to steal the Palladium.

Yet the problem of how to enter the city—in force—remained. According to some accounts, it was Odysseus alone who came up with the winning stratagem. Others relate that he was aided in his scheming by Athena. In either case, it was Odysseus who ordered the artisan Epeius to build a massive wooden horse, hollow inside to accommodate a small band of elite soldiers. When the horse was completed, Odysseus and his warriors secreted themselves inside. Most daring of all, the entire Greek fleet set sail, withdrawing from Troy, thereby prompting the Trojans to believe that they had lifted the siege, given up, and gone home.

Just one Greek, Sinon, was left conspicuously behind. When the Trojans came out of their city to marvel at the great horse, Sinon was there to greet them. He spoke loudly and bitterly. The Greeks, he complained to the gawkers, had deserted him, leaving him behind with this great wooden horse. Sinon assured the Trojans that the marvelous statue would bring to Troy precisely what he lacked: luck.

Luck was something the Trojans had also long lacked. Yet two among them, Laocoön and Cassandra, warned against bringing the horse into the city. They were blithely ignored by the rest of the Trojan people, who were grateful at having been given a victory at long last. Surely the great horse was a wondrous token of their long-delayed triumph.

With light hearts, they dragged the heavy horse into the walled city, where it became the centerpiece of riotous celebration. By late night,

> "Like cicadas, which sit upon a tree in the forest and pour out their piping voices, so the leaders of the Trojans were sitting on the tower."
>
> —Homer, *The Iliad*, Book III

all of Troy lay in drunken stupor, whereupon Sinon—the Greeks' outside man—opened the horse, letting Odysseus and his band out. They moved swiftly through the city, slaughtering the Trojans. Priam was slain as he cowered by the altar of Zeus. Cassandra was raped. Troy fell, and the war ended with the sacrifice of Polyxena, daughter of Priam, at the tomb of Achilles, and Hector's son, Astyanax.

The Trojan prince Aeneas managed to escape the city's destruction; his story is told in Virgil's *Aeneid*. Some sources claim that Aeneas was the only Trojan prince to survive the war, but other sources point out that Andromache later married Helenus, Cassandra's twin brother. Perhaps, then, two princes survived.

As for Helen, retaken by the Greeks, she nearly fell victim to the jealous rage of Menelaus, who, apparently assuming that she had been a

willing accomplice in her own abduction, swore to kill the faithless
woman. In the end, however, her beauty and seductive charms mollified
his passion for vengeance, and she

"Whatever it is, I fear Greeks   was allowed to live. The rest of the
even when they bring gifts."   women of Troy were apportioned

—Virgil, *Aeneid*   among the Greeks as the spoils of
war. Yet, as Homer relates in *The*
Odyssey, the return home of Odysseus and the others proved as difficult
and time-consuming as the Trojan War itself.

THE TALE OF THE TROJAN HORSE comes down to us as the archetypal parable
of folly: an object lesson in how thoughtless vanity prompts people to bring
about their own destruction. In the larger context of the Trojan War narrative, the episode of the horse is merely the crowning folly of an epic string
of follies that make up a ruinous struggle set into motion by a goddess
offended at nothing more than having been left off a wedding party's A-list.

As mythology, the story of the Trojan War invites our meditation on
the membrane-thin partition separating the most trivial of vanities from
the epic sacrifice of the greatest of heroes. For thousands of years, people
took some comfort in the fact that the story of the Trojan War was no
more than mythology. And it is true that the full narrative of this war is
known only through *The Iliad* and *The Odyssey* of Homer. Yet even in later
ages there were a few who insisted that the mythic poetry was founded on
historical fact, and, in the 1870s, the German-Russian treasure hunter
and amateur archaeologist Heinrich Schliemann excavated a site generally accepted as that of Troy. Despite ongoing controversies, Schliemann's
discoveries confirmed a basis of historicity to the Homeric account, and
in the twentieth and twenty-first centuries, subsequent archaeological
investigations have elaborated on this basis. The Trojan War—perhaps
really a series of Late Bronze Age conflicts—now appears less as the stuff
of poetry, myth, and parable than as an example of one of the innumer-

able, sometimes nameless, wars that mark the so-called progress of civilization, wars whose cost vastly outweighs the original cause and the potential gain.

In our own time, no less a warrior than General George S. Patton Jr., himself compounded of blended legend and fact, repeatedly observed that, next to war, all other human endeavor paled to puny insignificance. It is folly beyond the power of any mere parable to convey that this, though all history, should truly be so.

George Armstrong Custer and the Little Bighorn (1876)
THE DECISION TO ATTACK WITHOUT LOOKING

It is the most famous battle of the so-called Indian Wars and one of the most celebrated military engagements in American history, yet we really know very little about what happened near the Little Bighorn River in Big Horn County, Montana, on June 25, 1876. We do have a reasonably accurate body count from the June 25 engagement and the fighting that continued into the next day: 16 officers and 242 troopers of the 7th U.S. Cavalry killed, along with 10 civilians and scouts. Fifty-five were wounded—although from the principal encounter, the "last stand" of George Armstrong Custer, not a single officer or trooper emerged alive. Thus we have no battle report from the army combatants, and the Indian accounts are vague with great variation in the details. In the battle's main event, about 208 soldiers died, including Custer himself. Indian casualties are more difficult to determine. Chiefs Sitting Bull and Red Horse reported 60 killed and about 168 wounded, whereas modern U.S. government archaeological studies suggest that more than 200 Lakota (Sioux), Northern Cheyenne, and Arapaho warriors fell.

Whatever the facts of the Battle of the Little Bighorn may have been, two things are certain: It was just one among many bloody encounters in four centuries of North American white-Indian warfare, and its U.S. Army commander was among the most famous and controversial military leaders in American history.

Those four hundred years of racial warfare were marked by suffering, bravery, nobility, good intentions, tragedy, a lust for conquest, greed, racial mythology, racial hatred, cruelty, and sheer folly, the very ingredients of the Little Bighorn battle itself. As for the army commander, George Armstrong Custer represented both the best and the worst of American soldiery. Brave, bold, aggressive, and of unquestionably heroic mold, he was also reckless, bigoted, cruel, and blundering.

Custer was born in 1839 in New Rumley, Ohio, but spent most of his childhood with his half sister Lydia Reed in Monroe, Michigan. He enrolled at West Point, barely managing to graduate—at the very bottom of his class—on the eve of the Civil War. Despite his weak academic achievement and nearly scandalous record of conduct, in combat he found his calling. As a staff officer for General George B. McClellan and, later, General Alfred Pleasonton, Captain Custer leaped through the ranks, rapidly achieving promotion to brevet brigadier general and obtaining a Michigan cavalry brigade to command. At twenty-three, he was the youngest general officer in U.S. Army history, and the press—which dubbed him the "boy general"—loved him for his long golden hair, flamboyant velvet uniform of his own design, and, from Gettysburg to Appomattox, his slashing cavalry charges. Some of these actions were productive of nothing but bloodshed, but a number proved tactically decisive and earned Custer a reputation for personal fearlessness. By war's end, he had become a major general commanding a full division, but after the war, Custer was returned to Regular Army service and assigned the rank of lieutenant colonel in the newly authorized 7th Cavalry Regiment.

Custer set about doing in the Wild West what he had done on the battlefields of the War Between the States. Exchanging his Civil War black velvet and gold lace for fringed buckskin, he let his yellow hair grow longer—in the manner of a mountain man—transforming himself into the very embodiment of the dashing Indian fighter. Because the regiment's commanding colonel was often absent, Custer led the 7th in his stead, and, for all practical purposes, it became his regiment.

The popular press was primed for more Custer exploits. Yet his first experience fighting Indians, in Kansas in 1867, ended not only in the 7th's failure to defeat any braves, but also in the lieutenant colonel's court-martial on charges of taking unauthorized leave to visit his wife, the beautiful and worshipful Elizabeth "Libby" Custer, and mistreating his men by ruthlessly "overmarching" them. Sentenced to a year's suspension of rank and pay, he redeemed himself in the eyes of his military superiors in 1868 with a devastating surprise attack on Chief Black Kettle's Cheyenne village on the Washita River in present-day Oklahoma. The public, however, had a mixed reaction. After all, Black Kettle was an advocate of peace, and his village contained few warriors yet many old men, women, and children. The village was a civilian target. Some Americans were outraged, although many others subscribed to a mangled maxim attributed to Gen. Philip Sheridan shortly after Washita: *The only good Indian is a dead Indian.* In either case, the colorful Custer had made his reputation as an Indian fighter, and fighting the Sioux while guarding railroad surveyors on the Yellowstone River in 1873 embellished the image.

Although the public, especially easterners, saw Custer as the army's leading Indian fighter, he was actually no more successful than many of his peers and less effective than a few. Worse, his regiment was badly factionalized, compounded of idolaters on the one hand and nearly mutinous detractors on the other. Custer himself was a shameless self-promoter, who wrote popular magazine articles and a best-selling memoir, *My Life on the Plains.* In 1874, he led the 7th on patrol in the Black Hills of the Dakota Territory. Part of the Great Sioux Reservation, guaranteed to the Indians by the Treaty of 1868, the Black Hills had long been coveted by whites who thought its dark recesses harbored gold—which is precisely what miners traveling with the Custer expedition found. To no one's surprise, news of the discovery touched off a mad gold rush.

The U.S. government responded by offering to buy the Black Hills from the Sioux, but when the Indians refused to sell land considered sacred, the Sioux War of 1876 erupted. It was in this context that the Little Bighorn battle was fought. Despite enduring popular beliefs to the contrary, U.S. Indian policy never advocated genocide against the Indians, but it did call for tribal confinement to reservations. Most military operations against the Indians were, in effect, policing operations, designed to round up those who had left the reservations and to compel their return. So it was in 1876. General George Crook led nine hundred men out of Fort Fetterman, on the North Platte River in Wyoming Territory, on March 1, 1876, and, while battling winter storms, he searched the Powder River country for Indians. After three discouraging weeks without results, he finally found a trail and dispatched Colonel Joseph J. Reynolds with about three hundred cavalry troopers to attack a village of 105 lodges beside the Powder River. Although taken by surprise, the Oglalas (a Sioux band), under He Dog, and the Cheyennes, led by Old Bear, counterattacked so effectively that Reynolds was forced to withdraw back to Crook's main column. Crook's abortive campaign did nothing more than galvanize the Sioux and Cheyenne into a large and unified fighting force under the inspired leadership of Crazy Horse and Sitting Bull.

Late in the spring of 1876, Philip Sheridan devised a three-pronged campaign intended to round up the Sioux and return them to the reservations. General Alfred Terry would lead a force from the east (including Custer and his 7th Cavalry), while Colonel John Gibbon would approach

> "If I were an Indian, I would certainly prefer to cast my lot . . . to the free open plains rather than submit to the confined limits of a reservation, there to be the recipient of the blessed benefits of civilization with its vices thrown in."
>
> —George Armstrong Custer, 1874

from the west, and Crook would once again march out of Fort Fetterman. The three columns were to converge on the Yellowstone River, even as the Indians were traveling toward it. The braves would be caught in this convergence and duly battled into submission.

On the morning of June 17, Crook, with more than one thousand men, halted for a rest at the head of the Rosebud Creek. Crow and Shoshoni scouts attached to Crook's column sighted Sitting Bull's Sioux and Cheyenne as they descended upon the column. The scouts were able to give sufficient warning to avert outright annihilation, but, even so, the Indians withdrew only after a sharp six-hour fight in which Crook's column took a severe beating.

Unaware of Crook's defeat and retreat, Terry joined his column with that of Colonel Gibbon at the mouth of the Rosebud. The officers of both commands, including Custer, convened in the cabin of the Yellowstone steamer *Far West* to lay out a campaign strategy. They were confident that they would find the Sioux encampment on the stream that Indians called the Greasy Grass and that white men called the Little Bighorn. They had no notion, however, of the size of the camp, but they all operated on the cherished assumption that Indians were incapable of organizing large-scale attacks. It was an article of faith in the U.S. Army that Indian leaders lacked the logistical skill to maintain more than about five hundred warriors in the field at any one time. Even if an encampment contained many more than this number, it was believed that they could never be marshaled into an effective fighting unit—certainly not one to offer serious threat to well-organized army troopers.

The *Far West* plan called for Custer to lead his 7th up the Rosebud, cross to the Little Bighorn, then proceed down its valley from the south as Terry and Gibbon marched up the Yellowstone and Little Bighorn to block the Indians from the north. In this way, Sitting Bull would be caught between the pincers of a two-column flanking movement.

The operation stepped off on the morning of June 22. It was assumed that Custer's highly mobile cavalry would be the first to make contact and would therefore begin the fight, driving the Indians against the other column, so that the Sioux would be caught between Custer and the forces of Gibbon and Terry. Nevertheless, on the morning of the twenty-second, after Custer's six hundred men passed in review before Terry, Gibbon, and Custer himself—marching to the regiment's cheerful trademark tune, "Garry Owen"—Gibbon jauntily called after Custer as the lieutenant colonel rode off to join his men: "Now, Custer, don't be greedy, but wait for us."

Custer turned in his saddle. "No," he replied, "I will not."

Indeed, left to his own devices Custer almost immediately deviated from the plan of crossing to the Little Bighorn Valley south of the Indians' position. "Indian fighting" characteristically involved very little fighting but a great deal of marching and riding, so that troopers returned from an expedition exhausted and half starved with little of military value to show for their labors. When Custer determined that the trail was much fresher than anticipated, he decided to push the attack, even though Terry and Gibbon were still far away. He did not want another long ride for no result.

After a forced march by night during June 24/25, Custer awaited word from his Crow Indian scouts. At length, they reported a *very* large Sioux camp—a cluster of large camps, in fact. Apparently undaunted—if anything, more eager than ever to fight—Custer made no further attempt to ascertain the numbers of Indians in and around the camps. Focused solely on striking before the always-elusive enemy evaded him, Custer divided his forces four ways. He would personally lead Troops C, E, F, I, and L—13 officers and 198 troopers (seven of whom would be detached before the battle—and would therefore survive)—together with three civilians and two Indian scouts, along the ridge line on the east bank of the Little Bighorn so as to enter the encampment from the north. A second detachment, under Maj. Marcus Reno, was sent into the valley of the Little Bighorn to provoke a fight there. This detachment consisted of 11 officers and 131 troopers, plus some 35 Indian scouts. Capt. Frederick Benteen was assigned to lead the third detachment, the 5 officers and 110 men of Troops D, H, and K.

Benteen appears to have been given ambiguous orders. It is unclear whether he was supposed merely to scout the nearby valleys or to advance into the Little Bighorn Valley and make a drive into the village to coordinate directly with Custer's main column. Finally, the small regimental supply train was, quite properly, held in the rear.

Custer's overall plan was for each of the three combat detachments to attack and pin down any Indians encountered, holding them in place until both of the other detachments arrived as reinforcement. It was, in effect, a tactic of first to arrive, first to fight. Whatever detachment made initial contact would receive the support of the other two. Apparently, little or no thought was given to the possibility that two or all three of the detachments would fall under simultaneous attack—or that all three would simply be overwhelmed. All Custer knew was that he had used this tactic at Washita, and he had won. Of course, at Washita he had been fighting mostly old men, women, and children.

Most historians now estimate that the Sioux encampment on which Custer descended had about seven thousand inhabitants, of whom at least fifteen hundred (some estimates say much more) were warriors. Custer's combined strength was just six hundred—and this number had been divided four ways.

Reno's detachment of 142 soldiers plus 35 scouts was the first to make contact, sighting and then pursuing some 40 warriors. Reno dispatched a message to Custer, but, receiving no reply, he advanced on his own, driving the warriors before him. Despite—or perhaps because of—the ease with which he drove the enemy, Reno suspected a trap and stopped well short of the main Indian encampment. He resorted to the army manual, dismounting his men, and deploying precisely what standard doctrine called for: a skirmish line, in which every fifth trooper handled the horses for the four other troopers who took up firing positions. Highly mobile, cavalry could be very effective against the mounted Indians of the Plains. Once dismounted in the field, however, the cavalrymen's horses became burdens rather than assets. In effect, this conventional line of skirmish tactic reduced the fighting force by twenty percent, as one out of five troopers did nothing but hold horses.

And as Reno waited in his line of skirmish, the numbers of Indians multiplied. Soon he calculated that he was outnumbered five to one. As time passed and no reply—let alone reinforcements—came from Custer, Reno ordered a retreat, during which three officers and twenty-nine troopers were killed.

Reno managed to link up with Benteen's detachment, which had arrived from the south. Benteen reported to Reno that Giovanni Martini, one of Custer's buglers, an Italian immigrant who sometimes called himself John Martin, had delivered a message from Custer to him: "Come on . . . big village, be quick . . ." Martini's courier mission saved his life. He was the last white man to see George Armstrong Custer alive.

Benteen's fortuitous arrival saved Reno from meeting the same fate as Custer—but, in the aftermath of the Little Bighorn, few would praise Benteen for rescuing Reno and many more would condemn him for not riding to the aid of Custer. Benteen always claimed that he had followed Custer's orders, which, however, were so vague as to allow a wide range of interpretation.

In the meantime, Custer and his men were engulfed. He had led his troopers against a force he knew to be very large—though he did not know how large, and he had not tried to find out. Most modern authorities believe that, overall, Custer was outnumbered three to one, a ratio that, at times, was increased to five to one. Moreover, Custer made his stand on ground unfavorable to him. The Indians held the high ground, while he and his men occupied lower ground from which they often could not fire directly on their attackers. In contrast, the Indians could make use of indirect fire, launching volleys of arrows at high trajectory—from cover—so that they would rain down upon men huddled below. Not that the Indians were armed only with bows and arrows. Many warriors carried modern repeating rifles. In fact, their repeaters outclassed the single-shot Springfield carbines with which the conservative cavalry was equipped.

Thus the Indians occupied better ground and at least some of them fought with a better class of weapon.

Archaeological evidence suggests that Custer—at least initially—deployed his men much as Reno did: dismounted, in a line of skirmish. Some historians have concluded from this that the skirmish line would have disintegrated, fallen apart during the onslaught, and that the so-called "last stand" really did not take place. Instead, the Indians would have swarmed down upon the much-depleted line of skirmish and simply picked off survivors one by one. Yet the very latest archaeological evidence has led National Park Service researchers to conclude that some two hundred Indian warriors fell in the Battle of the Little Bighorn, a figure that indicates extremely strong—and effective—resistance on the part of Custer and his men. Indeed, various Indian participants in the battle reported that Custer had fought with extraordinary bravery. If Indian casualties were indeed so high—on a par with Custer's own casualties—it is almost certain that, even if Custer had begun with a line of skirmish, he ended the battle in a more effective, more cohesive "last stand," which may have held out as long as three hours.

> "The women . . . pushed the point of an awl into each of his ears, into his head. This was done to improve his hearing, as it seemed he had not heard what our chiefs in the south had said when he smoked the pipe with them. They told him then that if ever afterward he should break that peace promise and should fight the Cheyennes, the Everywhere Spirit surely would cause him to be killed."
>
> —Kate Big Head, Cheyenne, commenting on July 4, 1876, on the treatment of Custer's body as it lay on the field at the Little Bighorn

In the immediate aftermath of the battle, the combined forces of Reno and Benteen dug in along the bluffs and fought off a daylong siege, which was renewed on June 26, only to be lifted upon the approach of Terry and Gibbon.

The defeat and death of one of the army's most celebrated officers, along with his entire command, stunned the nation and prompted Congress to increase the army's strength and to give it military control of all the Sioux agencies and reservations. Despite this, the Custer catastrophe unnerved the army, which made little further attempt to engage the Indians until November, when the 4th Cavalry's Colonel Ranald S. Mackenzie won a significant victory in the Bighorn Mountains against a Cheyenne band led by Dull Knife and Little Wolf.

AN EFFECTIVE MILITARY LEADER is aggressive and even single-minded in focusing on his objective. Yet for Custer at the Little Bighorn, single-mindedness became a lack of imagination and focus turned to blindness. His absolute determination to attack drove him to reckless, heedless action, attacking without adequate reconnaissance, taking up a position on unfavorable ground, and failing to answer Reno's call for help. It is not known why Custer led his men north, into the main part of the Indian encampment, rather than abide by his own plan to reinforce the first detachment that made contact with the enemy. We can assume that Custer was afraid the Indians would run unless they were immediately encircled and cut off. Why he did not retreat once he finally saw the size of the forces confronting him is another mystery. Perhaps he believed—quite rightly—that he would suffer very heavily in a retreat. Perhaps he judged—incorrectly—that he would have a better chance making a stand and fighting it out.

Arrogance, blind ambition, recklessness, these were the elements of folly in Custer's Last Stand. They were, however, qualities that verge on what makes for greatness in a military leader: self-confidence, desire for glory, aggressive boldness. But there was another factor that doomed Custer at the Little Bighorn. It was his absolute conviction—both as an individual and as an army officer—that even a very large group of Indians was incapable of defeating the officers and men of the United States

Army. This conviction was born of a failure to understand the full military capability of the Indians and, even more, to appreciate the depth of their determination to hold the sacred Black Hills. For four centuries, whites and Indians had failed to comprehend each other. The Battle of the Little Bighorn was one more product of that long incomprehension.

André Maginot and His Line (1930–40)

THE DECISION TO HUNKER DOWN AND

HOPE FOR THE BEST

It was a masterpiece of military engineering, a multitiered fortified line extending from Switzerland to Luxembourg, with a sketchy extension all the way to the English Channel. The Maginot Line was the culmination of a tradition stretching back to ancient times, the idea that a great wall could hold back all enemies. Time honored, it was also a faith in fortification that, throughout time, had been repeatedly shattered. Yet, as with all who invest all they have in a single sovereign solution, the builders of the Maginot Line suffered from or indulged in a collective cultural amnesia, forgetting that a reliance on walls has always, sooner or later, proved to be folly.

In France, the notion of building a line of elaborate concrete fortifications, tank obstacles, machine-gun posts, and other defense structures along the borders with Germany and Italy originated with Marshal Joseph Joffre, the grandfatherly old soldier—he was universally known as "Papa Joffre"—who had led the armies of France into World War I.

> **"The foundations of the Maginot Line were the war cemeteries of France."**
>
> —Anonymous

For him, war between great nations meant and could only mean precisely what it had been on the Western Front: a static contest between huge armies fighting from trenches. Not that Joffre was so naïve as to believe that any fortification would prove forever impenetrable. Instead, he held that a great fortification could either hold off an invader long enough for France to mobilize a large counterforce or that it would discourage the Germans from making a direct attack, forcing them to attack via neutral Belgium, thereby bringing Britain (like France, pledged to defend Belgian neutrality) into war against Germany and also allowing France to fight inside Belgium rather than, as in the Great War, within its own territory.

The experience of the Western Front during the Great War fully supported this thinking, in which Joffre was hardly alone. That war's other top French commander, Henri-Philippe Pétain, also subscribed to the building of a line of fortifications, as did the writers of any number of government studies. A minority of French politicians—including Paul Reynaud, who would be the last prime minister of the Third French Republic, and Charles de Gaulle, at the time a forward-thinking military maverick—protested, arguing that the nature of warfare had radically changed, that aircraft and high-powered, fast-moving tanks ensured that the next war would be highly mobile, so that fixed fortifications would be rendered largely irrelevant. It would be much better, Reynaud and de Gaulle argued, to invest precious defense funds in the weapons of the next war: aircraft and armor.

In the end, it was another World War I veteran, André Maginot, from 1928 to 1931 France's minister of war, who persuaded the government to build the line. Like Joffre, he understood the true intention of the line of fortifications. In a speech on December 10, 1929, he disclaimed any "dream of building a kind of Great Wall of France," explaining that the fortifications would constitute a "powerful but flexible means of organizing defense, based on the dual principle of taking full advantage of the terrain and establishing a continuous line of fire everywhere." In short, the line would buy time to set up a credible defense and counterattack. Despite this expression of realism, Maginot and other advocates actually sold the fortification project to the French people as a means by which French borders would be rendered impregnable and France itself invincible. In private and among themselves, they appreciated the limitations of the proposed fortification system. And when they went to build it, they did indeed build something very real, but what they finally persuaded the French people they had built—and ultimately convinced themselves as well—was an illusion.

Maginot was born in Paris in 1877 but spent a good part of his youth in Alsace-Lorraine, the border region through which much of the Maginot Line would be built. He was a civil servant for most of his career, leaving his desk to enlist in the French army at the outbreak of World War I. Although he never rose above the rank of sergeant, he was decorated with the Médaille Militaire for conspicuous bravery at Verdun. Severely wounded in that battle, he walked with a limp for the rest of his life. Returning to government service after the war, he was deeply concerned that France put far too much faith in the provisions of the Treaty of Versailles, which, he believed, hardly ensured the nation's security. Accordingly, he became a vigorous advocate of increased defense funding.

It was a hard uphill battle. The great paradox of the Allied victory in World War I was that it had left the European democracies, chiefly Britain and France, exhausted, demoralized, gun-shy, and desperate to disarm, whereas the defeated Germany was increasingly determined to redeem what it saw as its national and even racial destiny by military means. Frenchmen did not want to spend money on arms, and most yearned to trust Germany's promises that it would not go to war again. Maginot, however, grew increasingly distrustful, and he therefore pushed all the harder for increased funding.

Investing that money in a series of defensive fortifications along the border seemed to him an answer not only to the nation's strategic needs, but it appeared to be precisely the kind of strategic project he could sell to his reluctant countrymen. Politicians who would vigorously resist buying offensive weapons—airplanes and tanks—might well be persuaded to invest in a defensive system intended not to make war, but, in effect, to stop war.

In 1926, Maginot persuaded the government to fund pilot sections of the line. Three years later, in 1929, during debate over the budget for 1930, Maginot made an all-out effort to complete the funding and succeeded in gaining an allocation of 3.3 billion francs. Later, he obtained even more money to improve the portion of the line running through Lorraine, the country of his youth. Although Maginot was the line's principal champion, the practical design was mostly the work of Paul Painlevé, who succeeded Maginot as minister of war after Maginot succumbed to typhoid on January 7, 1932. Shortly after his death, the defensive line was officially named for him, although it would not be completed until 1939, on the very eve of World War II.

As built, the Maginot Line was a series of fortifications linked by roads and, in some cases, by tunnels, which even included rail transport. The line was no mere trench, but a system of fortification in depth, with some complexes covering as much as fifteen miles from front to rear, east to west. The system combined strongpoints, fortifications, border guard posts, communications centers, barracks, weapons emplacements (for permanently installed artillery, machine guns, and antitank guns—all of the most advanced design), supply and ammunition depots, and forward observation posts. Various supporting structures were located to the rear of the main line of defense, which consisted of so-called ouvrages, or major forts. The Maginot Line included interconnected bunker complexes capable of accommodating thousands. Along the line at nine-mile intervals were 45 main grands ouvrages, or main forts. These were supplemented by 97 smaller forts (petits ouvrages) and 352 casemates (essentially machine-gun emplacements). Some of these elements were interconnected by tunnels—more than sixty-two miles of them.

Throughout, engineers took advantage of terrain, especially for the placement of observation posts. The planners also decided against extending the line through the Ardennes Forest, which was deemed impassable by any substantial invading force. As originally planned, there were no defenses along the Belgian border because, by treaty, the French army was free to operate within Belgium itself if Germany ever invaded Belgium. In 1936, however, Belgium declared neutrality, thereby abrogating the earlier treaty. The French hurriedly extended the Maginot Line along its border with Belgium, but not to the depth of the rest of the fortifications. This was less a political than a practical decision. The Belgian border was low-lying land, and tunneling through ground with a very high water table was risky and expensive.

By 1939–40, the Maginot Line was indeed formidable in the regions of Metz, Lauter, and Alsace, but it was unevenly manned and fortified elsewhere—and, of course, nonexistent through the Ardennes. Nevertheless, the thicker the war clouds gathered, the more French officials touted the impregnability of the Maginot Line, publishing elaborate cutaway illustrations showing vast, multilevel underground fortresses, storerooms, and barracks surmounted by powerful artillery mounted in turrets. According to the magazines, the subterranean soldier facilities even included fully equipped movie theaters. The picture was not entirely false—in some places, the line was almost as elaborate as the magazines and newspapers suggested—but the overall impression it was intended to create was an illusion.

> "The most dangerous aspect [of the Maginot Line] is the psychological one; a sense of false security is engendered, a feeling of sitting behind an impregnable iron fence; and should the fence perchance be broken, the French fighting spirit might well be brought crumbling with it."
>
> —British general Alan Brooke, diary entry for February 6, 1940

Fall Gelb—Case (or Operation) Yellow—the German plan to invade the West in the late spring of 1940, took the Maginot Line into account. There would be no head-on direct attack on the line. Instead, a decoy force was positioned just opposite the fortifications while the main German army sliced through Belgium, the Netherlands, and—most spectacularly—through the "impassable" Ardennes. The invaders coming through the Low Countries engaged and defeated substantial French forces there even as the forces that penetrated the Ardennes simply skirted the northern end of the Maginot Line and the other French defenses. Not only was the Maginot Line largely irrelevant in the invasion, it became something of a liability, since some four hundred thousand French troops were detailed to garrison the line and were therefore unavailable for combat up north, where they were desperately needed.

Few would contest the judgment that the Maginot Line was one of military history's most spectacular follies. Indeed, the very phrase Maginot Line has become shorthand for any system, whether a physical system or a system of belief, on which people blindly, heedlessly, and foolishly rely. Yet the Maginot Line itself did not fail. Built to discourage a direct invasion across the eastern border of France, it did just that, forcing the German invaders to take a different route. French strategists had anticipated that the Germans would march via the main roads through Belgium and so massed troops on the Belgian border. When the main assault came via the Ardennes, which the French had considered impassable by a large armored force, the French commanders were taken by surprise and never recovered.

French leaders signed an armistice with Germany on June 22, 1940, Adolf Hitler having ordered the signing ceremony to take place in the very rail car at Compiègne, France, in which German envoys had capitulated to the Allies in November 1918 at the end of World War I. France languished under German occupation until December 1944 and lost 250,000 military dead and nearly 400,000 wounded. At least 350,000 French civilians died in the war, including 107,874 killed in the resistance or in air raids and 90,000 Jews murdered in the Holocaust—26 percent of the nation's prewar Jewish population.

—

THE MAGINOT LINE DID NOT FAIL. The people who built it failed. They failed in imagination, leadership, logistics, troop management, flexibility, and courage. They clutched at an almost willful misunderstanding of what the Maginot Line could and could not do. It could and it did impede an invasion, but it could not and did not stop it. It could and did buy time. But it was not a sovereign defense. Building it had drawn funds and other resources away from the production of aircraft and tanks. That was bad enough. Far worse, however, was that this single weapon became an article of faith, allowed to trump all other strategy. Politicians and generals forgot that the Maginot Line was a tool to buy a little time, and instead they came to believe that it was an ultimate weapon, one that would enable France to win a war entirely by defensive means—even though, in all history, no war had ever been won by defense alone. The folly of the Maginot Line lay not in its concrete and steel, but in the insubstantial yet overwhelmingly powerful illusion that concrete and steel both engendered and reinforced.

Unsinkability and the *Titanic* (1912)

THE DECISION TO EMBRACE

TECHNOLOGICAL IMMORTALITY

Concerning the RMS *Titanic*, five facts are relevant. First: The largest and most advanced passenger ship of her time, she was considered either "practically unsinkable" or downright "unsinkable." Second: She sank. Third: Throughout history, most ships have not sunk. Fourth: Throughout history, some ships have certainly sunk. Fifth: The sinking of no other ship has so fascinated so many for so long. Much of the rest that we can say about *Titanic* and what befell her southeast of Newfoundland, on the final leg of her maiden voyage, between 11:40 PM on April 14 and 2:20 AM on April 15, 1912, is not fact, but speculation and interpretation. We will begin with a consideration of the five facts.

First: RMS *Titanic* was built for the British-based White Star Line at the Harland and Wolff shipyard in Belfast, Ireland (today, Northern

Ireland). Her keel was laid on March 31, 1909, and she was launched on
May 31, 1911, her extensive outfitting completed on March 31, 1912.
Intended to compete with—and, indeed, to outclass—the rival Cunard
liners *Lusitania* and *Mauretania*, *Titanic* was the somewhat heavier
and even more elegant sister ship of RMS *Olympic* (launched 1910) and
the precursor of the planned *Gigantic* (renamed *Britannic* and launched
in 1914).

Titanic was 882 feet 9 inches long, with a beam (maximum width)
of 92 feet 6 inches. From water line to boat deck, she was 60 feet tall,
had a draft of 34 feet 7 inches, and a gross tonnage of 46,328 tons. She
was powered by a pair of reciprocating four-cylinder, triple-expansion,
inverted steam engines and one low-pressure Parsons turbine. These
engines drove three giant screws. The steam produced by 25 double-
ended and 4 single-ended Scotch-type boilers, fired by 159 coal-burning
furnaces, gave *Titanic* a maximum speed of 23 knots, making her the
fastest large passenger liner of her day. Impressive though these specifications were, the ship's designers added a rhetorical flourish with a
fourth 63-foot-high funnel (smokestack), which provided extra ventilation but was mostly for show. Only three funnels actually functioned to
carry off steam exhaust.

Titanic had a capacity of 3,547 passengers and crew, with accommodations ranging from first class down to third, or steerage. The top-paying
passengers enjoyed accommodations of unprecedented opulence,
including a swimming pool, gymnasium, Turkish bath, and squash court.
Wood paneling and exquisite furniture abounded. Cuisine in the dining
room and Café Parisien rivaled the finest on the Continent. Well-stocked
libraries were provided not just for first-class passengers, but for all
classes. Although most celebrated as a conveyance for the rich and
famous between Europe and the United States, *Titanic* had also been
built to carry its second-class passengers in great comfort and its third-
class passengers with maximum economy. She was also an international
mail carrier and even had a cargo specialty: the rapid transport of frozen

meat from the United States to Europe, which could not produce enough livestock to satisfy its own needs. *Titanic* flew the British flag and was widely regarded as a British ship, but its principal owners were U.S. business interests.

Beyond its majestic dimensions, high speed, and luxurious appointments, the great selling point for *Titanic* passengers was the ship's technology and achievement as naval architecture. The highly respected *Shipbuilder* magazine pronounced it "practically unsinkable" because of its double-bottomed hull, its forty-four massive ballast and boiler water tanks (guaranteed to provide stability even in the worst of sailing conditions, or "sea states"), and its division into no fewer than sixteen compartments, whose watertight doors were operated electrically and could be closed by switches located on the bridge (the ship's main command and control center) or automatically, by means of float switches, which would be instantaneously activated in case of flooding. *Titanic* also featured a state-of-the art electrical subsystem throughout the ship and two wireless (radio) transceivers, Guglielmo Marconi having begun to develop the technology in the late 1890s. And, "unsinkable" or not, the ship boasted twenty lifeboats, a number that exceeded the sixteen-boat minimum specified by the prevailing law of 1894 (though, at that, sufficient to carry no more than half of the ship's passengers).

Now to the second fact: At 11:40 PM on the night of April 14, 1912, *Titanic*, cruising at 22 knots, struck an iceberg at 41°43″ 32″N, 49°56″ 49″ W, off the southeast coast of Newfoundland. Moments earlier, when the iceberg was sighted, the ship's first officer, William McMaster Murdoch, on duty at the time, ordered full stop and then reversal of the engines as

> **"I thought her unsinkable and I based my opinion on the best expert advice."**
>
> —Phillip Franklin, vice president, White Star Line, after the loss of RMS *Titanic*

well as a hard turn to starboard. It is likely that the ship was able to skirt the above-water portion of the iceberg, but sideswiped the submerged portion, tearing a long gash in the side of the hull and ripping out some plates from the double bottom as well. Despite the compartmentalized construction, flooding was so rapid that incoming water overtopped the watertight partitions, causing one compartment after another to flood. The "unsinkable" *Titanic* sank in just two hours, forty minutes.

Surprisingly, even at this late date, there is not universal agreement on how many people were lost that night. A U.S. Senate investigation reported 1,517 dead, whereas the British inquiry fixed the number at 1,490. Put another way, of 324 first-class passengers, 285 second-class, 708 third-class (steerage), and 891 crew members, approximately 705 survivors were accounted for.

The shortage of lifeboats certainly contributed to the heavy loss of life, which included such prominent figures as multimillionaire John Jacob Astor IV and his pregnant wife, Madeleine, the industrialist Benjamin Guggenheim, and Macy's department store owner Isidor Straus and his wife, Ida. The managing director of the White Star Line, J. Bruce Ismay, was on board and survived, but Thomas Andrews, one of the ship's designers, also on board, went down with his creation. Also a factor was the length of time that elapsed between the collision and the general order to abandon ship. A full hour was consumed in evaluating the damage and notifying first-class passengers (before any others were alerted). Only then was the first lifeboat lowered. In the eighty minutes that the ship remained afloat after this point, sixteen of twenty lifeboats were lowered—but the crew faced an unanticipated obstacle. Persuaded that the *Titanic* was unsinkable, many passengers refused to board the lifeboats, so that several were launched with far fewer occupants than the maximum they could hold. Lifeboat Number 1, for instance, with space for sixty-five, was launched with just a dozen passengers on board.

The reluctance to abandon ship was exacerbated by the traditional "women and children first" policy enforced by the officers and crew. Many wives did not want to leave their husbands or allow themselves to be separated from their children. Potentially, the *Titanic* had enough lifeboat space to accommodate slightly more than half of the passengers she carried. In the end, just under one-third of the passengers boarded the boats. Most modern analysts believe that if one man had been permitted to board for each woman or child evacuated, the number of survivors would have at least approached 50 percent. Moreover, the presence of boats filled to capacity would have encouraged more passengers to abandon ship as instructed. As it was, the women and children first policy created a great deal of time-consuming chaos on deck as crew members had to physically restrain—even at gunpoint—many panic-stricken men.

Within fifteen minutes of striking the iceberg, the *Titanic's* first wireless operator, Jack Phillips, began transmitting "CQD," the most widely used Morse code distress signal at the time. In 1908, a new signal—SOS—had been ratified by the international shipping community, but British wireless operators were slow to adopt it. Nevertheless, the second wireless operator, Harold Bride, suggested to Phillips that, in addition to CQD, he also "Send SOS; it's the new call, and this may be your last chance to send it." Phillips followed Bride's advice. The second wireless operator was right. It was his last chance to send the new signal. Phillips went down with the ship.

A number of ships within a two-hundred-mile radius received the wireless distress call and began steaming toward the stricken liner. At 7:30 on the evening of April 14, Cyril Evans, wireless operator aboard the small tramp steamer SS *Californian* had transmitted an iceberg warning, which Harold Bride intercepted and delivered to *Titanic's* bridge. Just before 11 PM, about forty minutes before the *Titanic* collision, officers on the *Californian* were close enough to *Titanic* to see her, but no one recognized the ship as the great liner. Nevertheless, *Californian* captain Stanley Lord knew *Titanic* was in those waters and ordered Evans to transmit to *Titanic* that his ship was stopped in an ice field. The *Californian* was so close that its signal blasted the ears of *Titanic* radio operator Phillips, who was swamped with incoming radio messages for his ship's passengers, which came by way of Cape Race, Newfoundland.

Annoyed, he shot back to Evans: "Shut up, shut up, I'm working Cape Race." Evans duly stopped transmitting and, at 11:30, shut down the wireless for the night and went to bed. A little more than half an hour later, Phillips began broadcasting his distress signal. Evans, the *Californian*'s only wireless man, was sound asleep.

At about the time Evans shut down, Captain Lord asked his third officer to use his Morse lamp to signal the ship he saw just four or five miles off. The *Titanic*—still unrecognized—did not return the signal. Shortly after midnight, the *Californian*'s second officer, Herbert Stone, tried his luck with the Morse lamp, but likewise received no reply. About forty-five minutes later, Stone saw a white flash on the horizon, followed by four more. It was 1:15 AM before he reported these to Captain Lord, who speculated that they were signal rockets—but since distress rockets were always red, not white, he assumed they were some sort of private steamship company signal. (Apparently, *Titanic* had left port carrying a stock of only white—no red—rockets.) Lord instructed Stone to keep signaling with the Morse lamp and to let him know if anything changed about the ship.

By 2 AM, it looked to Stone as if the ship was steaming away. What appeared to him as a vessel sinking below the horizon was, in fact, the *Titanic* sinking into the ocean. Only after Evans awoke at 5:30 AM and turned the wireless back on did Captain Lord learn of the sinking of the *Titanic*. He began steaming toward it, passing along the way the *Carpathia*, which had already picked up the *Titanic* survivors, leaving to the belated *Californian* nothing but a sea of flotsam and empty lifeboats. Except for the *Californian*, the *Carpathia* had been nearest to *Titanic*, but, even steaming dangerously at full speed, it had not reached the scene of the disaster before 4 AM.

The third fact relating to the loss of the *Titanic*, that throughout history, most ships have not sunk, makes the sinking of this extraordinary, technologically advanced ship—on its maiden voyage, no less—all the more shocking. And the fourth fact, that throughout history, some ships have sunk, does not seem to lessen the shock. These two facts lead to the fifth: the fact of the enduring fascination of the *Titanic* story. It has been the subject of countless books, of several motion pictures, of many television documentaries, and of several scientific and commercial underwater expeditions.

It is in thinking about the sources of that fascination that we must now turn from fact to speculation and conjecture.

Why did the great ship hit an iceberg? Partly, it was bad luck. Partly, it was excessive speed through waters known to be sown with dangerous ice. Captain Edward John Smith, eager to make exemplary time on his vessel's maiden voyage, heedlessly laid on the steam.

Why did the ship sink—and so quickly? Since the wreck was first discovered in 1985 by an expedition led by Dr. Robert Ballard, several teams have investigated the wreckage and have salvaged parts of it for analysis. Sideswiping the iceberg tore a very long gash in the hull below the waterline, and, in 2005, evidence of damage to the keel, the bottom of the ship, was also discovered, leading some to conclude that the *Titanic* had split in two before it sank, thereby hastening its demise. Others believe that the keel damage occurred as the doomed ship sank to the bottom—settling not at the stately rate of speed one might expect, but, pulled by the force of gravity, accelerating in a plunge through the water at a staggering eighty miles per hour.

> "I cannot imagine any condition which would cause a ship to founder. I cannot conceive of any vital disaster happening to this vessel. Modern ship building has gone beyond that."
>
> —Capt. Edward John Smith, master of RMS *Titanic*

Whatever the exact location and extent of the damage, the *Titanic* may have been doomed by shortcomings of design.

The gash made by the collision flooded several compartments, the weight of the water pulling *Titanic* down by the head (front first). This, in turn, allowed incoming water to flow over the top of the watertight bulkheads, which extended only three meters above the waterline and stopped far short of deck level. One by one, the compartments flooded—even those in areas undamaged below the waterline. It is possible that had the watertight bulkheads been sealed off with watertight decks, so that the incoming water would have been absolutely contained, the ship would not have sunk or, at least, would not have sunk nearly so rapidly. Given the size of the iceberg and the length of the gash it created, it is also possible, however, that the sheer weight of the water would have been sufficient to pull the ship down, even if a large portion of it had not flooded.

In promotion literature for its ship, the White Star Line touted the double bottom of *Titanic*. What was really needed, however, was a full double hull—one complete hull nested within another complete hull. This design feature might have spared the ship fatal damage because, even if the outer hull had been compromised, the inner hull would have remained watertight and intact. Certainly, White Star seems to have believed this after the accident. Following the loss of *Titanic*, the *Olympic* as well as the *Britannic* were both modified with full double hulls.

As a result of the analysis of material recovered from the wreck, there has been recent speculation that faulty steel and improperly tempered rivets were used in the construction of the ship. Some analysts believe that many rivets were brittle, making them highly vulnerable to fracture in a violent collision. This theory is still in question, but the possibility exists that the biggest passenger ship of its day was doomed by structural flaws on the submicroscopic molecular level.

Beyond design shortcomings and possible structural flaws, there is the question of ship handling. To be sure, it was reckless of Captain Smith to steam at high speed through an ice field. This was an arrogant error. But First Officer Murdoch also made a mistake. When, on sighting the iceberg, he ordered all engines back, he seems to have failed to understand the limitations of the *Titanic's* three-screw configuration. Reciprocating steam engines drove the two outermost screws, while the low-pressure steam turbine turned the center screw. Only the reciprocating engines could be reversed; the turbine could make revolutions in just one direction. Thus when he gave the order to reverse engines, Murdoch lost the use of the center screw. Positioned forward of the ship rudder, the idle screw reduced the ability of the rudder to steer sharply, thereby increasing the ship's turning radius. Murdoch's order meant that *Titanic* could not sheer smartly away from the iceberg. The more effective maneuver would have been to reverse only the port engine while maintaining both the starboard and center engines full ahead. This way the ship would have turned much more sharply and much more quickly. Indeed, Murdoch should have been aware of this maneuver, which was described and recommended in training instructions for large three-screw vessels. The skillful use of motive power might well have startled the passengers, but it could possibly have gotten the ship safely around the berg.

> **"Control your Irish passions, Thomas. Your uncle here tells me you proposed sixty-four lifeboats and he had to pull your arm to get you down to thirty-two. Now, I will remind you just as I reminded him these are my ships. And, according to our contract, I have final say on the design. I'll not have so many little boats, as you call them, cluttering up my decks and putting fear into my passengers."**
>
> —J. Bruce Ismay, director of the White Star Line, to *Titanic* architect Thomas Andrews

Some authorities have speculated that even though Murdoch had ordered all engines into reverse, *Titanic* still might have been saved had he simply maintained his course. Hitting the iceberg bow on, they theorize, would have caused less damage—or less fatal damage—than turning and sideswiping it. This, in fact, had been the case with some smaller ships that had collided with icebergs, but it is also true that *Titanic* was making twenty-two knots and was packing all the momentum of the heaviest ocean liner in the world at that time. A head-on collision might well have proved just as fatal as a glancing blow.

There are more what-ifs, of course. While the ship was still on the drawing board, the builders expected that the British Board of Trade would likely, sooner or later, raise the minimum requirement for lifeboats. With this in mind, special davits were designed, capable of handling four boats per pair of davits, thereby giving *Titanic* sufficient capacity to carry sixty-four lifeboats. That would have been more than sufficient to accommodate all passengers; however, the additional boats were never installed. Legend has it that White Star president J. Bruce Ismay blocked their installation, complaining that the extra boats would take up too much of the passenger promenade area on the boat deck. This allegation was denied at the British inquiry into the sinking, and it has never been proven one way or the other.

There is also the tragic incomprehension of those aboard the *Californian*, a ship in a position to rush to the aid of the stricken liner— though the small tramp steamer would have been hard-pressed to accommodate more than two thousand passengers and crew members.

———

THE WHAT-IFS ACCOUNT FOR MUCH of our enduring fascination with this now-distant disaster. But, even more, we are drawn by the tragedy and poignancy of sheer folly: a blind faith in the capacity of technology— purchased by the wealth of the most powerful among us—to afford sovereign protection against the forces and elements of nature and the trivial tyranny of chance by which, among other things, a radio operator retires to bed minutes before the broadcast of a desperate call for help. The enduring fascination of the *Titanic* is the flash of vision it conjures of the merest membrane that separates the mightiest achievement of industrial civilization from its utter and abject humiliation before a mass of unyielding ice and a black expanse of frigid and unforgiving sea. Through the ruined splendor of a great ship, it is a distance we are forced to see as tissue thin and infinitely more fragile than the most brittle of steel hulls.

Isoroku Yamamoto and Pearl Harbor (1941)

THE DECISION FOR TOTAL DEVASTATION

Every important military action has two dimensions, the tactical and the strategic: the short term and the long. It is folly to consider one without the other, to think in a single dimension. The Battle of Pearl Harbor was one of history's most lopsided tactical triumphs, yet it was also one of the greatest strategic catastrophes. In winning the battle, Japan doomed itself to a war it not only could never win, but a war in which defeat would be total and absolute.

The Battle of Pearl Harbor was born in the collision of two national policies, one that entailed war and another that sought to avoid war.

The war-bound Japanese national policy in effect on December 7, 1941, had its origin in virtually the first contact between the Western powers and Asia during the Renaissance, which initiated a long historical process by which most Asian nations became the economic, political, and cultural victims of white Christian racism. Japan made compromises with the Western powers beginning in the mid-nineteenth century, but it remained one of the very few Asian countries neither conquered nor colonized. Yet contact with the West was hardly without effect on Japan. It brought about a blending of Japanese and Western traditions, in particular a powerful synergy of modern Western military doctrine, tactics, and equipment with ancient Japanese warrior traditions. As a result of this blending and synergy, by the opening of the twentieth century Japan had become a formidable industrial power and, as the Russo-Japanese War of 1904–5 stunningly demonstrated, a major military power.

After Japan's victory over Russia, the Japanese military assumed an increasingly important role in Japanese government, and both industrialization and militarization proceeded at an accelerating pace. As Japan became more powerful economically and militarily, it sought not to integrate itself into the Western family of industrialized powers, but, rather, to expand its ancient empire in an effort to redeem all of Asia from Western imperialism and to put itself at the controlling core of an Asian ascendency.

Key to expanding what was now an industrial and military empire was control of what Japan's militarists were calling, by the 1930s, the Southern Resources Area. This encompassed Malaya, the Philippines, Indochina, and the Dutch East Indies. In contrast to the military planners, Japanese politicians dubbed this region the Greater East Asia Co-Prosperity Sphere in an attempt to rationalize its conquest—for non-Japanese Asians—as a mutually beneficial reclamation of territory that had been usurped by the West. Among Japanese rulers and militarists, however, the territory of the Greater East Asia Co-Prosperity Sphere was nothing more or less than the empire they believed was theirs by divine right. Considered less metaphysically, this "Southern Resources Area" contained most of the raw materials required by Japanese industry and the military, as well as abundant supplies of food and cheap labor. To possess the territory would make Japan autonomous and inordinately powerful.

Without possession of the Southern Resources Area, sustaining, let alone expanding, Japan's industrial empire required raw materials from some other source. That source, chiefly, was the United States, Japan's number-one supplier of oil, steel, and other strategic commodities. The administration of Franklin D. Roosevelt understood this and seized on trade pressure as an economic alternative to war to compel Japan to end its aggression against China, which erupted in 1937 as the Sino-Japanese War.

Yet if FDR saw embargoes imposed on Japan as an alternative to war, some others in the American government believed they were less an alternative than a provocation. As an alternative to outright embargo, therefore, U.S. Secretary of State Cordell Hull proposed a policy of "moral embargo," and on July 1, 1938, the Department of State notified American aircraft manufacturers and exporters that the government was strongly opposed to the sale of airplanes and aeronautical equipment to countries whose armed forces were using airplanes to attack civilian populations. In 1939, this nonbinding moral embargo was extended to raw materials essential to airplane manufacture as well as to plans, plants, and technical information for the production of aviation gasoline. Yet in September 1939 with the outbreak of World War II in Europe, U.S. policy makers—fearing that America would be drawn into a two-front war against Germany and Italy in Europe and Japan in the Pacific—grew increasingly wary of applying provocative economic sanctions, desirable as it might be to cut off essential materials to an aggressor. Despite the absence of legal sanctions, American manufacturers generally fell into line, effectively suspending export to Japan of aircraft, aeronautical equipment, and other materials.

In addition to the moral embargo on war matériel, the U.S. government began informally discouraging the extension of credit by U.S. banks to Japan. At last—and despite the trepidation of many of his fellow politicians, Roosevelt and his administration served notice to Japan in July 1939 that its long-standing trade treaty with the United States would be terminated, thereby paving the way for a full and formal embargo. This step motivated a series of high-level conferences during 1939 and 1940 in an effort to resolve the deterioration of relations between Japan and the United States. But as Japan moved against Southeast Asia as well as China, then added Tokyo to the Rome-Berlin "axis," Congress passed the Export Control Act of July 2, 1940, which initiated a massive embargo. By the winter of 1940–41, shipment to Japan of most strategic commodities, including arms, ammunition, and implements of war, aviation gasoline and many other petroleum products, machine tools, scrap iron, pig iron, iron and steel manufactures, copper, lead, zinc, aluminum, and other commodities important to any war effort, had completely ceased.

President Roosevelt now held the moral high ground, but, as many feared, the embargo served only to galvanize the efforts of Japanese militarists to seize raw materials and other resources in Asia and the Pacific, to continue the war in China, and to prepare for a wider war, even against the United States. The militarists operated from the assumption that, if Japan attacked decisively and destructively, the United States would back down and permit Japanese expansion. For his part, FDR only increased the pressure—and the provocation—by issuing an executive order on July 26, 1941, that froze Japanese assets in the United States and brought under government control all financial and trade transactions in which Japanese interests were involved. U.S.-Japanese diplomatic negotiations now became fevered and war seemed inevitable.

With all U.S. trade cut off, Japanese planners understood that they held no more than a six-month supply of fuel for the armed forces. The choice was between surrender—an immediate end to imperial expansion—or all-out war with the United States, Britain, and the Netherlands. The Japanese government, by now for all practical purposes a military dictatorship, chose war.

Admiral Isoruko Yamamoto, commander-in-chief of the Japanese Combined Fleet, understood that the U.S. Pacific Fleet created the most formidable obstacle to the continued Japanese conquest of Southeast Asia. This meant that the destruction of the fleet would have to be Japan's number-one objective. In addition, the action would have to be swift, sudden, and total—all in a single blow. Yamamoto explained to Navy minister Koshiro Oikawa, "We should do our very best . . . to decide the fate of the war on the very first day."

And he was quite serious about that. It would be necessary to find a way to hit American forces so hard that the United States, fearing—as it must—that it would soon be called on to fight against Germany, would seek a quick negotiated peace with Japan. To Oikawa, Yamamoto said only that, short of striking a war-winning blow on the first day, the Imperial Japanese Navy might purchase six months in which it could "run wild" in the Pacific, but, after that period, there was no telling how the war would turn out. Privately, Yamamoto despaired of both the consequences of failing to destroy the Pacific Fleet and of entering into war with the United States on any terms.

Yamamoto, born Isoruku Takano in Niigata prefecture in 1884, was adopted by the Yamamoto family and took their name in 1916 at the age of thirty-two. After graduating from the naval academy in 1904, he saw action at the epoch-making Battle of Tsushima in the Russo-Japanese War and was wounded on May 26, 1905, losing two fingers from his left hand—an injury that nearly caused his dismissal from the navy.

Yamamoto rose steadily through the officer ranks, and, as staff officer with the Second Fleet, he was sent to the United States for study at Harvard University from 1919 to 1921. He quickly came to admire America and the Americans and to marvel at the nation's staggering industrial capacity. It was this impression in particular that would weigh very heavily on him as Japan prepared to enter war against America.

After completing his Harvard studies, Yamamoto returned to Japan as an instructor at the naval war college there, serving in this post from 1921 to 1923, when he was promoted captain and sent on a tour of inspection and observation to the United States and Europe. He returned to the States again, in 1925, as naval attaché in Washington, D.C., then, in 1928, assumed command of the aircraft carrier *Akagi*.

Promoted to rear admiral in 1929, Yamamoto became chief of the technological division of the Navy Technological Department in 1930, and was promoted to vice admiral in 1934, then headed the Japanese delegation to the London Naval Conference of 1934–35. He was personally opposed to the official Japanese position, which demanded complete naval parity—ship for ship, ton for ton, gun for gun—with Britain and the United States, because he believed this position risked creating friction that might lead to war. Nevertheless, he understood his duty and, in obedience to his instructions, took a hard and unyielding line in treaty negotiations, rejecting any further extension of the restrictions established by the Washington Naval Treaty in 1922, and thereby freeing Japan to accelerate its naval expansion.

Named chief of naval aviation headquarters in 1935, Yamamoto championed the ascendency of the aircraft carrier as the principal offensive naval weapon, yet when he was appointed navy minister, serving from 1936 to 1939, he struggled to moderate the militarism of a government on the verge of a war he believed Japan could not win. Even as he spoke out against fomenting war, Yamamoto was reappointed chief of naval aviation headquarters in 1938, a position he held concurrently with his post as navy minister. In 1939, he returned to sea as commander of the Combined Fleet, adding First Fleet command in 1940.

He was now tasked with making preparations for the war he did not want, the planned war against Britain and the United States. Soon resigning himself to the inevitability of his nation's course, Yamamoto planned the Pearl Harbor attack as the only chance for victory. In January 1941, he wrote to Ryoichi Sasakawa, president of the nationalistic organization Kokusai Domei, explaining that, in "a war between Japan and America . . . our aim, of course, ought not to be Guam or the Philippines, nor Hawaii or Hong Kong, but a capitulation at the White House, in Washington itself." Only the instantaneous devastation of the U.S. Pacific Fleet, he believed, could create the level of demoralization necessary to bring about such a capitulation.

Yamamoto had first begun thinking about the feasibility of an attack on Pearl Harbor in the spring of 1940, as he watched his naval air fleet conducting aerial torpedo exercises. Yamamoto turned to Rear Admiral Shigeru Fukudome, chief of the first division of the naval general staff and remarked in a casual semi-whisper, "I wonder if an aerial attack can't be made at Pearl Harbor?"

In the eye of history, it seems a profoundly understated moment of great consequence. And so it was—though it was not an entirely new idea. In fact, both Japan and the United States had repeatedly war-gamed the scenario, and the top military planners of both nations dismissed it as impossible for two main reasons: First, it seemed impossible that a carrier fleet large enough to carry a sufficient number of planes to attack the base would escape detection—and destruction—long before it had come within flying range of Hawaii. Second—and even more important—Pearl Harbor was deemed too shallow for attack by torpedoes dropped from planes. The weapons of the day were heavy and would bury themselves in the harbor bottom and explode harmlessly instead of speeding along to their intended targets.

Then, on November 11, 1940, with the war raging in Europe, British torpedo bombers made a spectacularly successful attack against the Taranto naval base in southern Italy. Twenty-one obsolescent British Swordfish biplane torpedo bombers, launched from the aircraft carrier *Illustrious*, sortied in two waves spaced one hour apart. The raid achieved total surprise, and the British aircraft managed to hit two older battleships and a cruiser, and also damage the dockyard, forcing the rest of the Italian ships to evacuate Taranto for Italy's west coast, thereby eliminating a major threat to British convoys. British losses were trivial: just two aircraft. Yamamoto took special note of the striking topographical similarity between Taranto and Pearl Harbor, at the surface as well as below. Like Pearl, Taranto was a very shallow harbor.

The British pilots at Taranto had used sheer flying skill to ensure that their torpedoes would not bottom out. Yamamoto went a step further. Working with Japan's foremost aerial tactician, Comm. Minoru Genda, and First Air Fleet chief commander Mitsuo Fuchida, Yamamoto oversaw exhaustive maneuvers, which consumed nearly a year, in which shallow-water torpedo attacks were repeatedly simulated and refined. Because conventional aerial torpedoes plunged more than one hundred feet below the surface before leveling off and then running a long distance before arming themselves, Japanese engineers modified the torpedoes with wooden fins, which sharply reduced the underwater plunge to accommodate the forty-five-foot average depth of Pearl Harbor. They also set the arming mechanism to trigger in a much shorter distance, because a torpedo attack in the confined space of Pearl Harbor would require much shorter-than-normal runs.

As Yamamoto saw to the resolution of the tactical and technical aspects of the projected attack, he wrestled with even greater difficulty against many within the command of the Japanese navy, who continued to dispute the feasibility of an all-out attack on Pearl Harbor. In the end, it was Hideki Tojo, the army general who had recently been elevated as Japan's premier, who resolved all doubts with his customary swiftness.

Although Tojo was now a military dictator, his rise to power had not come about through masterful demagoguery in the manner of Adolf Hitler or Benito Mussolini. Because of his reputation as a brilliant bureaucrat who cut through red tape with decisive aplomb, Tojo was universally dubbed not Supreme Leader—the equivalent of Der Führer or Il Duce—but "The Razor." With U.S.-Japanese negotiations breaking down, he unilaterally authorized the "Hawaiian Operation" at an Imperial Conference of September 6, 1941. Japan would go to war with the United States.

To provide cover for the attack, Tokyo did not inform its ambassador to Washington of the finality of the decision, but instead authorized continued talks. In the meantime, a *kido butai* (strike force) consisting of two fleet carriers, two light carriers, a carrier that had been converted from a battleship, a carrier converted from a cruiser, two battleships, two cruisers, a screen of destroyers, and eight support vessels, all under the direct command of Vice Adm. Chuichi Nagumo, departed the Kure naval base during November 10–18 and rallied at Etorofu in the Kurile Islands on November 22. From here, at 6 AM on November 26, the *kido butai* steamed toward Pearl Harbor.

The strike force observed strict radio silence, which, in conjunction with decoy radio messages ("signals deception"), effectively prevented U.S. forces from detecting its movement. No American naval planners imagined that a mass ship movement would or even could be conducted in total radio silence. Moreover, U.S. naval intelligence assumed that any Japanese attack would have to originate from the Japanese-governed Marshall Islands, the Japanese territory closest to Hawaii. Contrary to much popular lore concerning the days before Pearl Harbor, the U.S. military was not oblivious to the likelihood of war with Japan. Pearl Harbor–based Pacific Fleet commander Adm. Husband E. Kimmel dispatched his limited fleet of reconnaissance aircraft to patrol the skies over the Marshalls—the place he and everyone else assumed an attack would originate from. Indeed, he viewed this as something of an abundance of caution, because, like other U.S. naval planners, he assumed that Pearl Harbor was too shallow for an aerial torpedo attack (the lessons of Taranto had clearly been lost on the Americans) and that, in any case, a Japanese first strike would almost certainly be made against the Philippines, not Hawaii. So confident were American planners that torpedoes could not be used at Pearl Harbor that they neglected to employ torpedo nets to protect the fleet. Moreover, discounting the likelihood of an air attack, Kimmel transferred of many of his P-40 pursuit planes—a first line of

> **"It is significant that despite the claims of air enthusiasts no battleship has yet been sunk by bombs."**
>
> —Caption published on November 29, 1941, with a photograph of USS *Arizona*, sunk by Japanese bombs at Pearl Harbor on December 7, 1941

defense against incoming enemy aircraft—from Hawaii to Wake and Midway islands to provide cover for bombers being flown to reinforce the Philippines.

What Kimmel and his U.S. Army counterpart on Hawaii, General Walter Short, did fear was ground-based sabotage at the hands of Japanese nationals and/or Americans of Japanese descent living in Hawaii. On November 27, 1941, U.S. Army chief of staff George C. Marshall issued to all commanders a "war warning," a message indicating that, based on the continued failure of negotiations, war with Japan was imminent. Kimmel and Short interpreted the war warning mainly as a reason to take precautions against sabotage. Kimmel accordingly ordered that only every fourth navy machine gun be manned, so that all "excess" ammunition could be locked away to secure it from saboteurs. Antiaircraft batteries were left without crews, and no special air reconnaissance was ordered. Indeed, about one-third of the fleet's captains were ashore, along with many other officers, rather than standing by, at alert, on their ships. For his part, Short put army troops on high alert—for sabotage. He took the extra step of informing Washington of his action. Receiving no reply, he assumed that high command concurred with his understanding that the only credible threat at present was sabotage. His opinion thus reinforced,

Short decided not to stock his antiaircraft batteries with ready ammuni-tion—preferring to lock it up—and he further ordered all U.S. Army Air Forces planes to be grouped together, wingtip-to-wingtip, so that they could be more easily guarded against saboteurs. By this action, he trans-formed his air fleet into a compact target for aerial attack.

Under normal circumstances, rough winter seas and the frequency of winter storms would have prompted Japanese naval commanders to avoid the northern approach to Hawaii. But Nagumo deliberately chose the route because the rough seas and storms would help to mask the fleet. Indeed, a winter weather front, moving at approximately the same speed as the fleet, provided a remarkably effective screen. In addition, Nagumo dispatched a force of submarines two hundred miles in advance of the striking force to furnish Tokyo with up-to-date intelligence, which was supplemented by reports from Japanese agents on Oahu. On December 2, the striking force received a message, "Climb Mt. Niitaka."

It was the code authorizing the attack.

As of 6 AM, Sunday, December 7, the striking force was 230 miles north of Oahu. Six carriers turned into the wind to launch the first wave of 183 planes. Two fighters dropped out, one plunging into the sea on takeoff and the other, suffering engine trouble, left behind on deck. No sooner had the first wave been launched than carrier crews prepared the second wave. One hundred sixty-seven additional aircraft were launched shortly after seven o'clock. A single dive bomber in the second wave devel-oped engine trouble, leaving a total of 350 planes to make the attack.

The aircraft included Nakajima B5N2 "Kate" bombers, which dropped both torpedoes and conventional bombs, Aichi D3A1 "Val" dive bombers, and Mitsubishi A6M2 Reisen "Zero" fighters, used both to escort the bombers and to make close attacks on ships and ground facilities.

Meanwhile, at 6:45 AM, the USS Ward, a destroyer on patrol, attacked and sank a Japanese midget submarine as it tried to enter Pearl Harbor. Although the submarine had been sighted three hours prior to its sinking, the skipper of the Ward did not report its presence until it was sunk. Worse, even after it received the report, the navy failed to pass it on to the army. In this way, a valuable opportunity for advance warning of the attack was lost. (In the end, Japanese submarines—there were sixteen full-size "I" types and numerous midget subs—failed to sink any American ships at Pearl Harbor.)

Between 6:45 and 7 AM, the Opana mobile radar unit, newly installed on Oahu, made contact with a Japanese reconnaissance float plane. The radar operator duly reported the contact, but no action was taken on the report. Of three operating radar on Oahu, two were shut down at 7 AM so that the operators could eat breakfast. The truck delivering breakfast to the third set of operators was late, so, on their own initiative, they killed time by continuing to operate their single instrument, which detected the approach of the carrier aircraft of the first wave. Alarmed, the men reported this, but failed to specify the number of aircraft detected. As a result, the duty officer who received the report assumed the targets were a flight of American B-17 bombers, whose approach was expected. Yet another warning of the impending attack was ignored.

The first wave of Japanese aircraft homed in on Pearl Harbor simply by following the signal of commercial radio broadcasts from Honolulu. The cloud cover, which had screened the fleet so effectively, now threatened the bombing mission. It was so thick that the flight leader, Commander Fuchida, had the sinking feeling that he and his men had overflown Oahu. His fear proved fleeting. Suddenly, the clouds that shrouded the island parted with a sunburst that struck all the fliers as resembling their nation's flag. It was not only a good omen—a sign, it seemed, of divine intervention—but revealed the target with crystal clarity.

Now the strike force aviators referred to the bombing grids that had been drawn up by the Japanese consul general stationed in Honolulu. Moored in the harbor that sleepy Sunday morning were seventy U.S. warships, including eight battleships and twenty-four auxiliaries. A scout plane had earlier reported, with exultation, "Enemy fleet in port!" But Fuchida now saw that the prime targets of the attack, the U.S. aircraft carriers, were not present.

The strike force had a plan B. Fuchida guided his torpedo planes to "Battleship Row" and began an attack on the battleships closely lined up there.

Torpedoes were launched beginning at 7:55 AM. Simultaneously, Zeros and Vals struck the airfields at Kaneohe, Hickam, Ewa, Bellows, and Wheeler. The closely parked airplanes made for a splendid target, and within the space of two hours, U.S. air power in Hawaii was all but totally destroyed. The first-wave assault by torpedo and dive bombers lasted from 7:55 to 8:25. Fifteen minutes after this attack, high-level bombers moved in, then at 9:15 the dive bombers of the second wave struck, withdrawing by 9:45.

> **"I feel all we have done is to awake a sleeping giant and fill him with a terrible resolve."**
>
> —Attributed to Admiral Isoroku Yamamoto, December 7, 1941

As the attacks began, U.S. sailors were raising morning colors or eating breakfast. Response to the attack was initially chaotic, but many ship gun crews managed to begin returning fire within the first five or ten minutes as the signal "Air Raid Pearl Harbor, this is no drill!" was relayed throughout the fleet. Nevertheless, the toll on the Pacific Fleet was devastating. The battleship *Arizona* was completely destroyed, and the *Oklahoma* capsized; the battleships *California*, *Nevada*, and *West Virginia* sank in shallow water. Three cruisers, three destroyers, and four other vessels were damaged or sunk. One hundred sixty-four aircraft were destroyed on the ground and another 128 were damaged. Casualties included 2,403 service personnel and civilians killed and 1,178 wounded. Japanese losses amounted to 29 aircraft (with 55 airmen) and 6 submarines—1 I-type and 5 midget subs.

Just before 10 AM, aircraft of the Japanese first wave began touching down on their carriers. By noon, all surviving planes had been recovered. Fuchida emerged from his cockpit, relieved to see that planes were being readied for a third-wave assault. Except for the unanticipated absence of the U.S. carriers—as well as the heavy cruisers—the attack had succeeded beyond all expectation; nevertheless, Fuchida was aware that many targets remained intact, including the all-important naval shipyard and oil-storage tank farm, not to mention a number of ships.

Soon, his relief turned to anxiety as the aircraft remained motionless on deck. He did not know that, on the bridge of the strike force flagship *Akagi*, Admiral Nagumo was arguing with his officers over what to do next. Nagumo, methodical and cautious, argued that the strike force was running low on fuel and that, surely, the American carriers and other ships that had not been in port were now on the hunt and would mount a massive counterattack. After so successful a blow, he could not risk losing the strike force. Indeed, Nagumo deemed his mission to have been accomplished. With that, he ended the debate and, at 1 PM, turned the strike force back toward Japan.

> "Yesterday, December 7, 1941—a date which will live in infamy— the United States of America was suddenly and deliberately attacked by naval and air forces of the Empire of Japan."
>
> —Opening of President Franklin D. Roosevelt's war message to Congress, December 8, 1941

The Americans had been guilty of tactical folly, having made one blunder after another. But, in failing to launch his third wave, Nagumo committed a tactical error that would ensure cataclysmic strategic consequences for Japan. If the third wave had destroyed the base's repair facilities and fuel installations, Pearl Harbor would have been knocked out of the war for a long time, if not permanently. As it was, the base returned to service quickly. Even the fleet's staggering losses did not prove fatal. Those battleships that had been damaged but not sunk were repaired, and all but two that had sunk in shallow water were later refloated. In all, six of the eight battleships attacked at Pearl Harbor were returned to service before the end of the war, along with all but one of the other major vessels sunk or damaged.

There was no salvaging the careers of Kimmel and Short, both of whom soon resigned in disgrace, some of it merited, some of it not. But the rapid resurrection of Pearl Harbor and the eventual repair of damaged ships were secondary to the effect Pearl Harbor had on the American people. Far from being demoralized, they were enraged. In his famous war message to a joint session of Congress on December 8, 1941, President Roosevelt would refer to it as "righteous might." The nation was immediately unified and committed in every conceivable way to exacting vengeance against Japan by achieving absolute victory over it.

—

YAMAMOTO HAD FEARED THAT INFLICTING anything short of an ultimate blow against Pearl Harbor would produce such an effect, but he had not anticipated just how far short the tactically brilliant attack would fall in achieving its strategic objective of disabling the Pacific Fleet and demoralizing America. He had also not anticipated—as how could he?—that the element of surprise, tactically so crucial, would prove Japan's ultimate undoing. Tokyo had planned to announce the severance of U.S.-Japanese diplomatic relations about one-half hour prior to the attack, thereby legitimating the attack as an act of war, yet without significantly compromising surprise. However, because of the complexities of decoding and transcribing the complex series of messages sent from Tokyo to the embassy in Washington, the announcement came *after* the attack. Yamamoto was appalled at what he—and the rest of the world—deemed a breach of honor. "A military man can scarcely pride himself on having 'smitten a sleeping enemy,'?" he wrote on January 9, 1941. "In fact, to have it pointed out is more a matter of shame." Americans labeled it a "sneak attack" and deemed no action against the perpetrators too extreme.

Having predicted that if the war were not won in the single day of the Pearl Harbor attack, the operation would at least provide six months in which the Imperial Japanese Navy could "run wild," Yamamoto followed up with lightning naval campaigns that captured the East Indies during January–March 1942 and that achieved significant success in the Indian

Ocean during April 2–9, 1942. In June 1942, however, his plan to lure the battered Pacific Fleet to its final destruction in the waters around Midway Island backfired disastrously. This naval battle turned the tide of the Pacific war, putting Japan on the defensive and drastically undermining Yamamoto's confidence. On April 18, 1943, acting on an intercepted Japanese radio message revealing that Yamamoto was flying to a tour of Japanese bases on Shortland Island, U.S. fighter aircraft shot down the bomber transporting him. Isoroku Yamamoto was killed near Bougainville. It was just one more blow from which the Imperial Japanese Navy could not recover as Japan conducted a long, bloody fighting retreat that would end in a pair of mushroom clouds in August of 1945.

NASA and the Space Shuttles (1986, 2003)

THE DECISION FOR COMPLACENCY AND
BUREAUCRATIC SCIENCE

All exploration is hazardous, and exploration by flight is perhaps the most dangerous of all. The Wright brothers became interested in manned flight when they read about the lethal crash of Otto Lilienthal in August 1896. They quickly realized that what had killed the German glider experimenter was his failure to solve what the brothers identified as the key problem of achieving human flight: control. They also realized that the only way to learn how to gain control in flight was actually by flying. Thus, to avoid death in flight one had to court death in flight, which is what aviation pioneers did from the very beginning, accepting the danger as part of the explorer's bargain.

Yet, when it came to manned space flight, Americans never quite bought into the bargain. To be sure, the original seven "*Mercury* astronauts" were hailed as heroes in the 1960s, intrepid adventurers willing to defy death, but they also seemed worlds apart from the goggles-and-leather-helmet aviators of human flight's first generation. Were there dangers? Of course. But, after all, the space race was "government work," and the nation's very best engineers and scientists worked very hard to ensure that multiple safeguards made sitting atop a giant rocket loaded with highly explosive fuels and packing megatons of propulsive force as safe as it could possibly be.

Novelistic journalist Tom Wolfe's 1979 history of the early manned space program, *The Right Stuff*, opened the eyes of some Americans, revealing just how much jeopardy NASA—the National Aeronautics and Space Administration—was willing to put its astronauts in. For public consumption, NASA has always presented as government policy a broad margin of safety. Wolfe revealed it as far, far thinner. Nevertheless, the nation was stunned when the space shuttle *Challenger* exploded off the coast of central Florida, at 11:39 AM (all times are Eastern Standard Time) on January 28, 1986, just seventy-three seconds into its flight, killing all seven astronauts on board. A quarter-century after Alan B. Shepard had become the first American in space, Americans did not marvel at the fact that no U.S. astronaut had ever been killed in space flight, but they were at a loss to explain how seven—including Christa McAuliffe, selected by NASA to be the first teacher in space—could be blown up. Seventeen years later (in 2003), when the shuttle *Columbia* disintegrated on reentry into the earth's atmosphere after nearly two weeks in space, they expressed similar disbelief. Naturally, space flight was dangerous, yes, but the government was supposed to make it . . . well . . . safe. In fact, that was a big part of what the space shuttle program was all about: making space travel a matter of routine.

On reflection, the real shock of the two shuttle accidents was not that they had occurred in spite of all that a government agency did to prevent them but that they were the result of that agency's very approach to space flight. NASA did not cause the *Challenger* and *Columbia* disasters, but NASA did make them possible.

The technical causes of the two accidents were quite different, but they both grew out of the institutional structure of the space agency. Together with its contractors, NASA is an economic-political *and* scientific-technological enterprise. Prior to each accident, personnel from the scientific-technical side of NASA and the scientific-technical personnel employed by its contractors expressed concern about potential problems. In both cases, those in the economic-political side of the agency and the management wing of the contractors either failed to understand or chose to ignore these concerns. Moreover, the bureaucratic structure of NASA—the clumsy interface between the agency's two sides—actually hobbled attempts at communication and action. The economic-political administrators refused to take any steps that might lead to economic and political consequences—the postponement of a mission, the investigation of inherent flaws—without absolute, objective proof of a scientific-technological problem. That is, the judgment or suspicion of the engineers was insufficient to trigger action because NASA administrators did not charge the agency's engineers with proving that all shuttle systems were safe. They charged them with proving any system unsafe. And the only absolute proof of that would be disaster.

It was national public folly to believe that a benign government bureaucracy had rendered space travel safe when that bureaucracy had actually multiplied the dangers inherent in space travel. It was folly on the part of the leaders of the government's agency of space exploration and space exploitation to put precisely the wrong burden of proof on its technical and scientific experts. And, as we will see, there was even more folly to go around.

Challenger was scheduled to lift off at 3:43 PM on January 22, 1986, but the launch was pushed back to the twenty-third, then the twenty-fourth, yet again to the twenty-fifth, and finally to 9:37 AM, January 27. One of the national selling points of the shuttle program was that it would make space travel nearly routine and highly reliable. Having to postpone a launch was therefore especially embarrassing. On the morning of the twenty-seventh, there were problems with the exterior access hatch, and by the time these were fixed, crosswinds had kicked up at the Shuttle Landing Facility, their speed exceeding safety limits. When the winds failed to die down, the launch was again postponed.

But January 28 did not look very promising. Central Florida was in the grip of a cold snap, with predicted temperatures approaching 31°F, the minimum permitted for launch. The prohibition against launching at freezing temperatures was not merely a matter of NASA policy. Engineers at Morton Thiokol, the contractor that had built the solid rocket booster (SRB) component of the shuttle, were so deeply troubled that, on the evening of January 27, they convened a telephone meeting with NASA managers at Kennedy Space Center in Florida and at the Marshall Space Flight Center in Huntsville, Alabama. Since 1977, a number of the Morton Thiokol engineers had expressed concerns over a design flaw in the SRBs, arguing that low temperatures would greatly reduce the resilience of the rubber O-rings that sealed the SRB joints. Nor did the temperature have to be very low. If it fell below 53°F, some engineers predicted that the rubber would lose sufficient resilience to potentially compromise its ability to create a reliable seal. No other part of the shuttle's many systems was more important than the O-ring equipment, a fact reflected in its designation as a "Criticality 1" component. This designation was reserved for system features whose failure would destroy the spacecraft and kill its crew. Yet, even though the design issue had been raised nearly a decade earlier, no manager at NASA or Morton Thiokol had ordered a fix. After all, the shuttle had already flown nine missions without any evident O-ring problem—although it had never been launched in temperatures as cold as those on this January day.

The January 27 teleconference did not directly pit NASA managers against NASA engineers or NASA managers against Morton Thiokol engineers. It was the Morton Thiokol managers, who also participated in the conference, who overruled their own engineers, recommending to NASA managers that the launch proceed as scheduled. Responsible for running one of NASA's major shuttle subcontractors, they apparently did not want Morton Thiokol to take the blame for yet another scrubbed launch.

Fully armed with hindsight, a chronicler of the tragedy could call this the "decision for disaster." But it was not simply that. To the misplaced priorities of the managers at Morton Thiokol and NASA must be added another layer of negligence, heedlessness, and institutional breakdown. The crew responsible for deicing the launch structure that stands beside the shuttle accidentally pointed their infrared camera at the booster itself, discovering that one of the joints sealed by an O-ring was at only 8°F, the result of very cold air blowing on the joint from a liquid oxygen tank vent. This should have greatly alarmed the ice crew, since it was a temperature very far below the design specifications for the O-rings. But measuring the temperature of the booster was not the assigned job of the ice crew, and so their observation was never conveyed to engineers, managers, or any other decision makers.

Even without knowledge of the ice team's temperature reading, another set of engineers, those working for Rockwell International, the prime shuttle contractor, voiced concerns as well, not about the integrity of the O-rings, but about the ice that might shake loose during launch and hit the shuttle, seriously damaging it. Yet again there was a disconnect between engineers and managers. Rockwell's own managers passed on the engineers' concern, but simply noted that the safety consequences of these concerns were unknown. Without any conclusive, urgent recommendations from the contractors' management team or NASA managers, NASA administrators decided to proceed with the launch—although they ordered an additional ice inspection. The ice team reported that the ice now appeared to be melting, and thus *Challenger* was okayed for launch at 11:38 AM.

The public and the media took a greater interest in the launch of *Challenger* than in any number of recent space shots. The reason was the presence on the seven-person crew of Christa McAuliffe, a civilian, a mother, a high school social studies teacher, and the first member of the

Teacher in Space Project. She was to be the first "teacher in space." In classrooms all across the country, schoolchildren gathered before television sets to watch the launch.

Six and six-tenths seconds before the spacecraft lifted off the launch pad, the three space shuttle main engines (SSME) ignited. At 11:38:00.010, the engines were at 100 percent power and then were automatically throttled up to 104 percent. With this, the two SRBs were ignited and explosive hold-down bolts were released, freeing the entire vehicle from the launch pad.

The only indication of trouble at launch time—visible at T+0.678, to be precise—were heavy puffs of dark gray smoke emanating from the right-hand SRB. A review of launch film revealed that the final puff occurred at T+3.375. The smoke came from the opening and closing of the aft field joint of the right-hand SRB, the casing of which had bulged out under the stress of ignition, creating a gap at the joint through which gases, superheated to 5,000°F, escaped. Such stresses were normal and were precisely what the SRB's primary O-ring was designed to compensate for, expanding as the metal bent and thereby keeping the gap sealed. But, in this case, the rubber was too cold and too brittle to close the seal in time. A secondary O-ring, also cold, failed to seal properly as the metal bent. Without any barrier to contain the hot gases, a large portion of both O-rings vaporized. Aluminum oxides produced by the burning solid-fuel propellant oozed through the damaged joint, temporarily sealing it. This effect would not last long.

As programmed, at T+28, the SSMEs throttled down to reduce velocity through the dense lower atmosphere of Earth. At T+35.379, the SSMEs throttled back to 65 percent, then, at T+51.860, the engines automatically returned to 104 percent. Seven seconds after this, as revealed by postlaunch study of a tracking film, a plume of flame blossomed near the aft "attach strut" on the right SRB. By this time, high-velocity wind shear had torn away the aluminum oxide "seal," and gas, fully aflame, had started burning through an expanding hole in one of the joints of the right-hand SRB. After one more second, the burning gas plume was plainly visible, and at T+64.660, the pressure of the liquid oxygen tank dropped due to the leak. Other systems compensated for the reduced pressure, and, four seconds later, mission control radioed the crew that all was well: They were "go at throttle up."

"Roger, go at throttle up," *Challenger* Commander Dick Scobee replied. It was the last radio message from the shuttle.

At T+72.284, the right SRB pulled away from the aft strut attaching it to the external tank. The crew cabin recorder, later recovered from the wreckage, recorded pilot Michael J. Smith's exclamation a half second after this event: "Uh oh."

At T+73.124, the aft dome of the liquid hydrogen tank catastrophically failed, initiating the breakup of the shuttle vehicle, which began at T+73.162 seconds at an altitude of 48,000 feet. The vehicle veered sharply and was instantly sheered apart by tremendous aerodynamic forces.

Television pictures beamed to the world showed a massive cloud of smoke where *Challenger* had been.

Even as these images appeared on television screens, all remained coolly professional at mission control. Flight director Jay Greene asked his flight dynamics officer for data.

"Filters"—that is, radar—"got discreting [separate, multiple] sources," came the reply.

To Greene, this meant only one thing. *Challenger* was now in pieces.

"Negative contact, loss of downlink," the ground controller reported, meaning that all radio and remote telemetry data from *Challenger* had suddenly ceased.

"Watch your data carefully," Greene ordered, cautioning controllers to look for any sign that the shuttle, with the crew on board, had escaped the disintegration.

It was T+110.250 before the range safety officer transmitted radio signals to initiate the self-destruction of the solid rocket boosters, which were still intact. One of these falling on a ship or other structure would be catastrophic.

Speaking to the world's television audience, who had witnessed what appeared to be a massive explosion, public affairs officer Steve Nesbitt was at first almost absurdly understated: "Flight controllers here looking very carefully at the situation. Obviously a major malfunction. We have no downlink." His tone changed as he next relayed what seemed to all the blunt and terrible truth: "We have a report from the Flight Dynamics Officer that the vehicle has exploded."

> "The crew of the space shuttle *Challenger* honored us by the manner in which they lived their lives. We will never forget them, nor the last time we saw them, this morning, as they prepared for their journey and waved goodbye and 'slipped the surly bonds of earth' to 'touch the face of God.'"
>
> —President Ronald Reagan, television address following the *Challenger* disaster

In fact, *Challenger* had not exploded, but had been torn apart by aerodynamic forces. The rapid disintegration of the external fuel tank gave the appearance of the eruption of a gigantic fireball, but the crew cabin and both SRBs had survived the breakup of the launch vehicle. The man in charge of maintaining safety for those on the ground, the range safety officer, destroyed the SRBs, which was standard operating procedure, but the crew cabin, intact, had gone ballistic and was seen emerging from the massive cloud of gases at T+75.237. It reached a maximum altitude of 65,000 feet while the rest of the shuttle broke apart at 48,000 feet.

To television viewers across the nation and around the world it seemed obvious that the *Challenger* crew had met with instantaneous death—terrible yet also merciful.

This was not the case. As the shuttle broke apart, the crew cabin detached, briefly undergoing 12 to 20 *g*'s of force, but soon experiencing no more than 4 *g*'s or less. Some or all of the crew would have remained alive and at least briefly conscious as the crew cabin plummeted toward the ocean surface. It is not known if anyone was conscious when the cabin hit the water with a crushing impact of more than 200 g's, far beyond the possibility of structural or biological survivability.

Theoretically, escape and survival might have been possible immediately after the breakup—had the shuttle been equipped with an ejection system. Designers had thought about installing something of the kind, but NASA concluded that the shuttle was so reliable a system, that an escape system, which offered only "limited utility" and threatened great "technical complexity and excessive cost in dollars, weight or schedule delays," was unnecessary.

The *Challenger* disaster killed seven astronauts and threatened to kill the shuttle program as well. For thirty-two months there were no further launches as a special presidential commission investigated the accident. The Rogers Commission concluded that the organizational culture and decision-making processes at NASA had been central to the accident. Neither NASA nor Morton Thiokol managers, the commission reported, had responded adequately to a clearly identified design flaw: the vulnerability of the O-rings.

In response to the Rogers Commission report, NASA authorized a redesign of the shuttle's solid rocket boosters (to eliminate problems identified as early as 1977) and established a new Office of Safety, Reliability and Quality Assurance. NASA also decided to slow down its launch rate by scheduling fewer missions. The changes were welcomed by NASA's growing legion of critics, but many persisted in pointing out that the disaster had not prompted essential changes in management structure and organizational culture.

The critics notwithstanding, between September 29, 1988, when the next shuttle mission, number twenty-six, was launched, and January 16, 2003, when *Columbia* lifted off, eighty-six successful space shuttle missions were completed. Except to those few who continued to insist that NASA's corporate culture was essentially flawed, there seemed no reason to expect that mission number 113 would be any different.

Yet this *Columbia* mission, originally scheduled to launch on January 11, 2001, also seemed plagued. Over the next two years, its launch would be postponed eighteen times, each scrubbed launch triggering protests from scientists as well as politicians, who pointed out that not only had the space shuttle program failed in its purpose of making travel nearly a routine matter, it was a waste of resources. More than a hundred shuttle flights had staked out no new territory in space, they said, but had only drained cash from the development and launch of any number of unmanned instrument probes, which could explore the truly unexplored and produce far more and far more important scientific data.

Even more than in 1986, the shuttle program found itself under political, administrative, and scientific pressure. Yet when a number of engineers pointed to inherent flaws in the shuttle design, including the possibility that foam used as external insulation for the shuttle's giant propellant tanks was subject to breaking off during launch and could cause impact damage to the shuttle's airframe, NASA responded ambiguously. On the one hand, the agency published a set of safety regulations stating that external tank "foam shedding" and subsequent debris strikes on the shuttle were important safety issues that had to be resolved before any launch was cleared. On the other hand, launches were repeatedly authorized even as engineers continued to study the foam shedding problem. Indeed, most shuttle launches recorded foam strikes and thermal tile scarring—all in blatant violation of safety regulations. As with *Challenger's* O-ring problems, NASA management tacitly accepted the foam strikes, as if they were inevitable. The managers even had a name for this willful blindness: "normalization of deviance."

When *Columbia* was finally launched on January 16, 2003, engineers studied video of the launch two hours after the event and found nothing unusual. The high-resolution film images of the launch processed overnight, however, clearly showed that a piece of insulation foam about the size of a briefcase had been shed from the external fuel tank 81.9 seconds after the initiation of the launch sequence. It appeared as if it had struck the shuttle's left wing, which engineers feared could have damaged the shuttle's thermal protection there.

While *Columbia* went about its mission, NASA managers and engineers conducted a series of "risk-management" conferences. Engineers made no fewer than three requests that Department of Defense equipment be used to image the shuttle while it was in orbit so that they might be able to assess possible damage. NASA management not only failed to honor the requests, but even actively intervened to prevent the Department of Defense from assisting. When NASA's chief engineer in charge of the shuttle's thermal protection system asked NASA management whether one of the shuttle astronauts would be tasked with visually inspecting the wings, the managers simply avoided response.

Management stonewalling was the product of two factors. First, shuttle after shuttle had suffered foam hits on launching and none had suffered fatal damage. Second, even if damage were detected, NASA managers could imagine no way to do anything to fix it. They did not ignore the problem, but, led by manager Linda Ham, chair of the Columbia Mission Management team, decided that, instead of attempting an actual inspection for damage, they would conduct a hypothetical "what-if" scenario study using a damage-prediction software program called Crater.

On the face of it, this was bizarre. In response to an actual and immediate problem, the space agency took only hypothetical action. Nevertheless, the results of the Crater simulation were not comforting. The program predicted serious penetration of a number of the shuttle's vital thermal protection tiles.

This time, it was not management, but some of the engineers themselves who downplayed the results. The Crater software was designed to predict damage not from foam insulation, but from small, hard projectiles, especially ice. Some engineers believed that foam insulation impacts could not create as much damage as the software predicted. Others, however, believed that, at high velocity, even the "soft" foam was sufficiently dense to create the kind of damage Crater predicted. Faced with two interpretations, NASA managers chose to agree with the engineers who discounted predictions based on denser materials. The managers decided to reduce the predicted damage from "total penetration" to "slight damage." Using this decision, they issued a definitive denial of engineers' requests for the Department of Defense images.

Were NASA managers justified in assuming that, with rescue or repair impossible, there was no point in inspecting the shuttle for damage while it was in orbit? The first question to ask is whether they were correct in assuming that either rescue or repair was actually impossible. The *Columbia* Accident Investigation Board (CAIB), convened after the disaster, did conclude that a rescue mission or in-orbit repair would have been risky, but might nevertheless have been possible if NASA had successfully verified the damage within the first five days of the mission.

On February 1, 2003, when *Columbia* began its reentry, coming back into the earth's atmosphere, superheated gases produced by friction with atmospheric molecules penetrated the leading edge of the wing, which had, in fact, been severely damaged by the foam impact. These gases destroyed the internal wing structure, first causing a loss of control and then the breakup of the shuttle in flight.

The fatal consequences of the foam impact that had occurred days earlier began to unfold at 8:44 AM, when *Columbia* entered the atmosphere at 400,000 feet. Four minutes later, a sensor on the left wing leading edge spar showed exceptionally high strains. By 8:50, the spacecraft was reentering at Mach 24.1 (more than 24 times the speed of sound), and debris began to come off the left wing, the leading-edge temperature of which was approximately 2,650°F. At 8:53, as *Columbia* crossed the California coast west of Sacramento en route to a Florida landing, the leading-edge temperature rose to more than 2,800°F. It was at this time that ground observers saw the first glowing signs of superheated debris.

At 8:54:24, the Maintenance, Mechanical, and Crew Systems officer based in Houston mission control reported that four hydraulic sensors in the shuttle's left wing were indicating "off-scale low"—a sign of total hydraulic systems failure.

Columbia now crossed from California into Nevada airspace. Ground-based witnesses reported seeing a bright flash, which was followed by at least eighteen more flashes over a span of four minutes. As *Columbia* crossed from Nevada into Utah, then into Arizona, and then into New Mexico, the temperature at the leading edge of the wings was nearly 3,000°F.

At 8:57 National Weather Service radar reported echoes of debris from the shuttle. A minute after this, *Columbia* crossed from New Mexico into Texas at Mach 19.5 and an altitude of 209,800 feet. At this time, one complete Thermal Protection System (TPS) tile was shed, falling on Littlefield, Texas, just northwest of Lubbock. A minute later, the Maintenance, Mechanical, and Crew Systems officer reported that pressure readings had been lost on both left main landing-gear tires. Apparently, the tires had burned up—even though the landing gear was fully retracted within the structure of the spacecraft.

> **"My fellow Americans, this day has brought terrible news and great sadness to our country. At 9:00 AM this morning, Mission Control in Houston lost contact with our Space Shuttle *Columbia*. A short time later, debris was seen falling from the skies above Texas.**
>
> **"The Columbia is lost; there are no survivors."**
>
> —President George W. Bush, televised address from the White House Cabinet Room, February 1, 2003

Now the Houston-based flight director instructed his Capsule Communicator (CAPCOM) to relay to the shuttle crew that Mission Control was evaluating the indications it was receiving.

"Roger, uh, bu—" crackled in Houston headphones seconds later. It was the last communication from the crew of space shuttle *Columbia*.

By 9:00 in the morning, Texans were seeing a lot more glowing debris. Five minutes later, a number of reports came from north-central Texas of a loud boom, a minor concussion wave, smoke trails, and multiple pieces of debris. At 9:12:39, the NASA flight director declared a "contingency,"

alerted search-and-rescue teams, and instructed the Houston ground
controller to "lock the doors," imposing a security lockdown on Mission
Control in order to preserve the integrity of mission data for later
investigation.

At 2:04 in the afternoon, President George W. Bush appeared on
television to announce what was by now obvious: *Columbia* had been lost
and "there are no survivors." He continued: "The cause in which they died
will continue. Our journey into space will go on."

As it turned out, that journey was delayed by two years, during
which the CAIB made its study and issued a report lashing into NASA
for complacency both before and during the mission. The agency, it
said, had failed to address design problems its own engineers had identified, and then, when damage was suspected, it had chosen not to
investigate it on the highly questionable assumption that no rescue or
repair was possible.

—◆—

AS HAD OCCURRED IN THE WAKE of the *Challenger* disaster, the loss of
Columbia brought not only criticism of NASA, but of the shuttle
program. Frustration among many scientists ran high. It was bad enough
to underestimate and even disregard the dangers of space exploration,
but far worse to risk those dangers to achieve highly dubious goals. The
space shuttle, many judged, had certainly failed in its key objective of
reducing the cost of access to space. Per pound, the space shuttle costs
as much to launch as a conventional expendable rocket. The shuttle also
failed to furnish reliable access to space. Delays and even multiyear
interruptions were common. Worst of all, the costs of the shuttle
program kept NASA from making any manned space flight beyond low
earth orbit since the *Apollo* lunar missions. Devoting so much money and
effort to repetitive shuttle missions also greatly curtailed far more
productive space exploration using unmanned vehicles and probes.
Sadly, too, the sameness of the shuttle flights failed to excite the

American public, which lost interest in the space program. Scientifically, technologically, and even spiritually, the space shuttle had come to seem a dead end, the product of science fossilized by a heedless bureaucracy, and surely not worth the lives or the missed opportunities it has cost. Despite these concerns, shuttle missions have been scheduled to fly through 2010.

PART TWO

The Decision to Manipulate

William McKinley, the USS *Maine,* and the Spanish-American War (1898)

THE DECISION TO FIND A FIGHT

At 6,682 tons, the USS *Maine,* commissioned in 1895, was one of the last of the pre-Dreadnought-class battleships. Its heaviest armament consisted of four ten-inch guns, whereas the Dreadnought-class battleship, displacing some seventeen thousand tons, would mount ten twelve-inch guns, plus a battery of secondary weapons nearly as heavy as the *Maine's* primary ten-inchers. The *Maine* was obsolescent from the day she was launched, November 18, 1889, her ten-inchers arranged so awkwardly that they projected off to either side—the forward turret to port, aft to starboard—which would have made it impossible for her to fire a full broadside. But she never had to. The closest she came to battle was her assignment, beginning on January 25, 1898, to "protect American interests" in Havana while Cuba was wracked by insurrection against its colonial master, Spain.

A symbol of American military might, *Maine* had been riding at anchor in Havana Harbor for some three weeks when, at 9:40 local time on the evening of February 15, the explosion of more than five tons of powder for the vessel's six- and ten-inch guns tore through the battleship. In an instant, nearly a hundred feet of the forward section, about a third of the *Maine's* entire length, were instantly reduced to shrapnel, sending the aft two-thirds rapidly to the bottom of the harbor.

Most of the *Maine's* 374 officers and men were drowsing or sleeping that warm tropical evening—the enlisted sailors, for the most part, bunked down in their forward quarters. Because so many men were packed into the front of the ship, the loss of life was devastating: 266

killed immediately, and eight severely wounded men succumbed later. Captain Charles Sigsbee and most of his officers survived, only because their quarters were well aft. That night, Sigsbee sent the following telegram to the secretary of the navy:

HAVANA, February 15, 1898.
SECRETARY OF THE NAVY,
Washington, D.C.:

Maine blown up in Havana Harbor at 9.40 tonight, and destroyed. Many wounded and doubtless more killed or drowned. Wounded and others on board Spanish man-of-war and Ward Line steamer. Send light-house tenders from Key West for crew and the few pieces of equipment above. No one has clothing other than that upon him. Public opinion should be suspended until further report. All officials believed to be saved. Jenkins and Merritt not yet accounted for. Many Spanish officers, including representatives of General Blanco, now with me to express sympathy.
Sigsbee.

Sending the *Maine* to Havana Harbor had been the culmination of an increasingly bellicose U.S. policy toward Spain, the colonial "overlord" of Cuba. On December 7, 1896, Grover Cleveland, in his final address to Congress as president of the United States, advocated the exploration of peaceful means to resolve the "Cuban crisis," as Americans called the ongoing Cuban Revolution. At the time, Cuba's struggle for independence from Spain was hardly a major issue for most Americans, but U.S. political leaders believed that the policies and activities of a colonial power just ninety miles from the United States would, sooner or later, have an impact on the nation. Cleveland acknowledged that Cuba "lies so near to us as to be hardly separated from our territory." He also noted, at least from $30 million to $50 million of American capital are invested in plantations and in railroad, mining, and other business enterprises on the island. . . . The insurgents are undoubtedly encouraged and supported by the widespread sympathy the people of this country always and instinctively feel for every struggle for better and freer government and which, in the case of the more adventurous and restless elements of our population, leads in only too many instances to active and personal participation in the contest. The result is that this government is constantly called upon to protect American citizens, to claim damages for injuries to persons and property, now estimated at many millions of dollars, and to ask explanations and apologies for the acts of Spanish officials, whose zeal for the repression of rebellion sometimes blinds them to the immunities belonging to the unoffending citizens of a friendly power. It follows from the same causes that the United States is compelled to actively police a long line of seacoast against unlawful expeditions, the escape of which the utmost vigilance will not always suffice to prevent.

"Entanglements," Cleveland called U.S. interests in Cuba, declaring that they had "led to a vehement demand in various quarters for some sort of positive intervention on the part of the United States," including official recognition of "the independence of the insurgents." It was, however, a notion Cleveland flatly rejected, observing that "imperfect and restricted as the Spanish government of the island may be, no other exists there." To those who advocated outright war with Spain so that the United States might assume the governing of Cuba, Cleveland responded that the "United States has . . . a character to maintain as a nation, which plainly dictates that right and not might should be the rule of its conduct." Moreover, the nation's "own ample and diversified domains satisfy all possible longings for territory, preclude all dreams of conquest, and prevent any casting of covetous eyes upon neighboring regions, however attractive."

Most of Cleveland's fellow Democrats were of like mind with the president, sharing his belief that the United States had no business engaging in imperialist ventures. The Republican voters who put Cleveland's successor, William McKinley, in the White House thought otherwise, and for that very reason were disappointed by their new president's first message to Congress, delivered on December 6, 1897. In the twelve months since Cleveland's final speech, the Cuban situation had become (in McKinley's estimation) the "most important problem with which this government is now called upon to deal." That hardly meant going to war, however. "The instructions given to our new minister to Spain before his departure for his post directed him to impress upon that government the sincere wish of the United States to lend its aid toward the ending of the war in Cuba by reaching a peaceful and lasting result, just and honorable alike to Spain and to the Cuban people." McKinley told Congress that the Spanish government had made an encouraging reply to the U.S. message, a reply that was "in the direction of a better understanding" and that appreciated "the friendly purposes of this government." Spain promised "political reforms" and the conduct of military operations that would be "humane and . . . accompanied by political action leading to the autonomy of Cuba while guarding Spanish sovereignty." If these reforms brought an end to the insurrection in Cuba, McKinley suggested that the interests of U.S. security would be satisfied and that there would be no need for any American intervention whatsoever.

By the time of McKinley's rational response to the developing situation in Cuba, the so-called "Yellow Press" had been covering the anti-Spanish insurrections in Cuba and the Philippines for months, raising popular American interest in these events. "Yellow journalism" took its name not from serious news reporting, but from an innovation in newspaper entertainment. In 1895, Richard Felton Outcault, a cartoonist for the *New York World*, introduced a single-panel comic featuring a slum child costumed in a garment that was tinted yellow by a new color printing process, which the paper was eager to showcase. "The Yellow Kid of Hogan's Alley" (as the strip was called) was a great success, allowing publisher Joseph Pulitzer to close the gap in his circulation contest with the *New York Journal*, published by rival William Randolph Hearst. Hearst quickly retaliated by hiring young George Luks (later a major American painter) to create a competing comic he called simply "The Yellow Kid." The dueling comics were but a single battle in the circulation war between Pulitzer and Hearst, who vied to outdo each other with increasingly sensational news stories. While these stories were, without doubt, of more consequence than the comics, it was the yellow ink used in those features that gave this style of newspaper reporting, writing, and publishing the name by which it is still known.

The Yellow Press produced some landmark stories exposing social injustice, corruption, and public fraud, which significantly contributed to the age of reform that produced the Progressive policies of Theodore Roosevelt and Woodrow Wilson. But yellow journalism also relentlessly drove publishers to find bigger and more sensational stories and, when necessary, to enhance those stories to make them even bigger and more attractive to readers. Accordingly, beginning in the mid-1890s, both Hearst and Pulitzer dispatched reporters to Cuba and, shortly thereafter, to the Philippines as well. To Cuba went skilled reporters as well as able artists, including the great painter of life in the American West, Frederic Remington. The news dispatches demonized Spanish authorities, who emerged for American readers as villains of melodrama, especially as personified in General Valeriano Weyler, sent by Spain in February 1896 to impose martial law on Cuba. Hearst's paper branded him "Butcher Weyler" after he created outrage in Cuba as well as in the United States by incarcerating those identified as rebel sympathizers in what he called "reconcentration camps." These were stockades in which the unruly were confined after having been removed from their farms and homes. Conditions in these camps ranged from poor to inhumane. As many American newspapers portrayed the situation, Spain was a barbaric, medieval, and simply incompetent nation incapable of administering

Cuba with enlightened efficiency. According to the papers, this presented not only a moral affront—on America's doorstep, no less—but a menace to U.S. business and financial interests in Cuba.

The role Hearst's and Pulitzer's yellow journalism played in pushing the United States to declare war on Spain has often been exaggerated. In one often-quoted exchange, Frederic Remington telegraphed Hearst asking to be sent home because it seemed to him that all was relatively quiet in Cuba. "There will be no war," he wrote, to which Hearst reportedly responded, "Please remain. You furnish the pictures and I'll furnish the war." A shocking story to be sure, but no source for it has ever been found. Just the same, there was a very real barrage of sensational news stories from the island, and, partly by dint of these, American public opinion was inexorably converted from patient forbearance (as advocated by the outgoing Grover Cleveland as well as by the incoming William McKinley) to war fever.

President McKinley had sent the *Maine* to Havana as a stopgap military response to the public and political clamor. After the *Maine* exploded in the harbor, the president refused to yield to the growing war cry of "Remember the *Maine!* To hell with Spain!" and convened a U.S. Navy court of inquiry to investigate the explosion. Early in March, the court released its findings,

"Spanish 'Justice and Honor' be darned!"

—Headline from the Hearst papers, 1898

concluding that contact with a submarine mine had caused the explosion. Over the years, subsequent inquiries into the *Maine* disaster would all conclude that no mine had been involved at all, but that the explosion was an accident almost certainly resulting from spontaneous combustion in the ship's powder magazine. Ascribing the explosion to a mine was, therefore, an error of the gravest consequences, yet it is also true that the court did not assign responsibility for the placing of the mine, thereby leaving open the question as to whether it had been placed by Spanish forces (with authorization from Spain), by Spanish loyalists (without authorization from Spain), or by Cuban rebels, who hoped to provoke U.S. entry into the war.

Even though the court of inquiry concluded—however mistakenly—that the *Maine* had been sunk by a military mine, its failure to assign blame for the action meant that it could not easily be used as a cause for war. That did not seem to bother the majority of American newspapers, which printed (as Hearst's papers did) such headlines as "Maine Was Destroyed by Treachery!" and "The Whole Country Thrills with War Fever!" In April 1898, journalist Albert Shaw wrote in the *Review of Reviews*:

> Quite regardless of the responsibilities for the Maine incident, it is apparently true that the great majority of the American people are hoping that President McKinley will promptly utilize the occasion to secure the complete pacification and independence of Cuba. There are a few people in the United States—we should not like to believe that more than 100 could be found out of a population of 75 million—who believe that the United States ought to join hands with Spain in forcing the Cuban insurgents to lay down their arms and to accept Spanish sovereignty as a permanent condition under the promise of practical home rule. It needs no argument, of course, to convince the American people that such a proposal reaches the lowest depths of infamy. . . . The people of the United States do not intend to help Spain hold Cuba. On, the contrary, they are now ready, in one way or in another, to help the Cubans drive Spain out of the Western Hemisphere. If the occasion goes past and we allow this Cuban struggle to run on indefinitely, the American people will have lost several degrees of self-respect and will certainly not have gained anything in the opinion of mankind.

Even after the explosion of the *Maine* and the findings of the board of inquiry, and always against the journalistic drumbeat, President McKinley still hoped to avoid war. On March 26, 1898, the U.S. Department of State sent a cable of instructions to the U.S. ambassador in Spain. "We do not want the island," the cable stated. "The President has evidenced in every way his desire to preserve and continue friendly relations with Spain. . . . For your own guidance, the President suggests that if Spain will revoke the reconcentration order and maintain the people until they can support themselves and offer to the Cubans full self-government, with reasonable indemnity, the President will gladly assist in its consummation. If Spain should invite the United States to mediate for peace and the insurgents would make like request, the President might undertake such office of friendship." On the next day, more specific instructions were cabled:

See if the following can be done:

First, armistice [between Spain and the Cuban insurgents] until October I. Negotiations meantime looking for peace between Spain and insurgents through friendly offices of President United States.

Second, immediate revocation of reconcentrado [reconcentration] order so as to permit people to return to their farms and the needy to be relieved with provisions and supplies from United States cooperating with authorities so as to afford full relief.

Add, if possible, third, if terms of peace not satisfactorily settled by October I, President of the United States to be final arbiter between Spain and insurgents.

If Spain agrees, President will use friendly offices to get insurgents to accept plan. Prompt action desirable.

The fact was that Spain clearly wanted to avoid war with the United States. The Madrid government instructed Cuba's governor-general to revoke the reconcentration policy and, on April 9, the military commander of Spanish forces in Cuba was instructed to grant an armistice to the rebels in preparation for peace talks. In short, McKinley was given everything he asked for.

Yet events somehow outran him. Propelled by public, political, and commercial pressure, he capitulated to those who would settle for nothing short of combat. On April 11, he finally appeared before Congress to ask for a declaration of war. He made little mention of Spain's recent conciliatory measures, but instead recounted events since 1896, claiming that the American people had patiently endured economic and general security hardships and calling the continued armed chaos in Cuba, so close to American shores, intolerable.

He concluded with the explosion of the *Maine*. The president did not lie about it. Indeed, he made it a particular point to note that the naval court of inquiry "did not assume to place the responsibility" for the explosion, yet he used the event just as the press and a growing majority of the public had been using it: as the last straw, *the* pretext for war. "In any event," he said, the destruction of the *Maine*, by whatever exterior cause, "is a patent and impressive proof of a state of things in Cuba that is intolerable. That condition is thus shown to be such that the Spanish government cannot assure safety and security to a vessel of the American Navy in the harbor of Havana on a mission of peace, and rightfully there." It did not matter, then, who blew up the battleship. The very fact that the Spanish government could not prevent its having been blown up was sufficient cause for war.

In response to President McKinley's request, Congress voted up a resolution on Cuban independence on April 20, 1898, recognizing the independence of Cuba and authorizing war on Spain with the object of forcing that country to a similar recognition. In tying the war resolution to the recognition of independence, Congress gave the president more than he had asked for—yet the resolution did not come without a rancorous debate from a sizable Senate minority, which questioned the administration's motives. To placate this anti-imperialist element, Senator Henry M.

Teller of Colorado drafted an amendment to the war resolution, by which the United States disclaimed "any disposition or intention to exercise sovereignty, jurisdiction, or control over said Islands except for the pacification thereof, and assert[ed] its determination, when that is accomplished, to leave the government and control of the Island to its people."

The Teller Amendment went a long way toward immersing the war in a cleansing bath of collective national altruism, yet, as a war of choice rather than of necessity, and despite patriotic and economic zeal in most quarters for a fight, there lingered a general uneasiness about the conflict, which prompted the apologists to spill many gallons of ink. Typical was "The Right of Our Might," published in the *Louisville Courier-Journal* of April 20, 1898, by editor Henry Watterson. The war, he wrote, is a struggle "for Americanism, for civilization, for humanity. . . . It is not a war of conquest. It is not a war of envy or enmity. It is not a war of pillage or gain. From the material side it is a war of tremendous loss to us, involving burdens of millions, not one cent of which can we hope to recover. There are those who diet on rice and peer through blue goggles, who whine that on legal grounds we have no right to interfere with Spain's belaboring her own ass, to dispute her sovereignty over Cuba, her own territory. If they had prevailed, America today would be a slave-holding nation." In our "warrant for this war," Watterson declared,

> we find it in the law supreme—the law high above the law of titles in lands, in chattels, in human bodies and human souls—the law of man, the law of god. We find it in our own inspiration, our own destiny. We find it in the peals of the bell that rang out our sovereignty from Philadelphia; we find it in the blood of the patriots who won our independence at the cannon's mouth; we find it in the splendid structure of our national life, built up through over a hundred years of consecration to liberty and defiance to despotism; we find it in our own giant strength, attained in the air, and under the skies of freedom and equality, which has not only won and guarded the world's bulwark of liberty and law in

our republic, but which has laid down and enforced the decree that liberty and law on this hemisphere shall not be further trespassed on by despotism and autocracy, and which now, in the sight of the powers of the earth and the God of nations, takes one step more and says that liberty and law shall no longer be trampled upon, outraged, and murdered by despotism and autocracy upon our threshold.

That is the right of our might; that is the sign in which we conquer.

The cause of war quickly escalated from vengeance over the loss of the *Maine* to a kind of holy crusade. Few Americans could see through the purple prose of patriotic fervor to the hard fact that U.S. ground forces were ill prepared for war. The regular army was tiny, and the reserves—the National Guard—though larger, was inadequately equipped and trained. Fortunately, the U.S. Navy was more prepared for war than it had ever before been. For this reason, senior military planners advocated a naval blockade as the principal strategy of war, at least for some months until a sufficient invasion force could be organized. But this strategically sound proposal was loudly overruled by politicians and the public, both of which criticized war by blockade as both too slow and unworthy of so noble a cause. They insisted on a full-scale invasion as the only manner of combat befitting a crusade undertaken by the righteous might of the American republic. Large numbers of Americans answered the call for volunteers, but the army lacked the transportation and logistics to mount an effective large-scale operation outside of the continental United States. The ground war, as a consequence, got off to a slow start and was plagued not only by delay and disorder, but by tropical diseases endemic to Cuba.

The Spanish-American War was the first American war fought overseas. Although shortly before the war the army's quartermaster General, Brigadier General Marshall I. Ludington, had begun investigating the feasibility of chartering commercial vessels as troop transports, Congress created a roadblock by barring U.S. registry of foreign vessels. For the Cuban expedition, therefore, the army could hire only U.S. vessels. By

July 1, it had chartered forty-three transports, four water boats, three steam lighters, two ocean tugs, and three decked barges for Cuba and another fourteen transports on the Pacific coast for the Philippines expedition. More were added in July and August. Discovering that it could not charter enough vessels, the army purchased outright fourteen additional steamships. Nevertheless, by the time the expedition left Tampa, Florida, on June 14 aboard thirty-eight vessels, faulty estimates of carrying capacity meant that only seventeen thousand out of a planned force of twenty-five thousand could be transported. Worse, the transports had been fitted out to accommodate troops for the short run from Tampa to Havana, the originally planned destination, not for the much longer voyage to Santiago de Cuba, which, the generals decided, was a more feasible spot for landing an invasion force.

Conditions on board the chartered ships were overcrowded and unhealthy. The absence of cooking facilities meant that soldiers had to eat canned beef almost exclusively, rations that, in all too many cases, proved to be spoiled or tainted. Cases of food poisoning, some minor, some debilitating, some fatal, were plentiful. Once landed in Cuba, troops continued to be poorly supplied. Little thought had been given to problems of food spoilage, especially in tropical climates. In the end only 369 soldiers would die in combat on Cuba, whereas 2,565 succumbed to such diseases as typhoid and yellow fever.

The fighting began in Cuba on June 10, 1898, and was concluded there, in Puerto Rico, and the Philippines by a peace protocol on August 12, 1898, followed by the Treaty of Paris signed on December 10. Thanks to the Teller Amendment, U.S. treaty negotiators did not seek to acquire Cuba, but only to oblige Spain to recognize the island's independence. The Teller Amendment did not apply to other Spanish possessions, however, and President McKinley eagerly pressed his negotiators to obtain Spanish cession of Puerto Rico, Guam, and the Philippine Islands. This sparked a bitter fight in the Senate over ratification of the Treaty of Paris, proponents arguing that it was America's duty to serve the world as the agent of Christian civilization whereas opponents decried American imperialism. In the end, the treaty was ratified by a margin of fifty-seven to twenty-seven—just two votes more than the two-thirds majority required.

WAS THE SPANISH-AMERICAN WAR NECESSARY? Flatly, no. Spain had already been "defeated" by American diplomacy. Yet countervailing and overcoming much of the controversy surrounding and following the conflict was the sense of the war as a triumphant demonstration of American arms. Secretary of State John Hay famously characterized the conflict "a splendid little war," because in less than a hundred days the American navy and army had "liberated" 13 million people living on some 165,000 square miles of what had been colonial territory, acquiring in the process a considerable degree of American control over Cuba, and outright possession of Puerto Rico as well as important Pacific territories. True, the brief Spanish-American War gave rise to a costly, bitter, and drawn-out four-year guerrilla insurrection against American dominion in the Philippines, but, from this point on, the United States would be regarded as a world power—a significant power in the Far East and the dominant power in the Caribbean. And for this reason, most Americans took away from the Spanish-American War the taste of victory. It was, at first, sweet—and yet there was, even from the beginning, an undertone of bitterness, the sickly savor of strained legitimacy. Since then, the legacy of the "splendid little war" has been a cocksure conviction of the right of American might, a sense that it must by definition always be unpatriotic to question the motives of any American administration for going to war, provided that the war could be justified as sowing the seeds of a heavenly decreed democracy or inoculating an oppressed people with the blessings of liberty. The brief war with Spain cast a shadow from which American foreign policy has yet to emerge.

Captain Alfred Dreyfus and the Honor of France (1894–1906)

THE DECISION TO DEFEND A BIG LIE

The birth of democratic France was long and difficult. The French Revolution overthrew Louis XVI in 1789, creating a republic of chaos and terror, which provided fertile ground for the rise of Napoléon Bonaparte. Bonaparte assumed dictatorial powers in 1799, then crowned himself emperor of France five years later. After Napoléon's final defeat in 1815, he abdicated in favor of his son, who reigned for little more than two weeks before the allies of the Seventh Coalition—including the United Kingdom, Russia, and Prussia—forced him from the throne. The Bourbon monarchy, from which Louis XVI had ruled, was then reestablished in France, albeit on a constitutional basis, and in 1830, a minor revolution ushered in a monarchy even more tightly circumscribed by constitutional limitations. This was replaced in 1848—a year in which revolution swept Europe—by the Second French Republic. Reactionaries brought about the end of the republic in 1852 when they backed Louis-Napoléon Bonaparte's proclamation of a Second French Empire. Louis-Napoléon, the nephew of Napoléon I, called himself Napoléon III. After an eighteen-year reign, he lost the throne when France suffered a crushing defeat in the Franco-Prussian War of 1870. In his place the Third Republic was established.

From the beginning, a sizable and powerful French minority sought the overthrow of the Third Republic and the restoration, yet again, of the monarchy. Many of these reactionaries were senior military officers or those who had connections with the military. Yet the defeat at the hands of Prussia in 1870 had been so costly and humiliating that the military lacked widespread prestige among French citizens. As a result, the reactionaries could get little traction for their monarchist movement, so that, by the final decade of the nineteenth century, they took a new tack. If the

French people could not be united in *support* of the cause of monarchism, they might well be united *against* a people that cultural and religious tradition had long portrayed as the common enemy: the Jews. Right-wing zealots turned from the forlorn task of overthrowing the Third Republic to rallying the nation in the cause of anti-Semitism. The Jews, whom the reactionaries deliberately confounded with the left-wing fringe of the republican movement, were portrayed as a force bent on weakening and destroying France. Wild accusations were leveled at Jewish political leaders, who responded with disdain, refusing to stoop to answer what they deemed mere slander. Many French men and women chose to interpret such refusals as tacit admissions of guilt. In particular, Édouard Drumont, who founded the Antisemitic League of France, and Paul Déroulède, founder of the League of Patriots, accused French Jews of being Jews first and French citizens second. The anti-Semites argued that, at best, the loyalty of a French Jew was divided and, at worst, to be Jewish was to be a traitor to France.

> "I see just one figure and it is the only one I wanted to show you: the figure of Christ, humiliated, insulted, lacerated by thorns, crucified. Nothing has changed in 1800 years. . . . He is everywhere, hanging in cheap shop windows, abused by caricaturists and writers in Paris full of Jews, as obstinate in their deicide as in the time of Caiaphas."
>
> —Édouard Drumont, *La France Juive*
> *(Jewish France)*, 1885

Over a continually swelling and receding chorus of anti-Semitism, the government of the republic pursued a policy that treated Jews without discrimination. Indeed, French Jews enjoyed greater equality of opportunity than did Jews in virtually any other European country. They held important positions in the government as well as in the army.

Alfred Dreyfus, the son of a Jewish textile manufacturer, was just eleven years old when his native Alsace—he was born in the Alsatian town of Mulhouse—was annexed by the German empire in 1871. He and his family remained in Mulhouse but chose to retain their French citizenship after the annexation. Flushed with both patriotism and images of Prussian soldiers marching triumphantly into his hometown, Dreyfus decided on a career in the French army. In 1877, he enrolled in the prestigious École Polytechnique, where he received military training as well as an education in science. He graduated in 1880 with the rank of sublieutenant and attended advanced artillery school at an academy in Fontainebleau from 1880 to 1882. After completing a course of advanced study, he joined the 32nd Cavalry Regiment and, in 1885, was promoted to lieutenant. Promoted next to captain in 1889, he was assigned as adjutant to the director of the pyrotechnical school in Bourges.

Like some other promising young Jewish men in the liberal climate of the Third Republic, Alfred Dreyfus relished the early fruits of a promising career. He married Lucie Hadamard on April 18, 1891, and, just three days after his wedding, received the welcome news that he had been appointed to the École supérieure de guerre (Superior War College), an institution reserved for the most promising of officers who were earmarked for the highest commands. When he graduated in 1893, standing ninth in his class, he was presented with a certificate of honorable mention and was given a coveted berth as an army headquarters trainee.

Headquarters, however, was a bastion of right-wing politics and, therefore, of anti-Semitism as well. Dreyfus had risen rapidly in the army, but headquarters was a world apart from the rest of the army. Here he was the only Jew. Despite his distinguished academic record, which amply merited a prestigious assignment to the general staff, one of the members of the jury that made such assignments—having expressed his opinion that Jews were undesirable on the general staff—inserted a negative report in Dreyfus's file, thereby lowering his cumulative école grade. When Dreyfus discovered that this officer had also treated another Jewish candidate, one Lieutenant Picard, similarly, both men formally protested to the director of the École supérieure de guerre. General Lebelin de

Dionne responded to the two young men by conveying his profound regrets, but he went on to plead that he had no authority to question the judgment or motives of a senior French officer sitting on the school's jury.

Worse, much worse, was to come. In October 1894, Dreyfus was suddenly arrested on charges of passing military secrets to the German embassy in Paris. The physical evidence against him consisted of a single item, a *bordereau*, or detailed note, listing the specifications of the French army's newest field artillery piece, the Modèle 1890 120-mm Baquet howitzer. An Alsatian cleaning woman in the undercover employ of French counterintelligence had found the *bordereau,* torn up, in the wastepaper basket of Major Max von Schwartzkoppen, the German military attaché based in the embassy. She collected the pieces of the paper, which found their way to the office of France's minister of war, General Auguste Mercier. Suspicion was immediately focused on Dreyfus because he was an artillery officer and an Alsatian, who, until the death of his father in 1893, had returned every year to Mulhouse— now a German town—to visit him. This flimsy circumstantial evidence colored the perception that the handwriting on the *bordereau* looked like that of Dreyfus.

At first, many high-ranking officers were thrilled to be able to brand a Jew as a traitor. On sober reflection, however, it occurred to most of them that the evidence against Dreyfus was tissue thin. By the time this realization set in, a shudder of fear passed through high command and the office of the ministry of war. If the charges were withdrawn, the powerful rightist anti-Semitic press would scream in blazing headlines of a cover-up. No one in the army's inner circle wanted to be accused of defending, let alone covering up for, a Jew. Accordingly, the commanders urged a speedy trial and a prompt conviction, which is precisely what they obtained in December 1894. Summarily, Alfred Dreyfus was packed off to France's infamous Devil's Island, the desolate prison colony off the coast of French Guyana from which there was neither escape nor—most likely—return.

By the time the Dreyfus court-martial got under way, its outcome was a foregone conclusion. Entirely unknown to the defense, prosecutors had prepared a secret dossier, which was presented to the tribunal judges. This was entirely illegal. But that was hardly the worst of it. Prosecutors knew, but did not reveal, that the discarded *bordereau*—the only piece of physical evidence presented in the trial—was written and delivered not by Dreyfus, but by Major Ferdinand Walsin Esterhazy, a French-born infantry officer of Hungarian descent. It has been theorized that Esterhazy, chronically short of cash, sold the information to the German attaché. In 1984, however, a French military historian, Jean Doise, presented evidence that Dreyfus was merely a pawn in a French counterintelligence disinformation scheme aimed at misleading the Germans with phony artillery specifications. Doise claimed that the information written on the *bordereau* was a fabrication and did not reflect the specifications of the actual new weapon, a revolutionary 75-mm field gun then under top-secret development. By publicly prosecuting Dreyfus for revealing a "crucial" military secret, counterintelligence sought to heighten the German perception that it was in possession of an extremely valuable piece of information. Moreover, since Dreyfus was a Jew, his sacrifice in the charade was counted no great loss and even a kind of bonus.

> **"Why are the snob, the German, the Italian, the half-breed for Dreyfus? Why is it that whoever is anti-French, or has a blemish, a sore, an intellectual deformity, a moral infection, sides with Dreyfus? Why is it that anybody who has sold out, been bribed, besmirched, contaminated, corrupted, is for Dreyfus?"**
>
> —Édouard Drumont, 1894

Doise and other recent French military historians have demonstrated that the French army's Bureau de statistique, its counterintelligence arm, operated at and even well beyond the fringes of legality, reporting only— and in absolute secrecy—to the minister of war, General Mercier. If the army and the government could cast Alfred Dreyfus very nearly out of this world in the hope that he would soon be forever forgotten, they could not stop others from keeping his name and his cause alive. Dreyfus's brother Mathieu worked tirelessly to keep the case before the public and government officials. In this he was aided by the Jewish journalist Bernard Lazare and Auguste Scheurer-Kestner, vice president of the senate, who doggedly argued for an official review of the Dreyfus conviction.

In addition, Dreyfus found a far less likely champion. Lieutenant Colonel Marie-Georges Picquart, a career cavalry officer, replaced Lieutenant Colonel Jean Sandherr as director of counterintelligence. Sandherr had a reputation for vigorous anti-Semitism, and, truth be told, Picquart probably had much in common with him in this regard. But Picquart nevertheless possessed a commodity in which Sandherr was clearly deficient: a sense of personal honor, a passion for the truth, and total innocence of any involvement in the court-martial and conviction of Dreyfus. Told in so many words to keep his hands off the Dreyfus case, Picquart earnestly reviewed the evidence. Instantly appalled by its insubstantiality, he pursued the matter of Esterhazy and, in 1896, definitively unmasked him as the real traitor. (Picquart did not suspect that Esterhazy may have been part of a deliberate counterintelligence disinformation scheme.)

Increasingly desperate to perpetuate the cover-up of the facts surrounding the Dreyfus conviction, army high command responded to Picquart's revelations by sending him as far away as possible. In December 1896, the lieutenant colonel was reassigned to a remote posting in Tunisia. Yet still the Dreyfus case would not disappear.

Acting on information provided by Mathieu Dreyfus, Lazare, Scheurer-Kestner, and Picquart, Émile Zola, one of the most popular, esteemed, and controversial writers of turn-of-the-century France, published an open letter to President Félix Faure. The document appeared in the debut issue of L'Aurore (The Dawn), January 13, 1898, under a headline chosen by liberal journalist, politician, and—later— premier of France, Georges Clemenceau: "J'accuse!" ("I accuse!").

"When it comes down to it, you no longer have republican blood in your veins. . . . It's a general you want in your bed. . . . France, if you're not careful, you're on the road to dictatorship. And do you know where else you're going, France? You're on the way to the Church, you're going back to the past, that past of intolerance and theocracy, which your children fought, which they thought they'd killed, by sacrificing their body and their spirit."

—Émile Zola, "Letter to France," published January 6, 1898, one week before his "J'accuse" letter

Zola's open letter named names, prominent names, in the government and military hierarchy. He hoped that doing this would provoke his prosecution for libel, thereby providing a spectacular public trial—outside of military control—in which the facts of the Dreyfus case could be fully exposed.

Zola got what he wanted. The novelist was convicted. Sentenced as he was to a substantial prison term, Zola fled to England, from where he continued to agitate on behalf of Dreyfus, ensuring that the case remained front and center in French life. Zola returned to France after the charges against him were dismissed and his sentence vacated. By that time, in June 1899, the government announced that the Dreyfus verdict would be reviewed.

Unlike the original tribunal, which took place entirely under military control, the review unfolded amid the international attention the world-famous Zola had generated. The most respected personalities of France and other countries were clamoring for justice. Among the French people, however, there developed a sharp division between the Dreyfusards, who believed in the innocence of Dreyfus, and the anti-Dreyfusards, who persisted in the belief that Dreyfus, a Jew, must also be a traitor, as the court-martial had determined.

A Court of Cassation, as the appeal body was called, overturned Dreyfus's conviction and ordered a new court-martial. The evidence Picquart had uncovered was presented, but the officers of the tribunal closed ranks and, amid much public outrage, reconvicted Dreyfus. His sentence was reduced to a total of ten years on Devil's Island. Before he could be returned to incarceration, however, President Émile Loubet pardoned him. Picquart and some others urged Dreyfus to stand on principle and refuse the pardon because it was not an exoneration. But, broken in health by the time he had already spent on Devil's

> **"I was only an artillery officer, whom a tragic error prevented from pursuing his normal career. Dreyfus the symbol . . . is not me."**
>
> **—Alfred Dreyfus, 1906**

Island, Dreyfus believed that returning there, even under shorter sentence, would mean his death. A full exoneration did come, but not until 1906, whereupon Alfred Dreyfus rejoined the army and was created a knight in the Légion d'honneur. He served honorably in World War I, attaining the rank of lieutenant colonel of artillery.

FOR ALL THAT ONE MAN SUFFERED as a result of his unjust conviction, the long cover-up that followed threatened to overturn the Third Republic, which struggled to survive by means of a gossamer web of compromise woven among its own jarring factions and its opponents. Whereas pro-Republic but fractious liberals, socialists, and anticlericalists were overwhelmingly Dreyfusard in their sympathies, the opponents of the Republic, including royalists, conservatives, and the Catholic Church, refused to shed their anti-Dreyfusard stance.

In the end, the Third Republic weathered the storm that was the Dreyfus affair, but the far right that opposed it fared worse. It was not destroyed, but it was for many years diminished and marginalized. In addition, the military endured a loss of public confidence, and for years, all talk of French military honor rang hollow. The Catholic Church likewise suffered a devastating blow with passage in 1905 of a law disestablishing the Church as a state religion and formally separating church and state. Amid the rising tide of French liberalism, however, a diehard core of anti-Dreyfusards became the nucleus of French fascism, the force that helped propel France to ignominious surrender in the early days of World War II and the creation of the collaborationist Vichy regime, which, among many other crimes committed against humanity, ordered the deportation of Alfred Dreyfus's granddaughter to a Nazi extermination camp. As for the French military, it refused to issue any official acknowledgment of Dreyfus's innocence—until it finally yielded in the year 1995, sixty years after Dreyfus's death.

Edward Bernays and the Campaign to Recruit Women Smokers (1929)

THE DECISION TO CREATE AN UNHEALTHY NEED

E dward L. Bernays was a dapper little man of five foot four with a thick but neatly trimmed black moustache and a taste for snap-brim hats and broad silk neckties. He had the look of success and was indeed successful, having become by World War I the youthful dean of American public relations, a field he was still very much in the process of inventing. Although he had been born in Vienna in 1891, the son of Sigmund Freud's younger sister Anna, he had lived in New York City since the age of one and was intensely American—not only a believer in the American dream, but determined to ensure his place as one of the shapers of that dream.

Patriotic to a fault, he tried to enlist in the United States Army on, April 6, 1917, the very day Congress declared war on Germany, but flat feet and poor eyesight kept him out of the service. Nor did it help that he had been born in the "land of the enemy."

Rejected by the army, Bernays tried the Red Cross, the Commission on Military Training (offering to recruit popular musicians to perform at camps), and his local draft board (presenting himself as a statistical manager). Rebuffed by all, he organized several patriotic programs on his own, then at last cadged an interview with journalist, author, and child-labor reformer Ernest Poole, an official with the Committee on Public Information, the government's newly created propaganda bureau. Poole was impressed, but cautioned Bernays that his Austrian birth might prove an insurmountable obstacle to his being hired.

Bernays was subjected to several months of investigation by military intelligence, which discovered, among much else, that, after graduating from high school at age sixteen, Bernays paid homage to his grain-merchant father by earning a degree in agriculture from Cornell University, even though the Manhattan-bred boy had absolutely no interest in farming. That done, he dipped a toe into the grain market, quickly withdrew it, and then began editing *The Medical Review of Reviews* and *The Dietetic and Hygienic Gazette* in 1912. For Bernays, this was hardly a more congenial vocation than buying and selling grain, but he always managed to find something to interest him in the work. For example, he used the pages of the *Review* to persuade physicians to prevail upon their women patients to abandon wearing corsets with stays. It was not so much that Bernays had a passion for liberating women from their whalebone corsets—although he made no secret of his admiration for the female form *au natural*—but that he had an emerging passion for what he would call, unapologetically, *propaganda.*

What was propaganda? As Bernays saw it, advertisers did their jobs crudely and more or less ineffectively, by pleading with prospective customers. In contrast, propagandists began by identifying the leaders—the trendsetters, the pacesetters, the tastemakers—in a given population, then focused their appeal on them, seeking to influence the very creators of influence. To tell women directly that they should shed their corsets might well produce some level of compliance, but Bernays believed it was far more efficient and effective to persuade their doctors to tell them.

Of course, the opportunities for such social leverage—propaganda—were few and far between for an editor of a "medical review of reviews." Nevertheless, just two months after he had begun editing it, that journal unexpectedly brought him something new. A physician submitted a review, not of an article reporting on some medical experiment, but a rave for a new play. Eugène Brieux's *Damaged Goods* told the story of one George Dupont, a man who, on the eve of marriage, is diagnosed with syphilis. Postpone your wedding, and you can be cured, Dupont's doctor tells him. But profound social embarrassment heedlessly propels him into the ceremony, he marries, fathers an infected child, and gives his wife a disease that renders her sterile.

Not only did Bernays publish the review—in itself a daring step at a time and in a nation which simply did not openly discuss syphilis and sex—he and his partner in the journal, a high school chum named Fred Robinson, decided to get *Damaged Goods* produced on the most public of American venues: Broadway. They discovered that Richard Bennett, one of the stars of turn-of-the-century American theater (and better known to later generations as the father of film actress Joan Bennett), had expressed interest in backing a production of the play. Bernays wrote to him: "The editors of the *Medical Review of Reviews* support your praiseworthy intention to fight sex-pruriency in the United States by producing Brieux's play *Damaged Goods*. You can count on our help." Bennett replied enthusiastically, promising to furnish a cast of marquee stars who would work without pay in this crusade against crippling Victorianism. However, it would be up to Bernays to raise money for renting a theater, hiring a crew, and myriad other expenses. It would also be up to him to persuade New York's watchdogs of decency not to shut the play down on opening night. After all, he aspired to Broadway, not the Bowery.

Bernays reflected on the nature of the project at hand. By presenting *Damaged Goods*, he hoped ultimately to effect social change. However, he reasoned that in order even to get the play to the stage, he would have to bring about some of that social change first. Controversy always poses a threat, but it also presents an opportunity, the very opportunity to convert controversy into a cause. This, Bernays understood, would not happen on his say-so alone, any more than women would cast off their corsets because he told them to. As with the corset crusade, he decided to identify and appeal to the leaders of influence in the community, and he did so not in the person of a twenty-one-year-old editor, but as the director of the "*Medical Review of Reviews* Sociological Fund Committee." To this organization, which had a name before it had a membership, Bernays drew Mrs. William K. Vanderbilt Sr.; John D. Rockefeller Jr.; Franklin and Eleanor Roosevelt; the Reverend John Haynes Holmes, a prominent Unitarian minister; and Dr. William Jay Schieffelin , who had developed a new drug treatment for syphilis. The participation of these leading figures transformed local society just enough to yield a flood of contributions to the fund. Moreover, it made the play, from its premiere, a hot ticket.

Most drama reviewers were, in fact, unimpressed. They did not find *Damaged Goods* obscene or offensive, but (in the words of one) "dull and almost unendurable." That hardly mattered. Drama critics are not society's leaders. They might be able to kill most plays, but not this one, which mounted the boards already anointed by society's moral, civic, and commercial luminaries, who created a social context in which the play simply could not be condemned or rejected. By the time *Damaged Goods* traveled to Washington, it was no longer a source of controversy but the focus of a cause. Rabbi Abram Simon, of the Washington Hebrew Congregation confessed, "If I could preach from my pulpit a sermon one tenth as powerful, as convincing, as far-reaching, and as helpful as this performance of *Damaged Goods* must be, I would consider that I had achieved the triumph of my life." Police Commissioner Cuno H. Rudolph remarked, "I was deeply impressed by what I saw, and I think that the drama should be repeated in every city, a matinee one day for father and son and the next day for mother and daughter." The surgeon general of the United States, Dr. Rupert Blue, pronounced it "a most striking and telling lesson. For years we have been fighting these conditions in the navy. It is high time that civilians awakened to the dangers surrounding them and crusaded against them in a proper manner."

So Edward Bernays had succeeded in making an impact on society. But just what impact had he made? On one level, he had found a way to open to discussion a sensitive subject of public health. That, however, was not the money-maker. What Bernays had really succeeded in doing was to find a way to get sex onto the American stage or, as one editorial put it, to make the hour strike "sex o'clock in America," *and* to do so with the blessing of society's religious, legal, political, and medical leaders. Such was the power of propaganda, which Bernays concisely defined as "a consistent, enduring effort to create or shape events to influence the relations of the public to an enterprise, idea or group."

> **"The only question is this: Is this play decent? My answer is that it is the decentest play that has been in New York for a year. It is so decent that it is religious."**
>
> —Review of *Damaged Goods* published in *Hearst's Magazine,* 1913

At length pronounced a loyal American by military intelligence investigators, Bernays duly contributed his expertise to the American propaganda effort for World War I. As much as he contributed, however, he learned even more, writing in his 1928 book *Propaganda,* that "the astounding success of propaganda during the war . . . opened the eyes of the intelligent few in all departments of life to the possibilities of regimenting the public mind." He and the other Committee on Public Information propagandists "not only appealed to the individual by means of every approach—visual, graphic, and auditory—to support the national endeavor, but . . . also secured the cooperation of the key men in every group—persons whose mere word carried authority to hundreds or thousands or hundreds of thousands of followers. They . . . gained the support of fraternal, religious, commercial, patriotic, social and local groups whose members took their opinions from their accustomed leaders and spokesmen."

World War I produced a host of new weapons that would both menace and shape the twentieth century, but none was more powerful than the modern concept of propaganda, and Edward Bernays emerged from the war effort as a pioneer and leading practitioner of a new American industry: public relations.

"We are governed, our minds are molded, our tastes formed, our ideas suggested, largely by men we have never heard of. This is a logical result of the way in which our democratic society is organized."

—Edward L. Bernays, *Propaganda* (1928)

Having employed propaganda to help America make "the world safe for democracy," Bernays wielded it after the war to sell everything from the purity of Ivory soap, to the economic message of the 1920 NAACP conference, the (apparently very well disguised) "warmth" of Calvin Coolidge, and the must-have desirability of General Motors automobiles. Then, in 1928, he was approached by a new client.

George Washington Hill was the hard-driving head of the American Tobacco Company, manufacturer of the nation's fastest-growing brand of cigarette, Lucky Strikes. By the 1920s, the cigarette business was booming. Before World War I, cigarettes had seemed somehow unmanly, and sales lagged far behind those of cigars, pipes, and even chewing tobacco. In the trenches, however, a cigarette came more easily to the hand than either a cigar or pipe, calmed the nerves, and provided a needed lift. The army even started issuing cigarettes with doughboys' rations. Then, after the armistice, when Johnny came marching home, he did so with a cigarette between his lips.

And that was just fine with George Washington Hill. But it wasn't nearly fine enough.

The war had made cigarettes popular with men, but, Hill pointed out, half the nation's population consisted of women. "If I can crack that market," he told Edward Bernays, "I'll get more than my share of it. It will be like opening a new gold mine right in our front yard."

Both Bernays and Hill recognized that among the many social changes wrought by the war was an increase in women's use of cigarettes; nevertheless, by 1928, women accounted for just 12 percent of the cigarette market. Hill's idea for getting more women to smoke was to present cigarettes as a way to get slim or to stay that way—at a time when a slender, streamlined figure was becoming more and more fashionable. He shared with Bernays the slogan he'd come up with, "Reach for a Lucky instead of a sweet," and the propagandist ran with it.

Bernays did not blatantly trumpet the slogan on billboards and in magazines. That was mere advertising. Instead, he sought nothing less than to reshape American society and culture, at least to the extent of changing the nation's habits of consumption by mounting an antisweets campaign. In this effort, he turned first to Nickolas Muray, a prominent photographer who was also a close friend. He asked Muray to praise the virtues of being svelte, and he asked him to enlist other photographers and artists to do the same. Soon, magazines and newspapers were carrying commentaries and interviews by these graphic tastemakers, all of whom promoted a slender figure as the standard of feminine beauty, a standard impossible to achieve if one habitually snacked on sweets.

Bernays fed editors and journalists a steady stream of "thin" propaganda, ranging from photographs of willowy Parisian models wearing the latest in haute couture to testimonials he had secured (and paid for) from physicians, including one George F. Buchan, M.D., retired chief of the British Association of Medical Officers of Health, who wrote an article advising that the "correct way" to end a meal was "with fruit, coffee and a cigarette." He explained that the fruit hardens the gums and cleans the teeth, the coffee stimulates "the flow of saliva [and acts] as a mouth wash," and the "cigarette disinfects the mouth and soothes the nerves."

That was not all. Bernays possessed a genius for finding and exploiting every possible portal of social opinion. He got the nation's dean of dancing instructors, Arthur Murray, to bemoan the sad "results of over-indulgence" in sweets as this was evidenced on the dance floor, "causing embarrassment not only to one's dancing partner but also to other dancers by encroaching on more than a fair share of space. . . . Dancers today," Murray advised, "when tempted to overindulge at the punch bowl or the buffet, [should] reach for a cigarette instead."

But Bernays was not content with mere testimonials. He combined these by altering the very environment, striving to create a world in which the cigarette was ubiquitous. He mounted a campaign to persuade hotels and restaurants to add cigarettes to dessert-list menus, and he provided such magazines as *House and Garden* with feature articles that included menus designed to preserve readers "from the dangers of overeating." Each of these menus concluded with advice that the reader "reach for a cigarette instead of dessert."

The idea was not only to influence opinion, but to remold life itself. Bernays approached designers, architects, and cabinetmakers in an effort to persuade them to design kitchen cabinets that included special compartments for cigarettes, and he spoke to the manufacturers of kitchen containers to add cigarette tins to their traditional lines of labeled containers for coffee, tea, sugar, and flour. The kitchen was the feminine domain par excellence, and Bernays's aim was to transform the perception of cigarettes from an occasional indulgence into a kitchen staple, the equivalent of coffee, tea, sugar, salt, and flour, and, like these, a staple no homemaker could afford to run out of.

The multifaceted campaign had an impact, both on cigarette sales and on the sales of sweets, prompting candy and snack makers to cry foul and raising howls of protest against what they called misleading and fraudulent propaganda. Bernays turned the outrage and accusations to the advantage of his client by persuading a prominent economist to send letters to professors of business touting the controversy as a prime example of "the new competition." While conventional advertisers assiduously avoided controversy, Bernays courted it as a means of generating media coverage. Soon "the new competition," as manifested

in the battle between the sellers of sweets and the purveyors of cigarettes, was winning precious column inches in the nation's magazines
and newspapers.

Hill was delighted and commissioned Bernays to expand the
campaign by promoting an elaborate national "moderation movement,"
which Bernays was to define narrowly as the substitution of cigarettes for
snacks. Headlining the movement was a team of six ultra-glamorous
Ziegfeld girls, who banded together as the "Ziegfled Countour, Curve and
Charm Club," united in signing a pledge to "renounce the false pleasure
of the table—fattening foods, drinks, and cloying sweets. But I make no
sacrifices: I shall smoke cigarettes."

By December of 1928, Hill was able to congratulate Bernays on
having helped American Tobacco achieve a $32 million increase in
revenues and growth in sales of Lucky Strikes that outshone the increase
in "all other Cigarettes combined."

Yet he wanted still more.

"How can we get women to smoke on the street?" Hill asked Bernays
early in 1929. "They're smoking indoors. But, damn it, if they spend half
the time outdoors and we can get 'em to smoke outdoors, we'll damn near
double our female market. Do something. Act!"

With cigarette use among women certainly climbing, Bernays asked
himself what social taboo discouraged women from taking the next step,
smoking in public. Then he stopped asking himself and decided instead
to consult America's most prominent disciple of his own uncle Sigmund
Freud, the psychoanalyst A. A. Brill.

Brill did not hesitate in his reply: "It is," he said, "perfectly normal for
women to want to smoke cigarettes." That was good news. But how could
one get them actually to do this "perfectly normal" thing?

Brill continued: "The emancipation of women"—the Nineteenth
Amendment had given American women the vote in 1920—"has suppressed
many of their feminine desires. More women now do the same work as men
do. Many women bear no children; those who do bear have fewer children.

Feminine traits are masked. Cigarettes, which are equated with men, become torches of freedom."

Torches of freedom! To Edward Bernays, the phrase was a gift of incalculable value.

Almost instantly, he decided to organize a parade of women—prominent, pace-setting women—who would stride the street ostentatiously igniting their *torches of freedom.* Moreover, there was already a parade ready-made: the celebrated "Easter parade"—that formalized informal annual promenade of the well heeled along Manhattan's most fashionable boulevard, Fifth Avenue.

Bernays called a friend who worked at *Vogue* magazine and obtained a list of thirty prominent debutantes. He then composed a telegram to be sent to each of them over the signature of Bertha Hunt, his own secretary:

> In the interests of equality of the sexes and to fight another sex taboo I and other young women will light another torch of freedom by smoking cigarettes while strolling Fifth Avenue Easter Sunday. We are doing this to combat the silly prejudice that the cigarette is suitable for the home, the restaurant, the taxicab, the theater lobby but never, no, never for the sidewalk. Women smokers and their escorts will stroll from Forty-Eighth Street to Fifty-Fourth Street on Fifth Avenue between Eleven-Thirty and One O'Clock.

Simultaneously, Bernays put a similar message in the form of advertisements in all of the New York newspapers, this time over the signature of Ruth Hale, wife of the influential *New York World* columnist Heywood Broun and one of the nation's best-known feminists.

Having ignited the "torches of freedom" parade, Bernays left to chance nothing about the event itself. The object of the parade, Bernays explained in a memo to Hill and his own staff, was to generate legitimate news stories equating outdoor smoking with women's rights. He advised his staffers to monitor the resulting stories carefully and to be prepared to answer and counter any that were negative. While Bernays could not tell reporters what to write, he took pains to orchestrate the parade so that they would be most likely to write the story he wanted. He arranged for women to join the parade at such strategic points as Saint Thomas's Episcopal Church and Saint Patrick's Cathedral, as well as "the Baptist church where John D. Rockefeller attends." They were emphatically not to light up on the church steps, but to do so as soon as they joined the parade. There should be at least three women at each church, "goodlooking [but] not . . . too model-y.'?" Bernays wanted no actresses—since their inclusion would seem a naked publicity stunt—but he did approve of the participation of prominent feminists and members of the Women's Party. Moreover, he asked the women to convene, in his office, on Good Friday afternoon, to be issued "their final instructions." Above all, he was anxious to ensure that all of the women were issued plenty of Lucky Strikes. The women were thoroughly coached in what Bernays called "business," a term he used in the theatrical sense of a choreographed routine. Such business "must be worked out as if by a theatrical director," Bernays advised his staffers, "as for example: one woman seeing another smoke, opens her purse, finds cigs but no matches, asks the other for a light. At least some of the women should have men with them." Finally, just to be safe, Bernays arranged for his own photographers to capture the event "to guard against the possibility that the news photographers do not get good pictures."

The "torches of freedom" parade succeeded even beyond Bernays's wildest dreams. It spawned newspaper stories not only in New York City, but all across the country. Women in one American town after another followed the lead of the New Yorkers, taking to the streets, and lighting their own torches of freedom. The women of the United States became smokers.

And Bernays did not let up—especially after stories began to appear concerning the harmful effects of smoking. Everyone was familiar with "smoker's cough," of course, which suggested that, at the very least, cigarettes were irritating to the throat. American Tobacco's Hill sought to counter that impression by recruiting famous opera stars to testify in print that not only were Lucky Strikes irritation-free, they actually *soothed* the throat. As early as the early 1930s, however, some medical authorities began linking cigarette smoking with cancer. Because mainstream medical opinion was very slow to support this view, however, Bernays took steps to counter the relatively few scare stories with what he called "a barrage" of favorable medical opinions concerning cigarettes. Bernays peppered the nation's editors with such pro-cigarette medical propaganda—"not so much with the purpose of getting this material printed," he wrote in a memo to American Tobacco, "but doing it rather to build up such a constructive picture of the cigarette in the minds of editors that when a [negative] story . . . comes along, they will hesitate to print it because they have been convinced of the contrary point of view." Thus Bernays frankly mounted a brainwashing campaign aimed directly at those who decided what news got printed and what news did not.

—

NO ONE KNOWS WHETHER EDWARD BERNAYS himself believed in the 1920s and 1930s that the cigarettes he promoted were, in fact, killers. It is known that he did not himself smoke and that he made a vigorous effort to get his wife, Doris, to kick her cigarette habit. Bernays's elder daughter recalled that her father "didn't think [cigarettes] were good for Mother," and his younger daughter remarked that he used to confiscate her smokes whenever he found them, pull them out of the packs, "and just snap them like bones, just snap them in half and throw them in the toilet. He hated her smoking." (Mrs. Bernays did not quit until the 1940s, and then only after her doctor told her that smoking was aggravating an old circulatory ailment and might lead to amputation of her leg.)

What is very well documented is the action that Edward Bernays took in 1964, some thirty-five years after his "torches of freedom" campaign, following the release of the U.S. surgeon general's epoch-making report definitively linking cigarettes with lung cancer and heart disease. Bernays attempted nothing less than to undo the results of his 1929 efforts by drawing up a massive PR push designed, he said, to portray smoking as "an antisocial action which no self-respecting person carries on in the presence of others." He envisioned enlisting filmmakers, celebrities, clergy, physicians, and captains of industry in a massive effort to "outlaw and eliminate cigarette smoking." Ultimately, such an all-out war on smoking was beyond even the genius of Edward Bernays, who had to content himself with contributing his expertise to far more modest educational and antismoking efforts sponsored by the U.S. government. The torches of freedom proved very, very difficult to extinguish. In the United States today, an estimated 25.1 million men (23.4 percent) and 20.9 million women (18.5 percent) smoke cigarettes.

Richard M. Nixon and Watergate (1973)

THE DECISION TO LOAD THE DICE

Historians seldom use the word "stupid." But they certainly could in this case. Whatever else Watergate was—illegal, unconstitutional, immoral, arrogant—it was stupid. That much is clear from the merest gist of the event.

On June 17, 1972, during President Richard M. Nixon's reelection campaign, five burglars were arrested in the headquarters of the Democratic National Committee at the Watergate office-hotel-apartment complex in Washington, D.C. It was a minor break-in, no shots fired, in a city swept daily by violent crime. So where was the news story?

As it turned out, these burglars were really "Plumbers." On July 17, 1971, the president's chief domestic advisor, John Ehrlichman, created this covert band, recruited and operating outside of the law, whose original mission was to plug "leaks"—security breaches—that had sprung or that might spring in the aftermath of the publication of the "Pentagon Papers." One of those assigned to the unit, a lawyer and former aide to Henry Kissinger named David Young, put a sign on his door—PLUMBER—reflecting the leak-plugging mission. The name stuck, although President Nixon claimed not to have heard the term until a year and a half after the unit had been put together.

The perceived need for the creation of the Plumbers takes some explaining, if only because the group's existence is a major part of the stupidity of the whole affair.

In June 1971, the *New York Times* published a series of articles on a secret government study officially titled "History of the U.S. Decision Making Process in Vietnam," popularly called the "Pentagon Papers." A massive forty-seven-volume document compiled between 1967 and 1969 by U.S. Department of Defense analysts, it revealed in agonizing detail how our nation's government had systematically deceived the American people as to its policies and practices in Southeast Asia from the 1950s through the 1960s. The most shocking revelations cut to the very core of why we were mired in Vietnam. For instance: The CIA had conspired to overthrow and assassinate South Vietnam president Ngo Dinh Diem, because he was uncooperative; the 1964 Gulf of Tonkin Resolution, ostensibly passed in response to purported North Vietnamese attacks on two U.S. destroyers, was actually drafted months in advance of the attacks, the authenticity of which were, in any case, highly dubious. With the Gulf of Tonkin Resolution, Congress handed President Lyndon Johnson virtually unlimited authority to wage war. The *Times* came by the document when, in 1971, one of its authors, Daniel Ellsberg, an MIT professor, government consultant, and former U.S. Marine, leaked it to the paper.

At first, President Nixon was almost pleased by the revelations of the Pentagon Papers. After all, the deceptions and misdeeds exposed were almost all those of Democratic administrations, from Harry S. Truman to Lyndon Johnson. Nixon and his administration weren't even touched. Now, here's the stupid part: The president could not resist looking this political gift horse in the mouth. He came to believe that this massive leak of a top-secret government document set a dangerous precedent. If earlier administrations could be breached, so could his own. Leaks—any and all leaks—had to be plugged, and so the Plumbers were born. Henry Kissinger, at the time Nixon's national security advisor, had known Ellsberg at Harvard and told the president that Ellsberg was "emotionally unstable." Nixon later claimed that what most alarmed him about the leaking of the Pentagon Papers was the fact that the Rand Corporation, the private, government-sponsored "think tank" that had employed Ellsberg, possessed 173,000 classified documents. "I wondered how many of these Ellsberg might have and what else he might give to the newspapers," Nixon wrote in his 1978 *Memoirs of Richard Nixon.* Yet, clearly, the threats that prompted Nixon to authorize the Plumbers did not exist directly against his administration; but even if we accept his rationale that Ellsberg might leak more documents, it was the creation of the Plumbers, an illegal, immoral, unconstitutional palace guard assigned to engage in criminal acts, that posed the far graver and more immediate threat to the nation, the Constitution, and to the president himself. Whatever danger Ellsberg might represent was pure theory, conjecture; the Plumbers were real, and they were against the law.

In an effort to discredit and intimidate Ellsberg, the Plumbers broke into the office of his psychiatrist, in search of embarrassing revelations, and then also planned, but never executed, a physical assault against Ellsberg himself. Then, very soon, the mission of the Plumbers expanded far beyond the mere plugging of leaks. Here's where things got even stupider.

As the 1972 elections approached, perhaps the only American who harbored doubts about the inevitable reelection of Richard Milhous Nixon was Richard Milhous Nixon. The Democrats were in disarray, President Nixon's top diplomat, Henry Kissinger, had just announced that peace in Vietnam was "at hand," international relations were generally improving, especially with Communist China, and the American people, as usual, were reluctant to do what Abraham Lincoln had advised against during his own reelection bid in 1864: change horses in midstream. Rarely has a second-term hopeful had more reason for realistic optimism.

Stupefyingly, this was not enough for Nixon. Determined to move the odds even more overwhelmingly in his favor, he directed his Committee to Re-elect the President—an organization universally known by the apparently unself-conscious acronym CREEP—to mount a campaign of sabotage against the Democratic Party and its presidential candidates, a campaign consisting of what CREEP operatives called "dirty tricks"—disinformation, rumors, lies, and outright forgeries aimed at smearing all challengers. The covert acquisition of intelligence was seen as a prerequisite to at least some of the sabotage, and so the Plumbers were dispatched to the Watergate to plant bugs (electronic eavesdropping devices) at Democratic National Headquarters.

The five Watergate burglars, Plumbers all, included anti-Castro Cuban refugees and James McCord Jr., a former CIA and FBI operative and now "security officer" for CREEP. McCord reported directly to the head of CREEP, Nixon's campaign manager, former U.S. Attorney General John Mitchell. The burglary he led was inept in the extreme, and the burglars amateurish to the point of slapstick. One of them actually carried in his pocket an address book that included the name of E. Howard Hunt. A former CIA agent who had been in charge of the infamously bungled Bay of Pigs operation, Hunt had made a living as the author of pulpy spy novels but now served as assistant to Charles Colson, special counsel to none other than President Nixon. As if the line from the Watergate burglars to the president had not been drawn quite directly enough, the address listed for Hunt was, simply, "The White House."

Until his dying day, the president claimed that the first he heard of the Watergate break-in was when he read a *Miami Herald* article (he was vacationing in Key Biscayne, Florida, at the time) headlined "Miamians Held in D.C. Try to Bug Demo Headquarters." In any case—also to the end of his life—Nixon failed to recognize any significant crime in the break-in and the bugging. "My reaction to the Watergate break-in was completely pragmatic," he wrote in his *Memoirs*. "If it was also cynical, it was a cynicism born of experience. I had been in politics too long, and seen everything from dirty tricks to vote fraud. I could not muster much moral outrage over a political bugging." Once the Watergate scandal broke, Nixon would appear on television to assure the American people, "I'm not a crook," yet his rationale for the break-in and bugging was that of a career criminal: *Everybody does it, so it can't be all that wrong.* As no judge or jury would accept such a plea from a criminal defendant, so the public would reject it from Nixon. Yet only as the Watergate crisis unfolded did the full extent of the administration's criminal conduct come to light. It was not a matter of a few "dirty tricks," a bugging incident, or even vote fraud. Testimony before Congress would reveal political espionage and sabotage, illegal wiretapping—including wiretaps on the press and ordinary citizens—and, to pay for a band of covert operators (including the Plumbers), a secret slush fund of money laundered through Mexico.

> **"I made my mistakes, but in all my years of public life, I have never, *never* profited from public service. . . . I welcome this kind of examination because people have got to know whether or not their president is a crook. Well, I'm not a crook."**
>
> **—President Nixon, press conference, Disney World, November 12, 1973**

The scandal that followed the Watergate break-in was slow to come to a boil, but it was kept simmering by the work of two enterprising young *Washington Post* reporters, Bob Woodward and Carl Bernstein. Although that simmering was insufficient to stop Nixon's landslide victory over Democrat George McGovern, the scandal hijacked the president's second term, beginning on March 19, 1973, when McCord, convicted on eight counts of conspiracy, burglary, and wiretapping—but clearly unwilling to fall on his sword to save his president—wrote a letter to U.S. District Judge John Sirica claiming that his original plea and testimony (a portion of which, he now admitted, was perjured) had been forced on him by White House counsel John Dean and former Attorney General John N. Mitchell.

McCord's was the first of many fingers that pointed, one by one, to the top. As one Nixon aide after another was questioned, tried, and convicted, they talked. Nixon and an ever-contracting circle of intimate advisors compounded the stupidity of the Plumbers' project—the criminal interference in an election already won—by desperate attempts at suppressing the Watergate investigation and covering up incriminating evidence. The president prevailed on the CIA—in his own words—"to intervene and limit the FBI investigation" into Watergate. This, of course, constituted a criminal obstruction of justice, but, remarkably, President Nixon did not see it that way. In his *Memoirs*, he admitted that at the end of June and beginning of July 1972, he "took the first steps down the road that eventually led to the end of my presidency," doing "nothing to discourage" the fabricated explanations that "were being considered to explain the break-in" and also approving the CIA's obstruction of the FBI. Nixon later claimed that he understood how his "actions and inactions during this period would appear to many as part of a widespread and conscious cover-up," but he himself claimed not to "see them as such." Nixon noted in *Memoirs*:

> I was handling in a pragmatic way what I perceived as an annoying and strictly political problem. I was looking for a way to deal with Watergate that would minimize damage to me, my friends, and my campaign, while giving the least advantage to my political opposition. I saw Watergate as politics pure and simple. We were going to play it tough. I never doubted that that was exactly how the other side would have played it.

His head freighted with words and phrases like "pragmatic," "strictly political," "minimize damage," "and play it tough," the president's heart had no room for the likes of character, principle, Constitution, oath of office, law, democracy, or even America. Because the actions he took were pragmatic and politically expedient, Nixon argued, they were somehow not illegal or immoral. Besides, that was "how the other side would have played it."

"I don't give a shit what happens. I want you all to stonewall, let them plead the Fifth Amendment, cover up or anything else, if it'll save it, save the plan. That's the whole point."

—President Nixon to White House counsel John Dean, March 22, 1973

Blinded by pragmatic expedience, the president broke the law and violated his oath of office. These were crimes. Whatever we may think of criminality, most of us admit, from time to time, the wit or even the sheer genius behind certain crimes—the multimillion-dollar heist in which everyone gets away. But the Watergate crimes were hardly evidence of genius, and the stupidity that crowned their immorality was the most damning evidence that came to light in the Senate investigations: hours of tape recordings Nixon himself had ordered in which he incriminated himself, not as author of the original crimes but of their cover-up.

In an effort to keep the tapes out of the hands of the courts and a congressional Watergate committee, Nixon clung to the first and last resort of cornered American presidents, a plea of "executive privilege," but he was rebuffed by the Supreme Court. Increasingly desperate, the president went after Archibald Cox, the special prosecutor in charge of investigating Watergate. Nixon ordered Elliot L. Richardson, who had replaced John Mitchell as attorney general when Mitchell resigned that post to head up CREEP, to fire Cox. On October 20, 1973, Richardson refused and resigned in protest, as did his deputy, William Ruckelshaus. Undaunted, Nixon found a willing headsman in his solicitor general, Robert H. Bork, a conservative stalwart with an untroubled conscience. The press dubbed the whole ghastly affair the "Saturday night massacre," and it served, of course, only to paint Nixon's guilt in darker hues and broader strokes. Nor did it help the image of the White House when Vice President Spiro T. Agnew, indicted for federal income tax fraud and for bribes taken when he had served as Maryland governor, abruptly resigned his office at about this time.

Faced with imminent impeachment, President Nixon appointed a new special prosecutor and, at length, released transcripts of some of the

White House tapes. The result was the final undoing of a doomed presidency. During July 27–30, the House Judiciary Committee issued a recommendation that Nixon be impeached on charges of obstruction of justice, abuse of presidential powers, and attempting to impede the impeachment process by defying committee subpoenas. This prompted the president to release the remaining White House tapes on August 5, 1974. Although they included an appallingly suspicious eighteen-and-a-half-minute gap, they contained enough to serve as what the press called "the smoking gun," irrefutably revealing that Nixon had attempted to block the FBI's inquiry into the Watergate burglary. Four days after the release of the tapes, Nixon became the first president in American history to resign from office. He made the announcement to the American people on television, on August 8, 1974:

> This is the 37th time I have spoken to you from this office, where so many decisions have been made that shaped the history of this Nation. Each time I have done so to discuss with you some matter that I believe affected the national interest.
>
> In all the decisions I have made in my public life, I have always tried to do what was best for the Nation. Throughout the long and difficult period of Watergate, I have felt it was my duty to persevere, to make every possible effort to complete the term of office to which you elected me.
>
> In the past few days, however, it has become evident to me that I no longer have a strong enough political base in the Congress to justify continuing that effort. As long as there was such a base, I felt strongly that it was necessary to see the constitutional process through to its conclusion, that to do otherwise would be unfaithful to the spirit of that deliberately difficult process and a dangerously destabilizing precedent for the future.
>
> But with the disappearance of that base, I now believe that the constitutional purpose has been served, and there is no longer a need for the process to be prolonged.

I would have preferred to carry through to the finish whatever the personal agony it would have involved, and my family unanimously urged me to do so. But the interest of the Nation must always come before any personal considerations.

From the discussions I have had with Congressional and other leaders, I have concluded that because of the Watergate matter I might not have the support of the Congress that I would consider necessary to back the very difficult decisions and carry out the duties of this office in the way the interests of the Nation would require.

I have never been a quitter. To leave office before my term is completed is abhorrent to every instinct in my body. But as President, I must put the interest of America first. America needs a full-time President and a full-time Congress, particularly at this time with problems we face at home and abroad.

To continue to fight through the months ahead for my personal vindication would almost totally absorb the time and attention of both the President and the Congress in a period when our entire focus should be on the great issues of peace abroad and prosperity without inflation at home.

Therefore, I shall resign the Presidency effective at noon tomorrow. Vice President Ford will be sworn in as President at that hour in this office.

———

THE STUPIDITY OF THE WATERGATE FIASCO was multifaceted, culminating in a plot device that might have been drawn from Greek tragedy. Recall that the very steps Oedipus took to avoid his fate brought that fate about. So it was with Nixon. Intent on winning an election whose conclusion was foregone, he took steps to secure his victory that assured his undoing.

For most of his career, Richard M. Nixon was one of the most personally despised men in American politics, but even his most ardent detractors never called him stupid. Watergate was stupid. Nixon was not. This paradox may never be explained more adequately than by blandly observing that smart people sometimes do stupid things. But maybe the folly of Watergate has deeper roots, more deeply tangled roots, roots that partake more profoundly of Greek tragedy—and all that it implies about human nature—than a superficial resemblance between a plot drawn by Sophocles and the plot of the Watergate affair. The Greek philosopher Heraclitus identified the essence of life and of history as one and the same with the essence of tragedy. "Character," he said, "is destiny." Harry Truman called Nixon "a shifty-eyed goddamn liar . . . one of the few in the history of this country to run for high office talking out of both sides of his mouth at the same time and lying out of both sides." Barry Goldwater pronounced him "the most dishonest individual I have ever met in my life. He lied to his wife, his family, his friends, his colleagues in the Congress, lifetime members of his own political party, the American people and the world." Henry Kissinger, first Nixon's national security advisor and then his secretary of state, admired him deeply, yet even he understood that Watergate, in all its folly, flowed directly from the character of its author. "It was a Greek tragedy," Kissinger said. "Nixon was fulfilling his own nature. Once it started it could not end otherwise."

Metropolitan Edison and Three Mile Island (1979)

THE FAILURE TO UNDERSTAND

At about four o'clock in the morning on March 28, 1979, the cooling system of Unit Two reactor at the nuclear power generating plant on Three Mile Island, near the Pennsylvania capital of Harrisburg, malfunctioned. The main feedwater pumps stopped running, which prevented steam generators from drawing off heat. The skyrocketing temperatures caused the steam turbine and then the reactor itself to shut down. These failures all occurred in the "secondary," or nonnuclear, portion of the plant, but they created abnormal pressure in the "primary," or nuclear, portion of the plant. In response, a relief valve automatically opened, relieving the pressure buildup, but then malfunctioned by failing to close after the pressure had been relieved. The result was an out-gushing of radioactive water from the reactor's cooling system. Without water to cool them, more than half of the reactor's thirty-six thousand nuclear fuel rods would rupture in a partial-core meltdown, potentially the prelude to a full meltdown: a doomsday scenario.

> "I first learned of the accident on Wednesday morning, March 28, 1979, at about 10 minutes before 8:00 when I received a phone call from our director of emergency management. My first thought was that, even though I knew little of nuclear technology, no accident at a nuclear plant could be anything but serious."
>
> —Pennsylvania governor Richard Thornburgh, *Washington Post* interview, March 29, 1999

Events moved quickly, but plant workers, inadequately trained and saddled with a plant design that provided too little information and control, moved nearly in slow motion. It was not until 7:00 AM that supervisors declared a "site area emergency." Twenty-four minutes later, this was escalated to a "general emergency." Yet the first public announcement of a "problem with the plant" came a full hour later, at 8:25, over Harrisburg radio station WKBO. The Associated Press announced the general emergency at 9:00 AM. During the course of the day, Pennsylvania's Lieutenant Governor William Scranton III appeared on local TV to warn residents to stay indoors and close their doors and windows. Many took this as a call to evacuate, more than one hundred thousand people fleeing the Pennsylvania capital and surrounding areas.

That evening, Walter Cronkite, the gold standard among broadcast anchormen, opened his nightly CBS newscast by pronouncing the disaster "the first step in a nuclear nightmare."

Over the next five days, Pennsylvania and the nation feared a full-scale meltdown. As if that weren't bad enough, there were also fears that a giant bubble of hydrogen, which had apparently accumulated within the reactor containment building, might ignite and explode, catastrophically releasing even more radiation, which could render a large portion of Pennsylvania permanently uninhabitable. Moreover, in a coincidence even Hollywood would never have dared to script, a movie called *The China Syndrome* had been released just twelve days before the accident. Starring Jane Fonda and Michael Douglas, the film dramatized the consequences—along with a sinister corporate cover-up—of a nuclear power plant accident that was eerily similar to what was happening at Three Mile Island. The film's title was a darkly ironic allusion to the theory that a full-scale meltdown of a reactor's core would burn so intensely that superheated molten radioactive material would sear its way through the reactor floor and deep into the earth—in effect, clear down to China.

About nine hours after the initial malfunction, the hydrogen that had collected within the reactor building did ignite and burn, but produced an explosion so small that it was largely unnoticed. A full sixteen hours passed before plant workers restarted pumps that deliver water that began to cool the reactor's core temperature. This was far too late to have prevented about half the core from melting, and the whole system remained dangerously radioactive. After four more very scary days, the emergency was declared to have ended—although steam and hydrogen continued to be removed from the reactor using methods that included venting the radioactive gas and vapor directly into the atmosphere, which caused great concern among many local residents.

Even though half the core melted down, the reactor vessel that shielded the core held, remaining intact and successfully containing the damaged, intensely radioactive fuel. In the end, despite the dumping of coolant water and the venting of gases, it was the sheer strength of the vessel itself that prevented a catastrophic release of radiation and widespread death. Government scientists later concluded that most people living within ten miles of the plant received just 8 millirems of radiation—8 millirems is equivalent to a chest X-ray, 100 millirems is about a third of the "background radiation" most U.S. residents receive in a year—and no one took a dose in excess of 100 millirems.

Although a major human disaster was avoided, the Three Mile Island accident did have at least one indisputably devastating effect: on the nuclear power industry. Before the accident, from 1963 to 1979, the number of reactors under construction worldwide had increased each year except in 1971 and 1978. After the accident, the number declined each year from 1980 to 1998. At the time of the accident, federal authorities had approved proposed construction of 129 nuclear power plants. Of these, just 53 were ever completed.

There is no denying that the Three Mile Island accident could have been much worse than it was. Plant workers did get the crisis under control—not quickly enough to prevent catastrophic damage to the reactor, but in good time to avert the "China syndrome" and a massively devastating radioactive leak or explosion. Yet it is also true that the accident could rather easily have been prevented altogether.

Look more closely at the sequence of events on March 28, 1979. It all began with the failure of the pumps; then the situation became more critical when the relief valve failed to close. Despite these malfunctions, the major accident could still have been prevented if the reactor, a massively complex monument to state-of-the-art technology, had been equipped with a few simple, quite unsophisticated gauges to indicate the water level in the reactor vessel. This, after all, was the critical measure of the reactor's safe operation. As long as the water level was high enough to cover and

"[My two daughters] had been standing out at the [school]bus stop that morning, so as soon as they come down with any sickness I start to worry about cancer."

—Patricia Smith, Harrisburg resident, speaking in 1983

cool the radioactive core, all would be well. Expose the core because of a drop in the water level, and the plant would quickly head into a super-heated cataclysm. Without the gauges, plant operators were blind to what they most urgently needed to see. All they knew was that they had sent the signal to close the relief valve. Having done that, they could only assume that the water level was normal.

Back when the plant was on the drawing boards, designers had real-ized the need for giving plant operators as much firsthand information as possible. They therefore included a control room indicator lamp to show not just that the relief valve had been open, but to give the actual position of the valve. It was decided that installing the indicator system was too costly and would take too big a bite out of the construction schedule. So it was scrapped. On the morning of the accident, without the indicator, plant operators could do no more than assume that the valve had closed. It had not, and the reactor vessel was being drained of its coolant water, sending the reactor toward meltdown.

Without gauges or any positive way of knowing the position of the critical valve, the operators relied on water-level readings in another plant component, the pressurizer, to guess at the level in the reactor vessel. Using instruments that permitted only an indirect picture of reality, the operators were dead wrong.

It was a perfect storm of bad design and human error that soon created yet another potentially catastrophic problem. The backup system for the main coolant feedwater system failed. Although the emergency feedwater pumps started automatically, as they were supposed to, valves on the emergency feedwater lines had been shut during a routine test that had been conducted forty-two hours before the accident. The problem? No one remembered to open them up again. With the valves closed, emergency feedwater could not get to the steam generators.

The accident was about eight minutes old before someone discov-ered that the valves had never been reopened. The discovery added to the mounting chaos in the control room, and although the valves were duly

opened, restoring the cooling flow of feedwater, bubbles of steam—
called "voids"—continued to block the transfer of heat from the reactor.
That was bad enough. Even worse, the blockages created by the voids
directed the badly needed coolant water away from the reactor core,
where it was so desperately needed, and to different parts of the system,
including the pressurizer. For this reason, the control room dials
correctly indicated an adequate water supply in the pressurizer. Lacking
gauges indicating the water level in the reactor vessel, operators assumed
that this also meant that there was sufficient water flowing throughout
the system. In reality, the water level was dropping everywhere except the
pressurizer. It was dropping drastically in the reactor vessel, exposing the
reactor core.

Water was urgently needed to cover and cool the core. But because
steam voids were sending so much water into the pressurizer, to control
room personnel it looked as if too much water was flowing through the
entire plant. Fearing an overflow, the technicians shut down the emergency core cooling pumps. Unable to see that their plant was starved for
water, they choked off what little was still coming through.

The instruments plant operators possessed told them they were
taking the right steps. Yet still the core temperature rose and the reactor
continued to gallop toward meltdown. In a bewilderment of chaos, no one
picked up on the clues to the real condition of the cooling system.

Because the relief valve had opened but then failed to automatically
shut, a "quench tank" that collected water from the still-open relief valve
soon filled to overflowing, disgorging contaminated water into the reactor
containment sump, which likewise filled, setting off a radiation alarm at
4:11 AM. In conjunction with abnormally high temperature and pressure
readings, this alarm should have alerted operators that the pressurizer
relief valve was stuck open.

Beleaguered, probably panicky, and certainly undertrained, the plant
operators missed the clues, and by 4:15 AM, the relief diaphragm that held
back water in the quench tank ruptured under pressure. The entire

containment building, the house in which the reactor lived, was now flooded with radioactive water. Automatic systems started pumping it from the relative safety of the containment building to an exposed auxiliary building until someone finally thought to shut off the sump pumps.

Plant operators neither knew what was happening nor what to do to find out. Some eighty minutes into the accident, they noted that steam instead of water was coming through the main pumps serving the lines to the reactor core. Sending steam to the core would only contribute to the crisis, so operators shut down the pumps, believing—or at least hoping—that the momentum of natural circulation would continue to move enough water to keep cooling the reactor core. They did not realize that the same steam that had prompted them to shut down the pumps was blocking the circulation of water. With water standing rather than moving through the superheated pipes, even more steam was generated.

It took about two hours and ten minutes after the beginning of the accident for the water to fall sufficiently to expose the top of the reactor core. The intense heat of this portion of exposed core triggered a reaction between the steam forming around it and the zirconium used to clad and protect the rods of nuclear fuel that powered the reactor. The chemical reaction quickly ate away at the cladding, exposing the rods raw and sending more radioactivity into the remaining reactor coolant water while also producing masses of hydrogen gas, which ignited and produced a minor explosion during the afternoon.

Not even the rapid unfolding of a potential nuclear holocaust could interfere with the change of shift at the Three Mile Island plant. At precisely 6:00 AM, the day shift entered the control room as the night shift left. Noting that the water temperature in the holding tank was high, one of the incoming operators closed a valve to stop the venting of coolant. By this time, however, a quarter-million gallons of radioactive coolant had already leaked. For some reason, the massive leak had failed to set off radiation alarms until an hour into the new shift. By then, the containment—site of the reactor—was wildly radioactive. Operators declared a

"Site Area Emergency" at 7:00 AM, followed by a "General Emergency" at 7:24. Another hour would pass before WKBO broadcast news of "a problem with the plant."

Even as the alerts were finally issued, the control room staff had yet to grasp the nature of the crisis: that water levels were so low that more than half of the reactor core was now exposed. By the time a group of technicians were suited up to venture into the contaminated containment areas to take manual temperature readings and draw samples of cooling water, seven hours had passed since the accident began. Based on these readings, engineers only now began pumping fresh water into the primary loop, the system that fed water into the reactor core; however, the primary loop pumps—the main source of coolant water—were not turned on again until nearly sixteen hours after the start of the entire accident. This began to bring the core temperature down; but although the immediate danger had passed, it would take the better part of a week to remove all the steam and hydrogen and thereby entirely contain the results of the accident.

> **"As a result of TMI, my level of skepticism about nuclear power was substantially raised and, like most Americans, I no longer took for granted the fact that this source of electric power was as risk-free as its promoters had indicated in its early years."**
>
> —Pennsylvania governor Richard Thornburgh, *Washington Post* interview, March 29, 1999

During the week of the accident, many Pennsylvanians and Americans came to believe that the utility company, Metropolitan Edison, and even the government were playing with their lives by failing to deliver timely, full, and frank information. The word "cover-up" was frequently spoken, and it did not help matters that Metropolitan Edison Company vice president Jack Herbein refused to call the accident an accident, but described it as "a normal aberration."

A concise masterpiece of corporate doubletalk, the phrase may not have been an attempt at cover-up many suspected it was. Instead, it may well have reflected a dangerous attitude toward technology, public service, and responsibility. It suggested a combination of incomprehension and arrogance, of assuming an intimacy with an awesomely powerful force of nature while failing to imagine and then pay for all the instruments of technology required to monitor it. It implied a blind reliance on inadequate technology and, even more, of a failure to train people sufficiently to understand and interpret the technology on which they so absolutely relied.

Yes, in the end, there was no China syndrome. Flawed in design and tended by poorly informed and insufficiently capable operators, the nuclear power station at Three Mile Island was ultimately designed well enough to contain a costly accident. In contrast to the holocaust that would occur at Chernobyl, Ukraine, in 1986, no one died, and most experts believe there were no lingering effects on health.

———

IT WAS THE NUCLEAR POWER INDUSTRY ITSELF that suffered most immediately and directly as a result of TMI. As many Americans saw it, that industry had it coming. Yet the effects were wider than a blow dealt to a single industry. Three Mile Island provoked a popular and political backlash of mistrust: mistrust of corporate America, mistrust of the government and its ability to inform and protect its citizens, and mistrust of technology itself. Some of this skepticism was doubtless healthy, but it also tended toward a lingering malaise of unthinking cynicism. Unconsciously, the bars defining acceptable corporate behavior and government performance were lowered. Over the next decade and beyond, Americans became increasingly numbed to news of one act of corporate greed and misconduct after another, and if the government was inept, wasteful, and even corrupt—well, what could you expect?

In the field of nuclear energy, Three Mile Island highlighted the need for more redundant safety technologies and for more thorough training of operators. These were good, positive results. But the accident also triggered an unthinking rejection of nuclear power as an alternative source of energy in a time of dwindling oil supplies and the necessary reliance on oil sources in volatile and even hostile parts of the world. Both before and after Three Mile Island, there was plenty of room for debating the risks and rewards of nuclear power and for finding ways to better balance those risks and rewards. Yet after Three Mile Island, the debate abruptly stopped. The American nuclear power industry did not die, but it threatened to, languishing for want of intelligent discussion. In the wake of the accident, cynical Americans grumbled as they waited in lines for gasoline, then paid more and more for it; struggled to heat their homes in winter; and eventually sent their sons and daughters to face death or dismemberment in a Middle East rich with the only source of energy on which the nation relied. Through all this, perhaps they found comfort in the prospect of having no more Three Mile Islands to worry about.

Ken Lay and Enron (2001)

THE BLIND EMBRACE OF GREED

Kenneth Lay was born in 1942 in the Missouri backwater town of Tyrone, the child of a tractor salesman turned Baptist preacher. As a boy, he did what other poor boys do, delivered newspapers and mowed lawns for nickels and dimes. He saw education as a way out of poverty, so he studied diligently at David H. Hickman High School and the University of Missouri, where he was an economics major and president of the Zeta Phi chapter of the Beta Theta Pi fraternity. In 1970, he earned a PhD in economics from the University of Houston, went to work for Humble Oil & Refining (which was subsumed by Exxon Mobil in 1972), then left the private sector to serve as a federal energy regulator. He rose in government service to become undersecretary for the U.S. Department of the Interior, then returned to business, first as a Florida Gas executive and then as president of Houston Natural Gas.

When President Ronald Reagan deregulated the energy industry, the former energy regulator was ideally positioned to take advantage of the new business environment. He engineered the purchase in 1985 of his Houston Natural Gas Company by the much larger Omaha-based Internorth to create Enron. Under his leadership, Enron revenues were claimed to be $111 billion in 2000,

> "I take full responsibility for what happened at Enron. But saying that, I know in my mind that I did nothing criminal."
>
> —Kenneth Lay

and Lay became one of America's highest-paid CEOs, bagging $42.4 million in compensation by the end of 1999. In December 2000, the transition team for President-elect George W. Bush mentioned Lay as a potential candidate for secretary of the treasury.

Four years later, on July 7, 2004, a Houston grand jury handed up a sixty-five-page indictment of Ken Lay on eleven counts of securities fraud, wire fraud, and making false and misleading statements. He was brought to trial on January 30, 2006, in Houston, over the protests of his defense team that he could not get a fair trial in his hometown. After all, the December 2001 collapse of Houston-based Enron was at the time the biggest bankruptcy in U.S. history, and it put twenty thousand Houstonians out of work, draining many of them of their life savings as well. Not that it would have been easy to find any venue free of hatred for Ken Lay. Nationwide—worldwide—the fall of Enron had cost investors a total of $74 billion, as measured from the point of the company's highest valuation, which was in 2000, when a single share of Enron sold for $90. During his trial, Ken Lay placed himself among the victims of the company's collapse, claiming that in 2001 Enron stock had made up about 90 percent of his wealth, so that his net worth as of 2006 was *negative* $250,000.

Few sympathized.

On May 25, 2006, a jury of eight women and four men found Lay guilty on six counts of conspiracy and fraud. In a separate subsequent bench trial, a judge found him guilty as well on four counts of fraud and making false statements. He was acquitted on only one of the counts originally charged against him. Sentencing was scheduled for September 11, 2006, then moved to October 23.

After his trials, Lay did not return to Missouri and poverty to await sentencing, but found time to vacation at one of his homes, at Old Snowmass, Colorado, near Aspen. There, on July 5, 2006, he died of a heart attack. His funeral was held privately and his ashes buried in a secret mountain location. One week after his death, some 1,200 guests—among them former president George H. W. Bush—gathered at Houston's First United Methodist Church for a memorial service. John "Mick" Seidl, a former Enron president, eulogized Lay as a "Boy Scout, if you will—who lived by Christian-Judeo principles." According to Seidl, his great misfortune was to have been the victim of an "overzealous federal prosecutor and the media" who together committed "total character assassination."

Indeed, Ken Lay died an innocent man, at least under U.S. law. Because he died before exhausting his appeals, Lay's conviction was "abated" on October 17, 2006. In the eye of the law, it was as if he had never been tried and convicted or even indicted.

In the eye of history, however, Lay was something else. Before it was the United States, America had been a collection of colonies belonging to the world's first industrialized nation, England. The child of capitalism, America would always be driven by capitalism, a force that first made the colonies and then drove them to fight for their independence from the mother country. For most of the nineteenth century, American capitalism grew unchecked; then, at the dawn of the twentieth century, a tide of Progressive reform swept the nation, bringing with it an escalating degree of government regulation to temper the buccaneering spirit of full-out market capitalism.

Regulation was propelled by a kind of egalitarian morality. Government was seen as the protector of the people against the inherently predatory forces of raw capitalism. That attitude ended in the 1980s, with the administration of Ronald Reagan, which ushered in a period of deregulation that was continued by Reagan's successor, George H. W. Bush. That the Republican administrations of Reagan and Bush were "pro-business" was hardly surprising, but then Democrat Bill Clinton defeated Bush in large measure by offering his own pro-growth agenda, which was advertised as the platform of the "new Democratic leadership." Under Clinton, during the 1990s, the small investor shared in a Wall Street boom, so that few if any Americans gave much thought to the way in which the regulatory safeguards so carefully assembled during Franklin Delano Roosevelt's Depression-era presidency were being exuberantly dismantled.

Ken Lay and Enron were very much part of this new era. As Lay brought himself up from penny-pinching working class paper boy to high-paid executive, so he exponentially grew his Houston-based company from the business of operating oil pipes to the status of energy broker, trader in electricity and other energy-related commodities. It was an entirely new kind of business, one that principally traded commodities produced by others, commodities ranging from electric energy and natural gas to pulp and paper to communications bandwidth. By the start of the twenty-first century, Enron was a colossal middleman, working, in the words of the *Washington Post*, "like a hybrid of traditional exchanges . . . instead of simply bringing buyers and sellers together, Enron entered the contract with the seller and signed a contract with the buyer, making money on the difference between the selling price and the buying price." From the looks of it, Ken Lay had performed a kind of capitalist miracle, creating a company that enjoyed the benefits of both buyer and seller.

Hundreds of thousands of investors wanted in on this miracle—who wouldn't?—driving Enron stock higher and higher.

The trouble was, Enron was no miracle. It was a trick, an illusion, a massive shell game. The millions and billions were there, all right, but they were not being *made*, only *exchanged*, washed this way and then that.

The company played it all very close to the vest, effectively closing its books to the public by ensuring that it and it alone was the only party privy to all sides of the astonishingly complex contracts it generated. Enron employed an army of PhDs in economics, mathematics, and even in physics to hammer into shape the appearance of limitless profit. Behind this finely fashioned facade, the shell game played out in a dumb show of buying and selling between parties that were ultimately connected to Enron and only to Enron. Much as the Hydra of Greek mythology grew head after head on a single body, Enron spawned a complex of partnerships, which enabled the company to shift its exponentially growing debt off one set of books and onto another and another and another.

At the core of any enterprise is the transformation of expenditure and debt into profit and wealth. At the core of Enron was not transformation, but presentation: the presentation of devastating loss as spectacular profit.

It did not require one of Enron's physics PhDs to explain something any high school physics student knows well. The Second Law of Thermodynamics, an expression of the universal law of increasing entropy (a measure of the unavailability of energy for work), states that the entropy of an isolated system not in equilibrium will tend to increase over time, approaching a maximum value at equilibrium. That is, even though energy is neither created nor destroyed, energy nevertheless becomes decreasingly efficient, less and less capable of doing useful work. Enron was the most isolated of isolated systems, and by early 2001, it was approaching the maximum value of entropy. The continual shifting of funds, a process in which no real profit was produced, was wearing the machinery down.

By February 2001 Enron executives and the company's accounting firm, Arthur Andersen LLP, glimpsed warnings of catastrophic problems ahead. Andersen even considered dropping Enron as a client, but hung on, presumably because Enron was such a lucrative customer. Nevertheless, by August 2001, one of Enron's own vice presidents, Sherron Watkins, alerted Ken Lay, at the time Enron's chairman, that the company "might implode in a wave of accounting scandals." Watkins was not part of Enron's inner circle, which orbited closely around CEO Jeff Skilling, but she had come to understand that, although massive amounts of money were changing hands, all the hands were attached to arms belonging to a single body.

By the time Watkins sent her internal e-mail warning to Lay, Enron entropy was nudging "maximum value." Even Arthur Andersen's account-ants had run out of hands to move the money into, and, on October 16, 2001, Enron management stunned Wall Street and the world by posting a $638 million loss for the third quarter. In that single day, stockholder equity in the company hemorrhaged value to the tune of $1.2 billion.

That was bad business news. The following month, on November 8, came news of a more sinister nature. Enron officials admitted they had overstated earnings for the past four years—by about $591 million—and also acknowledged liabilities of up to $3 billion in obligations to various partnerships. The closed system cracked, and what seeped and then flooded out was some-thing very ugly indeed.

> **"Was I [a] believer in Enron Corporation? Yes, sir, I was."**
>
> —Jeffrey Skilling

On November 28 Enron's many creditors downgraded the company's debt to junk-bond status. Even in this darkest of times, there had loomed on the horizon a white knight in the form of Enron's major rival, Dynergy, which had floated a $23 billion merger offer—money, *real* money from the outside, that would have gone a long way to staving off the final collapse. But with the announcements of November 28, Dynergy retracted its offer. Enron did not, as Watkins had warned, implode in accounting scandals. It simply imploded, period. What had seemed so substantial was revealed as so much vapor.

A series of congressional investigations rushed to fill the vacuum created by the implosion of Enron. Politicians on both sides of the aisle, along with George W. Bush in the Oval Office, rudely elbowed one another aside in a scramble to be among the first to deplore corporate crime and corporate criminals. To many Americans, nursing their bruised stock port-folios, this appeared to be an instance of politicians biting the hand that had fed them. During the 2000 elections, Enron had spent $2.4 million in individual, PAC (political action committee), and "soft-money" contributions to federal candidates and parties. Nevertheless, by the summer of 2002 no fewer than ten House and Senate committees were wallowing through a steamy swamp of documents and were jockeying to book hearing time.

While Washington churned, the larger financial community endured the aftershocks of the scandal. Markets shrank, pension funds went bust, and a substantial number of people found themselves suddenly unemployed. Talk of political reform grew strident, as those who had earlier clamored for deregulation now loudly demanded that government "step in" and "take a hand." Yet reform could hardly keep pace with the burgeoning toll of collapsing giants, each of which proved as hollow as Enron. There were Global Crossing in New Jersey and Worldcom in Atlanta, among others. In fact, no business seemed safe, as some of the more highly anticipated mergers of the new century—including AOL TimeWarner, DaimlerChrysler, and others—looked ready to be unraveled by the angrily clawing fingers of disillusioned and highly litigious shareholders.

—

AT TRIAL, KEN LAY PLEADED POVERTY. Like everyone else, he had been deceived, he said, made victim of crooked accounting and rogue underlings. But even those who had bought stock in a company that presented losses as profits put no stock in the pleas of Kenneth Lee Lay. Television news shows repeatedly broadcast videotape of the Enron chairman addressing an assembly of employees in the fall of 2001, urging them to buy more stock— especially now that it was so affordable—assuring them that Enron was basically healthy and would surely rebound. He did not mention that, during this very same period, he himself was frantically dumping shares he owned, rapidly accelerating the liquidation of some $300 million in stock (mostly in stock options) in a sell-off he had quietly begun back in 1989.

Ken Lay, PhD economist, top-earning CEO, potential secretary of the treasury: Was he really, at bottom, nothing but a thief? Perhaps. Or perhaps he was, for all his education and accomplishments, more fool than thief. Greed, after all, drives both thieves and fools, we know that; and greed also drives investors. The average American may have been raised to believe that businesses exist to make products and provide employment, but the manipulators of wealth, men like Kenneth Lay, believe that companies exist exclusively to enrich investors. In this, they are subscribers to what Gordon Gecko, the fictional tycoon played by Michael Douglas in Oliver Stone's 1987 movie *Wall Street*, tells a meeting of investors in a company he is about to liquidate: "Greed is good." They are words paraphrased from a real-life Wall Street manipulator, Ivan Boesky, who told the graduating class of the School of Business Administration at the University of California, Berkeley, on May 18, 1986: "Greed is all right, by the way . . . I think greed is healthy. You can be greedy and still feel good about yourself." Shocking? Well, most of us have been taught that greed is immoral. And probably it is. More important, however, greed as a motive is simply inadequate.

However humble their background, whatever their educational attainments, however great their net worth, the greedy care for nothing but money. And that is hardly enough. They do not care how money is made or what it can, in turn, be made to produce. All they see is the money itself and the movement of the money, not where it came from or where it goes. They see quantity without quality, motion without direction. Their vision wholly absorbed by the mere medium of business, they miss the meaning of business. Greed is blindness, and greedy men like the late Ken Lay are blind.

Dick Cheney and the Iraq War (2003)

THE DECISION TO INVENT A CAUSE

In 1898, Mr. Dooley, the Irish owner of a Southside Chicago bar, made his first appearance in the *Chicago Post* as a political and social commentator. Nationally syndicated almost immediately, Mr. Dooley—the fictional invention of newspaper reporter Finley Peter Dunne—became America's favorite pundit and remained as such well into the early twentieth century. Among Dooley's many celebrated rants was his explanation, in 1906, of the vice presidency. Whereas, he pointed out, the presidency is "th' highest office in th' gift iv th' people," the "vice-presidincy is th' next highest an' th' lowest. It isn't a crime exactly. Ye can't be sint to jail f'r it, but it's a kind iv a disgrace. It's like writin' anonymous letters." Years later, John Nance Garner, FDR's vice president from 1933 to 1941, remarked somewhat less hilariously that the office "isn't worth a pitcher of warm piss."

To be sure, the vice presidency has traditionally been a strangely feeble office. Except for the handful whom fate thrust into the presidency—and the single instance of Al Gore, who, narrowly missing elevation to the Oval Office in 2000, blazed another public career as a charismatic environmentalist—it is a stretch even for the most avid students of historical trivia to name more than a half-dozen vice presidents.

That was before Dick Cheney. Everyone, from popular political pundits to academic historians, agrees he is the most powerful vice president in American history. Some have even suggested that he is the nation's first shadow president.

He was born in 1941 in Lincoln, Nebraska, and moved with his family to Casper, Wyoming, while he was still a boy. He set off for Yale but, in his own words, "flunked out" and returned to Casper, where, after working for a year as a power company lineman, enrolled in the local community college in 1963, thereby securing the first of five student deferments that allowed him to avoid the draft during the Vietnam War—a conflict he avidly supported, despite his earnest and successful efforts to avoid fighting in it. He subsequently transferred to the University of Wyoming, from which he earned a BA and MA in political science.

In 1969, Cheney became an intern for Congressman William A. Steiger, then joined the staff of Donald Rumsfeld, director of the Office of Economic Opportunity. In the Nixon administration, he served as White

House staff assistant (1971) and assistant director of the Cost of Living Council (1971–73), then became vice president of Bradley, Woods, and Company, an investment firm (1973–74), before returning to the White House as deputy assistant to President Gerald Ford (1974–75). Cheney was Ford's campaign manager in his unsuccessful White House run against Jimmy Carter in 1976.

In 1978, Cheney was elected to the U.S. House of Representatives to replace resigning Wyoming Congressman Teno Roncalio. Reelected five times, he served until 1989 and compiled a record as a conservative on the far right, even supervising the composition of a minority report dissenting from congressional condemnation of the 1987 Iran-Contra affair, the Reagan administration's scheme to sell arms to Iran in order to secretly fund the Contras, which opposed the leftist Sandinista government in Nicaragua.

"I had other priorities in the sixties than military service."

—Dick Cheney, quoted in the *Washington Post*, April 5, 1989, in answer to a question about his multiple draft deferments

In 1989, Cheney joined the cabinet of George H. W. Bush as secretary of defense and played a key role in America's invasion of Panama (1989), Operations Desert Shield and Desert Storm, and the first Iraq war (1990–91). The defeat of Bush's reelection bid in 1992 sent Cheney back into the private sector, and from 1995 until 2000, he was chairman of the board and CEO of Halliburton, an energy, technical services, and major construction multinational corporation.

In 1997, with fellow conservatives Donald Rumsfeld and William Kristol, Cheney founded Project for the New American Century (PNAC), a neoconservative think tank dedicated to the promotion of "American global leadership." During the first Iraq operation, Secretary of Defense Cheney had supported George H. W. Bush's refusal to press military operations to the point of overthrowing Saddam Hussein, explaining in a 1994 interview that to have done so would have created a power vacuum in Iraq and led the United States into a hopeless quagmire. In 1997, however, his PNAC vigorously advocated a U.S. initiative to remove Hussein through "diplo-matic, political and military efforts." That aspiration remained uppermost in his mind when George W. Bush chose him as his running mate in 2000.

From the beginning of the Bush presidency, there were rumors that Cheney enjoyed extraordinary power in this traditionally lackluster office. Perhaps the most dramatic confirmation of such rumors came on September 11, 2001. The president was engaged in a photo op at a Sarasota, Florida, elementary school classroom when, at 9:05 AM, his chief of staff, Andrew Card, whispered in his ear the news of the first attack on the World Trade Center, which had occurred some twenty minutes earlier. Unaccountably, the president continued to visit with the schoolchildren, reading to them from *The Little Goat*, until 9:23 when he excused himself to call Vice President Cheney and others. Cheney remained on the line until, nine minutes later, Secret Service agents whisked him to a bunker in the White House subbasement.

At 9:37, American Airlines Flight 77 hit the Pentagon, and at 9:45, Bush's motorcade left the Emma E. Booker Elementary School, headed for the Sarasota-Bradenton International Airport. Fourteen minutes later, Air Force One departed, bound for Washington, D.C. At this very moment, 9:59, the south tower of the World Trade Center, which had been hit at 9:02, collapsed.

As his plane took off, the president called Cheney. Minutes earlier, a military aide had informed the vice president that another airliner was "eighty miles out." It was United Airlines Flight 93, headed toward Washington, perhaps targeting the White House. Conferring quickly with Secretary of Defense Donald Rumsfeld, Cheney asked Bush to order the airliner shot down. Condoleezza Rice, at the time the National Security Advisor, later recalled that the president "did give the order to shoot down a civilian plane if it was not responding properly," but White House photographer David Bohrer, present in the bunker with Cheney, had a different recollection: "The president gave the VP authority to make that call. It was a chilling moment, chilling moment."

Air Force One is often called the "Airborne White House" because, with its suite of advanced communication equipment, it is designed to allow the president to monitor all situations and issue any necessary orders. Yet President Bush chose to relinquish to his bunker-bound vice president the authority to shoot down a civilian airliner. Such was the relationship between Bush and Cheney, and such was the authority the president allowed Cheney to wield.

In the course of his exchange with Cheney from Air Force One, Bush angrily sputtered, "We're going to find out who did this, and we're going to kick their asses."

Even before the attacks of 9/11, Dick Cheney had made quite clear whose asses he wanted kicked. In the days before President-elect Bush's inauguration in January 2001, Cheney had communicated directly with Bill Clinton's outgoing secretary of defense, William S. Cohen, to request that the briefing he was to give to the incoming president should specifically include options concerning Iraq. Moreover, no sooner did the new president take office than he delegated to Cheney the work of exploring a variety of intelligence scenarios, with emphasis on what should be done if weapons of mass destruction (WMDs) fell into terrorist hands. Cheney presided over numerous national security meetings in the days before 9/11, all focused on bringing down the Hussein regime. At one of these meetings, Paul Wolfowitz, deputy to Cheney's longtime friend and ideological collaborator, Secretary of Defense Donald Rumsfeld, proposed a military invasion of Iraq for the purpose of seizing the country's southern oil fields. Secure this economically vital base, Wolfowitz argued, and indigenous Iraqi forces opposed to Saddam Hussein would be able to launch a coup d'etat to bring down the regime.

From the beginning, the Bush White House was notorious for the zeal with which it kept its secrets. Yet certain prominent journalists, most notably Bob Woodward (*Plan of Attack*, 2004) and James Bamford (*A Pretext for War*, 2004), were given remarkable access to insiders. Woodward reported that Secretary of State Colin Powell responded to the Wolfowitz plan by calling it "lunacy" and cautioned President Bush that he did not "have to be bullied into this." (Bush himself later denied ever having seen a "formal plan" for the rapid strike Wolfowitz proposed, but he did tell Woodward that the "idea may have floated around as an interesting nugget to chew on.")

Just why Colin Powell worried that the president would allow himself to be "bullied" is not clear. Did he sense that Cheney, Rumsfeld, and their circle wielded inordinate influence over the president? We don't know. It is clear, however, that the president became increasingly focused on bringing about regime change in Iraq, either by diplomacy or war, and that, in the aftermath of 9/11, it was war planning, not diplomacy, that gathered momentum, a momentum provided not by outside forces, but by those from within, particularly by Vice President Cheney, whom Woodward described as a "powerful, steamrolling force." Building on intelligence and intelligence analysis supplied by George Tenet's CIA, which suggested that Hussein could be removed only by force and that the dictator possessed a massive secret stockpile of the dreaded WMDs, Cheney kindled within the Bush administration what some colleagues (Woodward reported) called a "fever" for military action against Saddam Hussein.

Events proceeded rapidly. On February 16, 2002, President Bush signed an "intelligence finding" ordering the CIA to assist the military in overthrowing the regime of Saddam Hussein and to conduct operations inside of Iraq. He was acting on scant data gathered by no more than four informants in the entire country. By July, however, the CIA recruited some eighty-seven informants, giving the agency so substantial a stake in Iraq that the CIA turned from intelligence gathering to outright advocacy of war. At first, CIA Director Tenet argued that covert action against the Hussein regime would fail, so outright military action was the only viable alternative. Next, he added what he deemed another good reason for war: that the extensive new network of eighty-seven spies in the country would be imperiled if the United States failed to attack.

In the summer of 2002, President Bush approved preparations for combat, funding the upgrade of military bases and other strategic infrastructure in the Persian Gulf area. To maintain secrecy, the administration did not request the funds from Congress, but instead siphoned off the necessary money from existing projects as well as from a supplemental appropriations bill passed to fund the war against the Taliban and al Qaeda in Afghanistan. Yet during this same period, Secretary of State Powell came into increasing conflict with the vice president. Powell did not want America going it alone against Iraq, and he argued strenuously for appealing to the United Nations. Cheney dismissed such an effort as a waste of time.

As Woodward reported it, relations between Powell and Cheney became strained beyond civility. The two barely spoke with each another. Increasingly Powell came to believe that Cheney's efforts to establish a link between Iraq and the al Qaeda terrorist network—the terrorist organization responsible for the 9/11 attacks—had become obses-

> "My belief is we will, in fact, be greeted as liberators."
>
> —Dick Cheney, prediction on the Iraq War, March 16, 2003

sive to the point of magically transforming inconclusive and even entirely ambiguous intelligence into solid fact. Powell came to believe that the circle that orbited about the vice president, including Cheney's principal aide, I. Lewis "Scooter" Libby, Deputy Defense Secretary Wolfowitz, and Undersecretary of Defense for Policy Douglas J. Feith, constituted a kind of separate, shadow government.

Even as he worked secretly within the White House, Vice President Cheney started taking his case public as well, making speeches—always to conservative audiences—in which he represented as "conclusive" the connection between Hussein's Iraq and al Qaeda as well as Hussein's possession of WMD stockpiles. Crushed under the Cheney steamroller, Powell finally could do no more than offer President Bush the now-famous "Pottery Barn rule" concerning Iraq. If we invade the country, he warned, "you're going to be owning this place." That meant it was just like shopping at Pottery Barn: "You break it, you own it."

This admonition, however, was as far as Colin Powell was willing to take his opposition to the headlong journey toward war. A lifelong soldier, he remained loyal to the man he apparently perceived as his commander in chief. When Bush personally asked him to make the case against Saddam Hussein before the United Nations in February 2003, Powell did so, presenting to that body several discrete items of evidence, every one of which would be utterly discredited—albeit only after the war was well under way and the United States of America found itself the owner of a badly broken Iraq.

—

IN JANUARY 2004, THE BUSH ADMINISTRATION'S top weapons inspector in Iraq, David Kay, issued a report concluding unequivocally that Saddam Hussein had possessed no weapons of mass destruction when the United States invaded Iraq. In an interview with NPR's *Morning Edition* on January 22, 2004, Vice President Cheney announced that, despite Kay's report, the hunt in Iraq for weapons of mass destruction would go on, adding that he was also certain of ties between al Qaeda and Saddam Hussein. In September 2006, however, the vice president stunned viewers of NBC's *Meet the Press* by admitting that "clearly, the intelligence that said [Saddam Hussein had WMDs] was wrong." Host Tim Russert then asked him if the invasion would have proceeded had the CIA reported in 2003 that Hussein did not have the weapons. The vice president responded: "He'd done it before. He had produced chemical weapons before and used them," and Cheney concluded by saying that the invasion "was the right thing to do, and if we had to do it again, we would do exactly the same thing."

Having invented a cause for war with Iraq after 9/11, Dick Cheney no longer needed the invention—long since discredited in any case— since the United States was already deeply involved in the war. The only pretext he offered now was that, *fifteen years earlier,* Saddam Hussein had used chemical weapons. No matter that he had not possessed them in

2003. Having abandoned even an invented cause, the vice president was nevertheless as vigorous as ever in asserting that the Iraq War "was the right thing to do" and "and if we had it to do over again, we'd do exactly the same thing." He spoke to Russert using the plural pronoun, "we," presumably confident that he spoke for the president as much as for himself. It was a reasonable assumption, inasmuch as Bush had, back in 2001, delegated to him the authority to kill a planeload of people. Yet we are left to wonder if even the president still shares Cheney's belief in doing "exactly the same thing." George W. is a famously stubborn man, but even he must be familiar with the common-sense definition of madness: the repetition—"exactly"—of what you know has failed before.

PART THREE

The Decision
to Leap
(Without Looking)

King George III and the American Revolution (1775–83)

THE DECISION TO TYRANNIZE

"An old, mad, blind, despised, and dying king," Percy Bysshe Shelley called George III in his "Sonnet: England in 1819," and the characterization, through history, has stuck. But is it a fair assessment? That question requires more than a little discussion.

It is beyond dispute that, by 1819, the reigning British monarch had been "mad" for some time—or at least behaved that way. As early as 1765 there may have been a brief episode of erratic behavior, but that passed, and the king seemed perfectly sane until 1788, when he suffered bizarre hallucinations, paranoia, and depression while also speaking for hours on end in streams of nonsense, raving, soiling himself, making sexual advances to all and sundry at court, and generally breaking down. Because his behavioral symptoms were often accompanied by excruciating abdominal pain, vomiting, neuropathy (numbness, pain, strange sensations), seizures, skin eruptions, and discolored urine (his physicians reported the presence of a blue or purple pigment in the king's chamber pot), modern physicians believe George suffered not from insanity as such, but from porphyria, an enzyme disorder. It may have been hereditary or at least the king may have inherited a predisposition to porphyria, the acute onset of which was probably triggered by arsenic, a major ingredient in many eighteenth-century medicines. Nevertheless, and fair or not, Shelley left to posterity a portrait of George III as the embodiment of all that was wrong with English government:

"Sonnet: England in 1819"

An old, mad, blind, despised, and dying king,—

Princes, the dregs of their dull race, who flow

Through public scorn,—mud from a muddy spring,—

Rulers who neither see, nor feel, nor know,

But leech-like to their fainting country cling,

Till they drop, blind in blood, without a blow,—

A people starved and stabbed in the untilled field,—

An army, which liberticide and prey

Makes as a two-edged sword to all who wield,—

Golden and sanguine laws which tempt and slay;

Religion Christless, Godless—a book sealed;

A Senate,—Time's worst statute unrepealed,—

Are graves, from which a glorious Phantom may

Burst, to illumine our tempestuous day.

—Percy Bysshe Shelley

George's sanity was seriously in question during 1788–89, and Parliament was on the verge of voting his son regent when the king suddenly recovered. George continued to rule, but by 1810 he had become (as Shelley's sonnet portrays him) almost totally blind because of cataracts, and had slipped into a profound depression following the death of his youngest daughter, Princess Amelia. By 1811, insanity returned with a vengeance, and George himself assented to the elevation of his son the Prince of Wales to the regency. The king's son served in this capacity until George died in January 1820.

There is, then, historical truth in Shelley's characterization of George III, certainly the George of 1819, when he was old, mad, and dying. But it is also true that the king had ruled for a long time in apparently sound physical and mental health, including during the period of the American Revolution.

But what of the other adjective—"despised"? Was this an accurate description of the attitude toward George?

It was. But one has to identify just who did most of the despising.

The first of the English kings to bear the name George was a German, the elector of Hanover, who was deemed the rightful heir to the throne of England because he was the grandson of a bona fide English king, James I. Accordingly, George I ascended the British throne in 1714 and reigned for thirteen years, never troubling himself to learn English, but, then, never really troubling himself to govern the nation, either. He passed most of his time agreeably enough in the company of a succession of mistresses.

The king's son George II did manage to learn English, but failed to shed the heavy German accent with which he spoke it. He did possess sufficient command of his adopted tongue to give eloquent voice to his feelings about his subjects: "No English cook could dress a dinner, no English confectioner set out a dessert, no English player could act, no English coachman drive, no English jockey ride, nor were any English horses fit to be ridden or driven. No Englishman could enter a room and no English woman dress herself."

If George II bore little enough affection toward his subjects, he had even less love for his firstborn son, Frederick Louis, the Prince of Wales, whom he once described as "the greatest beast in the whole world," adding "I most heartily wish he were out of it." His father's hearty wish to the contrary notwithstanding, Frederick Louis grew to adulthood and married a German, Princess Augusta of Saxe-Gotha, on whom he begat, in 1738, George III, just one of eight other offspring, none of whom their parents counted as very promising.

The British historian J. H. Plumb pilloried the young George as "a clod of a boy whom no one could teach." He was, it is true, eleven years old before he read his first word, and his own mother grew weary with admonishing him "George, be a king!" but Frederick Louis, his father, was spared the spectacle of his

> **"Had he been born in different circumstances, it is unlikely that he could have earned a living except as an unskilled laborer."**
>
> —**J. H. Plumb (1911–2001),**
> **British historian, about George III**

son's ascension to the throne because he was beaned by a the wild return of a tennis ball in 1751 and never recovered from the blow. Thus are kings sometimes crowned for the most trivial of reasons. After the death of George II, his grandfather, twenty-two-year-old George III ascended the throne on October 25, 1760.

Plumb is typical of the many historians and others who, over the years, have condemned George III with such adjectives as "lethargic," "apathetic," and "childish." Yet the fact is that these descriptors all have their origin in his childhood and youth and were voiced principally by George's parents. Maybe he really was a stupid boy, and maybe he was also an unlovable boy, but what is certain is that he was an unloved boy, and it is the assessment of those closest to him, who did not love him, that seems to have influenced others, historians included, to condemn George III roundly and without reservation.

In recent years, however, one prominent defender has emerged. In 2004, Prince Charles sat down with an interviewer on the British television program *Timewatch* to explain what he described as his long-standing fascination with his ancestor. He noted that, far from being dull or stupid, George III was highly cultured, with an intense interest in the arts as well as the sciences. He pursued hobbies that included astronomy, architecture, and clockmaking. He was an avid collector of books, and he supported a number of British painters by commissioning or acquiring their paintings and drawings. His most intense avocation was agriculture, which he considered vital to the well-being of the nation. Yet it was this preoccupation that his detractors—and some historians—used against him, deriding the king as "Farmer George."

As a direct descendant, Prince Charles, it is true, has a vested interest in standing up for George III, but it is also objectively the case that "Farmer George" was sufficiently skilled to have led his nation through the menacing years of the Napoleonic Wars and to have presided over England in a period of unprecedented scientific, industrial, intellectual, literary, and economic development and growth. Nor did his people give evidence of despising him. Despite instability in George's government—within his Cabinet and in Parliament—he himself was a remarkably popular king, a man perceived to have a common touch, and a monarch who, in sharp contrast to both his great-grandfather and grandfather, showed a frank and open affection for his subjects.

Why, then, has George III come down through history as what J. H. Plumb called him, a clod? The answer may be given in a single sentence. *He lost America.*

"George, be a king!" It was, perhaps, with his mother's scold ringing in his ears that, no sooner crowned, he made what he deemed

> **"The farmer grown familiar asked the gentleman, as he thought, if he had seen the King; and being answered in the affirmative, the farmer said 'Our neighbours say he's a good sort of man, but dresses very plain.' 'Aye,' said his Majesty, 'as plain as you see me now,' and rode on."**
>
> —Story often told about George III, who loved to tour the countryside incognito

a most kingly gesture by deciding to enforce, for the first time ever, a series of long-neglected Navigation Acts, the first of which had been on the books since the mid-seventeenth century. Ever since the first permanent English colony had been established at Jamestown, Virginia, in 1607, the British crown tended to treat both colonies and colonists with what historians have often called "salutary neglect," imposing few restrictions and extending little aid. The expense of the wars between the British colonists and the French as well as French-allied Indians beginning at the end of the seventeenth century and spanning the first half of the eighteenth century, culminating in the cataclysm of the French and Indian War (1754–63), persuaded the new British king that the colonies should be made to help pay for their defense. By imposing various duties on colonial commerce, the Navigation Acts would generate some of that revenue.

By no means was George's government unanimous in supporting the new application of the old Navigation Acts. His own prime minister, the Progressive-minded William Pitt, warned that the new economic policy would drive a wedge between colony and mother country. This elicited the young man's second kingly act. He ousted Pitt in 1761 and replaced him with Lord Bute (John Stuart), an archconservative. Bute was compliant to the king's will, but enjoyed little support in Parliament, which forced his resignation in 1763.

Menaced by the French and Indian War, the colonies, though provoked by the new laws, were not yet stirred to rebellion. Fighting between England and France ended in 1763, but this very year the Ottawa chief Pontiac led a violent Indian uprising, Pontiac's Rebellion. This revolt prompted the king to issue the Proclamation of 1763, by which he sought to appease the Indians by drawing a line marking the legal western limit of white settlement at the Appalachians. This did pacify the Indians—and therefore even pleased some colonists, especially those in the well-established coastal regions—but it caused outrage on the frontier. Western settlers freely violated the Proclamation line, provoking the Indians to resume warfare. Terrorized, the settlers demanded military aid from colonial authorities and then from the mother country. Little, however, was done for those who, after all, had violated the royal decree. The result of this indifference was increasing alienation between colonies and king.

> "We do hereby strictly forbid, on pain of our displeasure, all our loving subjects from making any purchases or settlements whatever, or taking possession of any of the lands above reserved [to the Indians], without out special leave and license."
>
> —From the Proclamation of 1763

In 1763, Lord George Grenville replaced Lord Bute as prime minister. Even as the Proclamation line chafed against colonial ambitions, George III urged Grenville to raise more money from the colonies. Whereas the Navigation Acts called for duties on certain imports and exports, Grenville upped the ante by introducing, for the first time ever, direct taxes on the colonies. While the duties had created discontent, especially because the colonists were languishing in a postwar recession, taxation provoked outrage. It was not so much the idea of paying the Crown that stung as it was the notion of being taxed without Parliamentary representation.

This concept became the central cause of the American Revolution. No one, not Parliament, prime minister, or even king, disputed that representation was a basic English right, guaranteed in the Magna Carta of 1215. Even conservative British officials conceded that the king had no right to tax the colonies or anyone else. Parliament alone had the authority to levy taxes. The colonists, as well as liberal elements within the British government, argued that the inhabitants of the colonies were not represented in Parliament, whereas the people of the mother country were. The authority of Parliament to levy taxes flowed directly from its function as a representative body. It had no authority to tax those whom it did not represent. But neither George III nor Grenville accepted this. The king and his prime minister countered that Parliament did not actually represent *anyone*. Rather, it represented *estates*, socially and economically defined groups, such as physicians, lawyers, merchants, the landed gentry, and so on. In this sense, then, the colonists had as much representation as anyone in the mother country, inasmuch as the interests of a merchant in Philadelphia were no different from a merchant living in London.

It was a bold assertion that greatly pleased the king. In America, however, a growing majority rejected it—and angrily. One of these, a Boston attorney named James Otis, declared in a speech of February 24, 1761, that "Taxation without representation is tyranny," and that became the cry of an independence movement.

The king turned a deaf ear to that cry, throwing his full support behind Grenville, who resurrected more of the old Navigation Acts and added to these the enforcement of the Acts of Trade, which had been passed in the early eighteenth century. Then he engineered passage of a new tax in the Sugar Act of 1764, which increased duties on foreign refined sugar and products imported from countries other than Britain.

The so-called Grenville Acts occasioned the first serious, organized, and effective colonial protest against the mother country's taxation policy. On May 24, 1764, a Boston town meeting proposed that the colonies unite in a Non-Importation Agreement, unanimously pledging to boycott a wide variety of English goods. By the end of the year, a number of colonies had joined the boycott, though by their nature, the British North American colonies were competitive rather than cooperative. It was in opposition to external force, not of their own internal volition, that they first united.

George III failed to perceive the irony of his policies, which were not tying the colonies closer to the Crown, but driving them into a union against the Crown. What happened next should have served as the king's wake-up call. Grenville ushered through Parliament the Stamp Act, which was put into force on March 22, 1765.

The new law taxed all kinds of printed matter, including newspapers, legal documents, and even dice and playing cards. On all such items a government tax stamp was to be affixed. As with the earlier taxes, colonists were outraged by the injustice of taxation without representation; but the Stamp Act was regarded as even more egregious. The revenues it generated were specifically earmarked to defray the cost of maintaining British soldiers in the colonies, but now that the French and Indian menace had been ended, colonists grew to resent the presence of British soldiery among them, and many felt that they were being required to pay for nothing less than an occupying army. As if this situation were not inflammatory enough, the act contained an enforcement clause stipulating that any infringement of the new tax was to be tried in the vice admiralty courts—which answered to the royal government—and not by local magistrates.

The Stamp Act moved the colonies to the brink of revolution. In Boston, Samuel Adams, a failed businessman and brilliant political agitator, organized one of the first of many secret societies that sprang up in direct response to the Stamp Act. Adams's group, like others that followed, called itself the Sons of Liberty. Members pressured and intimidated the stamp agents and were so successful at it that every agent they approached resigned. Perhaps more important, the various Sons of Liberty cells communicated with one another and coordinated their activities. They became a network linking the colonies together.

In Virginia, passage of the Stamp Act moved Patrick Henry, a lawyer and member of the House of Burgesses, to introduce the seven Virginia Resolves of 1765, the last of which boldly asserted that Virginia enjoyed, by right, complete legislative autonomy. This was a vivid precursor of the Declaration of Independence, a document that would not appear for another decade. For the first time publicly in the colonies, Henry spoke out against King George III himself. "Caesar had his Brutus—Charles the first, his Cromwell—and George the third may profit by their example," he declared to his fellow burgesses. When some objected that such speech was treason, Henry replied: "If *this* be treason, make the most of it." The resolves were enacted on May 30, 1765.

Still the king and his ministers did not relent. The more the authority of king and Parliament was challenged, the harder king and Parliament pressed their authority. Even as the Stamp Act protest gathered momentum, Parliament passed the Mutiny Act of 1765, which included a provision for quartering British troops in private houses. When colonists argued that quartering should not apply to England's overseas possessions, Parliament replaced the Mutiny Act with the Quartering Act, which eliminated the provision requiring private homeowners to billet soldiers, but replaced it with one requiring colonial authorities to furnish, at public expense, barracks and supplies for British troops. Later, the Quartering Act was extended to require billeting soldiers in taverns and inns, again at the expense of the colonists. Colonial legislatures responded by refusing to vote funds for the troops.

Each new protest brought the colonies closer to a formal union, heralded by the Stamp Act Congress of October 7–25, 1765, which drew delegates from eight of the thirteen colonies. The Congress produced a Declaration of Rights and Grievances, which made the argument that Parliament had no authority to tax the colonies and that the crown's vice admiralty courts had no rightful jurisdiction in the colonies. The delegates then sent the declaration to King George III, who ignored it. Parliamentary liberals paid attention, however, moving to repeal the Stamp Act even before it was scheduled to go into effect. Parliament was being heavily pressured by English merchants, whose colonial trade had suffered badly because of the Non-Importation Agreement. Even as Parliament debated repeal of the Stamp Act, all the colonies chose simply not to enforce it.

Faced with rebellion in Parliament and abroad, Grenville refused to compromise and instead recommended deploying troops to force compliance with the Stamp Act, but Parliament overrode him and voted repeal on March 18, 1766. Any thrill the colonies felt at this was diluted by the Declaratory Act, passed on the very same day. It reaffirmed Parliament's authority to make laws binding on the American colonies. With one hand, Parliament had acknowledged colonial rights while, with the other, simultaneously denied them.

Grenville stepped down in July 1765 and was replaced briefly by the Marquess of Rockingham, who, in turn, was succeeded on July 30, 1766, by William Pitt, whom the king consented to reinstall in his Cabinet because he felt need for liberal support.

Under Pitt, in August, Charles Townshend rose to the post of chancellor of the exchequer—the equivalent of secretary of the treasury. The liberal and highly competent Pitt might well have guided the colonies toward a compromise with the government or to a peaceful independence, but a complete mental breakdown took him out of office and effectively catapulted the opportunistic Townshend into the position of acting premier. Under the approving gaze of George III, Townshend pushed through Parliament the so-called Townshend Acts, a whole new round of taxes, including substantial duties on lead, glass, paint, tea, and paper imported into the colonies for the specific purpose of supporting the military and paying the salaries of royal colonial officials. So far as these officials were concerned, the act took away from colonial legislatures the power of the purse, so that royal administrators became answerable only to the Crown. This tyranny was compounded by an act of June 15, 1767, suspending the New York colonial assembly because it had refused to authorize funds mandated by the Quartering Act. For its part, the Massachusetts General Court voted not only to oppose the Townshend Acts, but to inform the other colonies of what it was doing in the stated hope that those colonies would do the same. To this end, it issued the "Massachusetts Circular Letter" on February 11, 1768, urging the other twelve colonies to consider three revolutionary propositions: first, that the Townshend Acts were "taxation without representation"; second, that governors and judges must not be independent of colonial legislatures; and third, that Americans could never be represented in Parliament.

The idea that Americans could never be adequately represented in Parliament signaled a leap from the former position that taxation without representation constituted tyranny to the position that not only did this constitute tyranny, but a tyranny that could not be remedied simply by providing representation. For Parliamentary representation proportionate to colonial population was a practical impossibility. The people of Britain would never stand for it. This being the case, what alternative was left? Only one: independence.

The quartering of soldiers triggered a riot in Boston on March 5, 1770, the so-called Boston Massacre, which colonial firebrands such as Sam Adams tried in vain to fan into an immediate revolution. In the aftermath of the incident, however, on April 12, 1770, Parliament repealed all of the Townshend duties, save one, the tea tax, which remained in force because King George III insisted "there must always be one tax" to preserve Parliament's right to tax the colonies. In truth, the tea tax was not terribly burdensome on the colonists for the simple reason that it was so easily evaded. Colonial consumers loved their tea, but they did not feel compelled to buy it from English sources. Instead, they purchased smuggled tea from Dutch traders. The result was that the tea tax was harder on England's financially ailing East India Company than on the colonials. If this cartel of British merchants and shippers didn't soon pack off to America some of the seventeen million pounds of India tea lying in its London warehouses, the whole lot would go rotten. Fortunately for the company, its stockholders and ministers had strong ties to George's new prime minister, Lord Frederick North, who proposed a program of what today would be called corporate tax relief. North understood that the East India Company actually paid two taxes, one when it landed tea in Britain, and another when it landed a shipment in America. By means of the Tea Act (May 10, 1773), Lord North forgave the first tax and retained only the lesser three-penny-a-pound duty due on landing in America. This priced East India Company tea lower than the smuggled tea.

George and his prime minister were confident that the colonists would vote their pocketbooks and start obeying the law by buying only East India Company tea. Their mistake was in failing to understand that, while money was indeed an important dimension of the colonists' understanding of their rights, the rights, not the money, were at issue. The Tea Act set up an arrangement whereby East India Company tea would not be wholesaled to colonial merchants, but would be exclusively consigned to specially designated—and royally connected— brokers in the ports of New York, Charleston, Philadelphia, and Boston. The law drove American merchants out of the loop, and thus the Tea Act drove the hitherto moderate American merchants squarely into the camp of the radicals. Once again, the colonies drew together, uniting against their sovereign.

> **"I am not sorry that the line of conduct seems now chalked out. . . . The New England Governments are in a state of rebellion, blows must decide whether they are to be a subject to this country or independent. . . . The people are ripe for mischief. . . . We must either master them or totally leave them to themselves and treat them as aliens."**
>
> —George III to Lord North, November 18–19, 1774

Under the aegis of local committees of correspondence, colonial activists intimidated into resignation the royal tea consignees in Philadelphia, New York, and Charleston. Additionally, American captains and harbor pilots refused to handle the East India Company cargo, and tea ships were turned back to London from Philadelphia and New York. One ship was permitted to land in Charleston, South Carolina, but the tea was impounded in a warehouse, where it lay unsold until the Revolutionary government auctioned it off in 1776.

In Boston, after three Tea Act ships did land, activists prevented their being unloaded. Yet the royal governor, Thomas Hutchinson, refused to issue permits to allow the ships to leave the harbor and return to London. This stand-off spawned the event celebrated in history as the Boston Tea Party, in which 150 Sons of Liberty, their faces painted to simulate Mohawk war paint, climbed aboard the three ships and jettisoned in Boston Harbor 342 tea chests valued at $90,000 in colonial currency.

When word of the Boston Tea Party reached England, liberal voices rose in support of the Americans and called for the repeal of all taxes as well as all coercive restraint of trade, but George III declared, "We must master them or totally leave them to themselves and treat them as aliens." To find a declaration of war for the American Revolution, we need look no further than this statement. War was declared not by the colonists, but by their king.

In response to the Boston Tea Party, George's government effectively declared Massachusetts to be in rebellion, and Parliament passed what it called the Coercive Acts (the colonists called them the Intolerable Acts), which closed the port of Boston, abridged the colony's self-government, made most local officials answerable only to the *royal* governor, restricted town meetings, drastically reduced the jurisdiction and authority of colonial courts, and ordered the permanent quartering of British troops in Boston, which became an occupied city. The actions against Massachusetts motivated the convention of a "Continental" Congress. Yet again, coercion served only as a spur to colonial solidarity and the creation of a new national identity.

Through the rest of 1774 and into 1775, the revolution crystallized. Alarmed at long last by events, Lord North ushered through Parliament a last-ditch "conciliatory plan," by which Parliament would not renounce its right to tax the colonies, but did declare that it would "forbear" to levy all but regulatory taxes on any American colony that, through its own assembly, taxed itself for the support of defense and civil government. The colonies rejected North's Conciliatory Plan, but the Second Continental Congress, convening in Philadelphia on May 10, 1775, did weakly endorse the Olive Branch Petition, which reverently appealed to King George III to redress colonial grievances in the interests of avoiding war. The petition was put into the hands of the highly respected Richard Penn (descendant of Pennsylvania founder William Penn), and Arthur Lee, who took it to London, and, on August 21, sent a working copy of the petition to Lord Dartmouth, secretary of state for the colonies. This was followed by the original, which Penn transmitted to Lord Dartmouth on September 1. The king, however, refused to see Penn, Lee, or the petition. When Penn pressed Dartmouth for a reply, the secretary of state said: "As His Majesty did not receive the petition on the throne, no answer will be given." In fact, George III had already given his answer. Without so much as acknowledging the existence of the petition, the monarch proclaimed on August 23 that, "our Colonies and Plantations in North America, misled by dangerous and designing men," were in a state of rebellion. The king ordered "all our Officers . . . and all our obedient and loyal subjects, to use their utmost endeavours to withstand and suppress such rebellion."

Once again, it was George himself who declared a revolution. The colonies' own declaration of independence would not follow until July 4, 1776, by which time war had been underway for more than a year.

———

GEORGE III WAS NOT AN EVIL, BAD KING, or an inept king. But with respect to American independence, he did prove a foolish king. He believed—foolishly—that tyranny was an acceptable substitute for government.

It is one thing for a leader to resist a demand for novel rights and unheard-of privileges, but the American "revolution" made no such demands. Unlike any other revolution before or since, its proponents did not ask for what the motto later engraved into Great Seal of the United States says that they asked for, "a new order of the ages." Instead, they demanded nothing more than their ancient rights as Englishmen and -women and their even more primeval rights as human beings. As the colonists saw it—and as George III stubbornly refused to see it or simply could not see it—king and Parliament were denying them rights they already possessed. Such a denial is tyranny, and it is a wrong so essential—so "self-evident"—that any attempt to defend or perpetuate it is folly, a folly that some might even judge to be madness.

The "War Hawks" and the War of 1812 (1812)

THE DECISION TO PICK A FIGHT

"War is death's feast" says an English proverb from the seventeenth century, and it has always been hard to find people—political leaders, military leaders, and ordinary folk—who will speak up for war as a good thing. It is a "last resort," everyone says. Yet the Swiss historian Jean-Jacques Babel calculated that, in some 5,500 years of recorded history, the world has known no more than 292 years of peace. Judging from history, it seems that war is more rule than exception and hardly a last resort. For the United States, war has been a frequently chosen course, even in times and in situations that made war the very worst of courses to choose.

The United States declared war on England in 1812, when President James Madison was up for reelection on the ticket of a party variously known as the Democratic-Republicans or simply the Republicans (not the same as the GOP, which would be founded in 1854), which was opposed to the increasingly moribund Federalists. Whereas the Federalists had supported the buildup and maintenance of a strong military, the Republicans opposed doing so; yet, whereas the Federalists had generally opposed any drift toward war, the Republicans promoted, even urged it—this despite the peaceful alternatives available.

When Thomas Jefferson, first of the Republicans, took office as president in 1801, he began to turn back the policies inherited from the Federalists, namely George Washington (who never adopted the party name) and John Adams (who did). The nation's first two presidents sought friendly relations with the British, even if this involved some superficial compromises of independence. In contrast, Jefferson had no desire to maintain cordial relations with what he considered a backward-looking monarchy that, having lost its thirteen colonies, now endeavored to recolonize them economically through the trade compromises negotiated under Washington and Adams. Yet even as the Republicans increasingly defied and alienated the British, they slashed U.S. military spending, so that by 1810, Winfield Scott, destined to become an American hero in the War of 1812 and whose military endured until the Civil War, called the army's officer corps a band of "swaggerers, dependants, decayed gentlemen and others—'fit for nothing else,' which always turned out utterly unfit for any military purpose whatever."

Nathaniel Macon, a representative from North Carolina, declared that the "state of the Army is enough to make any man who has the smallest love of country wish to get rid of it." As for the U.S. Navy, which President Adams had built up, Jefferson tore down, canceling construction of major new warships and letting others rot.

While the United States was dismantling its armed forces, England and France were heavily engaged in the Napoleonic Wars, and Americans, as neutrals, engaged in a lucrative trade with both combatants. The British, however, were jealous of American trade and correctly accused the nation's merchant captains of flouting neutrality laws by freighting goods between France and France's colonies in the West Indies, thereby circumventing the British blockade of French ports. This not only aided the French war effort but, even more galling, put the United States in a position to reap the benefits of Britain's war effort. Having scourged French commerce from the Atlantic, the British now saw American ships usurping that commerce, capturing most of the trade between Europe and the Caribbean. In response, the Royal Navy was authorized to seize American ships suspected of violating neutrality by acting as transports for French goods.

Before 1810, American outrage mounted to the verge of war, but the British courts soon acted to release the seized vessels and to end, for the most part, the practice of seizure on the high seas. This should have removed at least one major impetus toward war, but though the offenses ceased, the bad feelings remained. Worse, the Royal Navy continued to practice impressment—the policy of intercepting U.S. merchant ships, boarding them, and seizing sailors deemed to be British subjects liable for service in the Royal Navy.

Impressment was driven by three factors. First: Because of the demands of the Napoleonic Wars, the Royal Navy was critically short of sailors. Second: Enjoying great commercial opportunity in the struggle between Britain and France, the American merchant fleet was also critically short of sailors and eagerly hired British sailors, including Royal Navy deserters. Third: British sailors much preferred sailing under American merchant captains, who treated them reasonably well, than languishing in the Royal Navy, which treated them like dogs. Most of the sailors seized and pressed into British service between 1803 and 1812 were in fact British subjects, but at least six thousand were U.S. citizens wrongly deemed British subjects by boarding parties. Most American captains and politicians did not dispute the right of the Royal Navy to arrest U.S.-flagged ships in international waters in order to inspect for the presence of British subjects—it was a right guaranteed by the Jay Treaty negotiated under President Adams—but the seizure of American citizens caused outrage. Even more outrageous were British seizures that occurred in U.S. territorial waters—a clear violation of American sovereignty.

Here, then, was another cause of war, and it is impressment that grade-school history lessons have traditionally cited as *the* cause of the War of 1812. Yet the fact is that the British made a series of concessions to the United States to reduce and regulate impressments, and in 1806 even agreed to a treaty negotiated by the Americans James Monroe and William Pinkney, promising to exercise "the greatest caution" in impressing British sailors and conceding to a great extent the right of American merchant ships to carry French goods from one French port to another.

It was a treaty lopsidedly favorable to the United States both commercially and politically, and it would probably have come into force had the British government refrained from appending to it at the last minute a note by which the Crown reserved the right to retaliate against France if the United States acquiesced in Napoléon's so-called Berlin Decree, a blockade that forbade the importation of British goods into countries allied with France. In fact, the French blockade existed on paper only because Napoléon did not possess the navy to enforce it. The appended note, therefore, was largely moot. But it stuck nevertheless in President Thomas Jefferson's craw, and he refused to submit the Monroe-Pinkney Treaty to the Senate. By this refusal, he rejected America's single most attractive alternative to war.

Like the displaced stone that triggers an avalanche, Jefferson's rejection of the Monroe-Pinkney Treaty initiated a catastrophic deterioration of Anglo-American relations. On June 22, 1807, HMS *Leopard* intercepted USS *Chesapeake*, an American warship, demanding the right to search for deserters from the Royal Navy. The American captain refused, whereupon *Leopard* opened fire, killing three U.S. sailors and wounding eighteen others. *Chesapeake* summarily struck her colors, a British party boarded, and four deserters were taken away. The clash brought the two nations once again to the precipice. As one Republican politician put it, "all distinctions between Federalism and Democracy are banished" as the nation was united in outrage. Yet, for its part, the British government drew back, denounced the attack, recalled the commanders involved, volunteered restitution, and agreed to return three of the deserters, who were found to be U.S. citizens (a fourth, confirmed to be a British subject, was hanged).

In the absence of the Monroe-Pinkney Treaty, Anglo-American relations were not only subject to crises such as the clash between the *Leopard* and *Chesapeake*, but to the commercial warfare that was a major component of the struggle between England and France. Each country sought to cripple the trade of the other, the British seizing neutral ships on the high seas, the French confiscating neutral cargoes in the continental European ports they controlled. In theory, if U.S. ships complied with French demands, they would be subject to seizure by the British; if they complied with British demands, the French would seize their cargoes. In practice, however, both England and France allowed U.S. merchants considerable wiggle room, but many ships and cargoes were nevertheless seized.

In rejecting the Monroe-Pinkney Treaty, President Jefferson had maneuvered the country very close to war. Yet even he understood that the United States—thanks to the policies of his own party—was unprepared for such a war, and he hit upon trade restrictions as an alternative to armed confrontation. Between 1806 and 1812, at the urging of Jefferson and his successor, James Madison, the Republican-dominated Congress passed a series of laws intended to impose a boycott on commerce with England as well as France, thereby forcing them to respect U.S. neutrality rights. The culminating legislation of this series was the Embargo Act of 1807, which simply prohibited American ships and goods from leaving port. Even Virginia senator John Randolph, a loyal Republican, was appalled by this economically ruinous legislation, which he likened to an attempt "to cure corns by cutting off the toes."

Intended by the Republicans as an alternative to a war that their own policies were inciting—yet inciting in the absence of the military capacity to carry out successfully—the embargo and its follow-up, the Non-

Intercourse Act of March 1809, were as economically devastating to the United States as the war that followed would be. However, on their intended targets, England and France, the laws had little effect. This was not only bad for the nation, but was also directly damaging to the Republicans because it served to rejuvenate the rapidly fading Federalist Party. Yet worse, in parts of New England, the economic crisis had started talk of secession, the dissolution of the Union. Steps intended to avert war with England now threatened to bring on civil war within the United States.

In the end, however, the crisis did not spark a civil war. Jefferson and, after him, Madison, managed to keep the focus of America's discontent on England. Created by economic depression and perceived affronts to U.S. nationhood and sovereignty, this discontent was intensified in 1811 by an outbreak of Indian hostility in the Old Northwest, the American frontier corresponding to the modern states of Ohio, Indiana, and Illinois. Because the Indians were supported by British trade interests based in Canada, American popular hatred of England boiled over as the frontier reeled under what newspapers were calling the "Anglo-Savage War."

Indian warfare in the Northwest added a powerful new incentive to the general drive toward war. As the population of the United States burgeoned, the hunger for new territory intensified. Not only did Americans want to ensure control of the Old Northwest and to push its boundaries ever westward, but they also hankered after so-called Spanish Florida, which extended below the Old Northwest from Florida and westward through the lower south as far as the Mississippi River. By 1812 Spain was allied with Britain against Napoléon; therefore, war with Britain would mean war with Spain, and victory in such a war would mean the acquisition of Florida as well as the redemption of the menaced Northwest. Nor was land hunger entirely separate from the issues revolving around interference with commerce on the high seas. The disruption of the Atlantic trade devastated not only the coastal economy, it brought depression to the West, whose abundant produce could be exported only if the sea-lanes were open.

As the year 1812 approached, the land-hungry westerners in Congress, led by Kentucky's Henry Clay, became the "War Hawks," a clique of about a dozen Congressmen ardent for war and around whom the often-fractious Republicans coalesced. War came to seem an answer to the nation's economic woes, to its insatiable hunger for land, and to its proud desire to uphold its sovereignty. Not least of all, it seemed to President James Madison a means of unifying the Republican Party and crushing once and for all the distressingly resurgent Federalists.

Up to June 19, 1812, the very day on which President Madison signed the declaration of war that Congress had voted him, the British government continued to offer conciliation, including new agreements to curb or even to end impressment, liberalized policies regarding trade, and promises to restrain British Canadians from inciting Indian depredations in the Old Northwest. But the momentum of war now exceeded the force of compromise. There were a good many dissenters in Congress, who warned that the United States was hardly prepared to fight the great army and navy of England, but they were roundly shouted down as unpatriotic. When Madison's own secretary of the treasury, Albert Gallatin, issued a report to the effect that waging war would require the imposition of new taxes—absolutely anathema to the Republicans—he was accused of attempting to "chill the war spirit." The War Hawks insisted that the British could be fought without any new taxes. And they kept insisting on this until war became a foregone conclusion, forcing Congress to vote up the dreaded taxes after all. Even then, it would take a lot of scrambling even to begin to build up the long-neglected army and navy.

The reality was that the United States proposed to go to war against the most powerful nation on Earth

> "The mad ambition, the lust of power, and commercial avarice of Great Britain have left to neutral nations an alternative only between the base surrender of their rights, and a manly vindication of them."
>
> —*Report of the House Foreign Relations Committee,* June 3, 1812, written chiefly by John C. Calhoun

with a regular army that consisted of just twelve thousand troops, widely scattered and led by inept officers, and with a navy that was tiny by any standard and downright miniscule in comparison with that of England.

The majority in Congress refused to confront these realities, comforting themselves instead with the fantasy that militiamen and privateers (state-sanctioned pirates) could compensate for the lack of a large federal army and navy. Some entertained the even wilder fantasy that the mere threat of war would intimidate the British into surrendering without firing a shot. And when a congressional minority threatened to slow the march to war by insisting on pointing out the hard reality, President Madison announced to Congress on March 9, 1812, that his administration had uncovered a British plot, centered on an Irishman named John Henry, to incite disunion in New England. The Madison administration paid $50,000 to acquire certain "incriminating" documents from Henry, who fled back to Ireland. Claiming that Henry's papers were "formal proof of the Cooperation between the Eastern Junto [New England dissidents] & the Br[itish] Cabinet," Madison sent the documents to Congress. But when they were actually presented there, they seemed completely inconsequential. As a cause of war, they simply evaporated, and the Federalists protested that the Henry documents were nothing more or less than "an electioneering trick" and a desperate attempt to raise the temperature of war fever.

Yet the revelation that the Henry affair was so much hot air failed to cool war fever. Both Congress and the American people were, in fact, divided on the issue of war, but the majority of both were sufficient to bring that war about. And so, amid much jubilation and solemn prayer, it came.

There were instant and abundant reasons for regret.

The first campaigns were uniformly disastrous. At Detroit, on the Niagara frontier, and in New York, American forces suffered one defeat after another. Despite its size, the U.S. Navy fared better, and in 1813, Captain Oliver Hazard Perry won control of Lake Erie and General William Henry Harrison defeated British and Indian forces at the Battle of the Thames. Despite these signal triumphs, an attempt to invade

Canada failed horribly, and, even worse, in 1814, with Napoleonic France in collapse, the British were able to turn their full attention to the war with the United States. They invaded from the north in a campaign that culminated in the burning of Washington, D.C., an action that sent both Madison and the War Hawk Congress fleeing the capital for their very lives. American fortunes revived a bit later, when

"It has become, indeed, sufficiently certain that the commerce of the United States is to be sacrificed, not as interfering with the belligerent rights of Great Britain . . . but as interfering with the monopoly which she covets for her own commerce and navigation."

—President James Madison, message to Congress, June 1, 1812

the British failed to capture Baltimore, and a splendid American naval victory on Lake Champlain forced the English invaders to retreat back into Canada, thereby prompting British diplomats in December 1814 to end the war by signing a treaty at Ghent, Belgium, in a peace conference that had been fitfully under way since August.

NEWS OF THE TREATY OF GHENT did not reach the United States until Americans also heard that General Andrew Jackson had stunningly defeated the British at the Battle of New Orleans. This American victory came after the war had officially ended, but before news of the treaty had been received. It served, therefore, to steep the whole struggle in an air of triumph, even though not a single one of America's war aims had been achieved. The Treaty of Ghent did nothing more than restore the "status quo antebellum"—the state of matters before the war.

Yet, for the United States, it would take more than a treaty to restore the status quo. Most of the public buildings of Washington lay in ashes. The United States economy was in deep depression. And westerners, the very people most directly represented by the War Hawks, had ample reason to believe that their nation had frankly lost the war, since the Treaty of Ghent barred all military activity in their part of the country until the United States had concluded treaties with the "Indian allies of the English." For the time being, this left the Indians free to roam the western territory at will, while local American authorities were hamstrung by an international agreement. It was a military hiatus many Indian leaders exploited to the fullest, using it to launch their most destructive raids of the period. A war of choice rather than necessity, the War of 1812 came very close to substantially reducing, if not destroying, the United States of America.

John C. Calhoun and Nullification (1832)
THE DECISION TO DISSOLVE A NATION

According to most accounts, the Civil War began in South Carolina at four thirty on the morning of April 12, 1861, when sixty-seven-year-old Edmund Ruffin, a rural Virginia newspaper editor, long-haired and wild-eyed "fire-eater" in the defense of slavery, pulled the lanyard on a cannon pointed against Fort Sumter. Through all the rest of that Friday and into Saturday, some four thousand more rounds followed, battering parts of the fort to rubble.

Thus most accounts. The truth is that the Civil War began—and the American union started to unravel—long before any shot was fired. Its beginning may be traced to the day in 1619 when a Dutch ship landed twenty Africans in Jamestown, Virginia, for sale as slaves there. Or it might be said to have started in 1789, when the U.S. Constitution came into force all but silent on the subject of slavery. But perhaps it is most accurate to say that the Civil War began on November 24, 1832, the day the state legislature of South Carolina passed an ordinance to "nullify" a federal law of the United States. On that day, all that was missing was the shooting.

Ever since the Civil War, and to this very day, it has been easy to find people willing to argue that the conflict had little or nothing to do with slavery, which, as a cause for war (they say), was secondary to issues of "economics" or "state's rights." But such responses are only dodges. The American people went to war for a variety of reasons in 1861–65, but the core truth is this: If there had been no slavery in the United States, there would have been no Civil War. Economics and state's rights were real issues, but they were part and parcel of the overriding issue that was slavery.

Slavery was the engine that drove the South's agrarian economic system, which was dedicated to producing raw materials for manufacture by others. Some of these raw materials, chiefly cotton, were shipped to textile mills in the North, but most of what the South produced was exported. The great bulk of Southern cotton was spun into cloth in the mills of England, which in turn exported the manufactured product back to the United States, and through the first quarter of the nineteenth century, Southern cotton exporters enjoyed trade with England and its other European customers mostly unfettered by U.S. tariffs and duties. This was a tremendous boon to the agricultural economy of the South, but it came at the expense of the embryonic industrial economy of the North. Each manufactured item Americans imported from abroad was one fewer item they purchased domestically. Without a market, homegrown industry struggled, stunted.

In an effort to foster American industry, Congress enacted a protective tariff in 1828, which levied a substantial duty on imported manufactured items. Naturally, the people of the Northeast hailed the legislation, even as Southerners howled with indignation over it. The purpose of the tariffs was to make European goods so costly in the United States that Americans would be compelled to buy from domestic manufacturers. But if U.S. consumers bought fewer European products, European manufacturers would purchase less of the raw materials produced by the South. Southern political leaders therefore took to calling the 1828 legislation the "Tariff of Abominations."

Foremost among these leaders was John C. Calhoun, a South Carolinian whose fiery nationalism had moved him to introduce in Congress the declaration of war against England in 1812. Indeed, Calhoun had promoted the War of 1812 so vigorously that a colleague christened him the "young Hercules who carried the war on his shoulders."

After the war, Calhoun's nationalist passion grew even stronger, and he advocated federal funding of a permanent national road system as well as the creation of a large standing army and a modern navy. Setting aside the parochial interests of his own region, he even voted for an early protective tariff, in 1816. Recognizing in young Calhoun an eloquent and energetic patriot, President James Monroe appointed him secretary of war in 1817, and John Quincy Adams, tapped as Monroe's secretary of state, pronounced Calhoun to be "above all sectional and factious prejudices more than any other statesman of this Union with whom I have ever acted."

Calhoun may have been, at the time, above sectional prejudice, but he was intensely prejudiced where his own ambition was concerned. He burned with a desire to become president, and although he would go on to serve as vice president first under John Quincy Adams and then Andrew Jackson, the office of chief executive eluded him. Doubtless resulting in part from his frustrated ambition, Calhoun became increasingly cantankerous as he aged. The passing years also brought a turn from what had been passionate nationalism to fanatical regionalism. In 1828, even as he served as Adams's vice president, Calhoun wrote and anonymously published the *South Carolina Exposition and Protest*, a pamphlet arguing that any state possessed the right to deem the Tariff of Abominations unconstitutional and unilaterally declare it "null and void."

It was a stunning idea—that any *state* could nullify a *national* law— but it was not an original idea of Calhoun's. No lesser figures than James Madison and Thomas Jefferson had introduced the concept when they wrote, respectively in 1798 and 1799, the Virginia and the Kentucky resolutions. Composed on behalf of the legislatures of Virginia and Kentucky, these documents had declared that the Alien and Sedition Acts— reactionary and repressive legislation sponsored by the Federalist administration of John Quincy Adams's father, John Adams, and voted up by a Congress fearful of French-inspired radicalism—violated the Bill of Rights. That assertion was hard to argue with, but what followed from it was downright inflammatory. On behalf of the two state legislatures, Jefferson and Madison argued that, because the acts were unconstitutional, they could and should be "nullified" by any state that chose to do so.

Yet even acting from a precedent established by two of the nation's founding fathers, Calhoun at first got little traction for nullification in 1828. Much as Southerners hated the Tariff of Abominations, they roundly repudiated Calhoun's nullification theory, and Jefferson Davis, the Mississippian destined to become the first and final president of the Confederate States of America, argued with particularly notable eloquence against the idea, emphatically denying that any state had the right to choose to invalidate a federal law.

Calhoun's campaign on behalf of nullification seemed destined to defeat when the entire issue of the Tariff of Abominations suddenly faded with the election of Andrew Jackson as president in November of 1828. A Southerner, Jackson ran in part on a platform of tariff reform, and that was sufficient to mollify the South—at least until Southerners saw how narrow in scope the actual reform was. The Tariff Act of 1832, passed during the Jackson administration, was potentially as damaging to Southern commerce as the Tariff of Abominations had been.

With enactment of the new tariff, Calhoun abruptly resigned as vice president to accept election to the Senate. In the meantime, on November 24, 1832, a special South Carolina convention revived Calhoun's earlier proposal by passing an Ordinance of Nullification, which barred the collection of federally imposed tariff duties in the state. Although the nullification option was most closely associated with John C. Calhoun, it was another South Carolina senator, Robert Y. Hayne, who actually presented nullification to the Senate. Hayne took Calhoun's theory to the logical conclusion Calhoun himself had avoided. He argued that not only could a state nullify an unconstitutional law, but that it could also, if necessary, secede from the Union.

This theory of state's rights did not simply entail the possibility of the dissolution of the United States; it was, in fact, the denial of a *United States*. If any single constituent of a nation could defy the law of the nation and even leave that nation at will, there was no nation—just a collection of constituent states.

Daniel Webster, senator from Massachusetts, rose in reply to Hayne, launching into an eloquent defense of the powers of the federal government as the basis of nationhood itself. "Liberty *and* Union," he declared, "now and forever, one and inseparable!"

Through Hayne, nullification was transformed from Calhoun's theory to the source of a critical showdown between the will of a state and the law of the nation. Everyone understood that the scope of the crisis reached far beyond the issue of the tariff. Hayne, Calhoun, and the newly won advocates of nullification said they were fighting for state's rights, but what that meant in this instance was a fight to protect and preserve slavery. Calhoun in particular foresaw the likelihood that, sooner or later, the antislavery North would achieve a majority in the Senate and when that day came, it would attempt to legislate slavery out of existence. This would happen, Calhoun believed, unless the doctrine of state's rights, the cornerstone of which was nullification, could be made to override the national will, which, Calhoun and other Southern leaders feared, would eventually be dictated by a more

> **"When my eyes shall be turned to behold for the last time the sun in heaven, may I not see him shining on the broken and dishonored fragments of a once glorious Union. . . . Let their last feeble and lingering glance rather behold the gorgeous ensign of the republic . . . not a stripe erased or polluted, nor a single star obscured."**
>
> —Senator Daniel Webster, reply to Senator Robert Y. Hayne of South Carolina, January 26–27, 1830

populous North. Calhoun passionately addressed the Senate with a speech in February 1837:

> If we do not defend ourselves, none will defend us; if we yield, we will be more and more pressed as we recede; and, if we submit, we will be trampled underfoot. Be assured that emancipation itself would not satisfy these fanatics; that gained, the next step would be to raise the Negroes to a social and political equality with the whites; and, that being effected, we would soon find the present condition of the two races reversed. . . . I dare not hope that anything I can say will arouse the South to a due sense of danger. I fear it is beyond the power of mortal voice to awaken it in time from the fatal security into which it has fallen.

With serenely arrogant confidence, Calhoun assumed that Jackson, as a Southerner, would yield to nullification by backing down on enforcement of the tariff. But Calhoun had badly misread Old Hickory. The combative president responded to the South Carolina nullification resolution on December 10, 1832, with an executive proclamation upholding the constitutionality of the tariff, denying nullification—the power of any state to block enforcement of a federal law—and concluding with a threat of armed intervention to support the collection duties. To make good on the threat, he quickly obtained from Congress passage of a Force Act, by which he was empowered to use the military to enforce the tariff.

Passage of the Force Act, which South Carolina promptly "nullified," seemed to many the inevitable prelude to a full-scale civil war, but early in 1833 Congress passed a compromise tariff, which South Carolina accepted. This rendered moot the state legislature's defiant nullification of the Force Act because the federal government no longer had reason to implement the act. There would be no confrontation of arms, and so the crisis passed—or, rather, receded. For states' rights and nullification had introduced secession, the dissolution of the Union, as a very real option, and civil war was surely just a matter of time.

Or was it? Little less than thirty years after the nullification crisis, and now on the very verge of the Civil War, Abraham Lincoln, speaking his first inaugural address, tried to persuade his fellow citizens that secession was neither more nor less than folly:

> If the minority will not acquiesce, the majority must, or the Government must cease. There is no other alternative, for continuing the Government is acquiescence on one side or the other. If a minority in such case will secede rather than acquiesce, they make a precedent which in turn will divide and ruin them, for a minority of their own will secede from them whenever a majority refuses to be controlled by such minority. For instance, why may not any portion of a new confederacy a year or two hence arbitrarily secede again, precisely as portions of the present Union now claim to secede from it?

As CALHOUN ESPOUSED IT, nullification was nothing less than the assertion that each state was a nation unto itself and that, therefore, the so-called United States could never be more than a collection of sovereign nations. Indeed, secession was the logical and inevitable end of nullification. Calhoun may have believed that a state could nullify some laws and choose to abide by others, but this was self-delusion. As with any pledge of loyalty, allegiance to the Union could be not be a halfway, occasional, sporadic, or selective matter. A state was either subordinate to the nation or it was not and, if not, it was either no part of the nation or there was no nation to be part of. Lincoln explained that to affirm the "right" of secession was to render the idea of nationhood forever absurd, impossible, and without meaning. Secession was political, social, and human folly, which, as it turned out, could be defended not by any rational argument but only by the greatest folly of all: civil war.

Russell, Majors, and Waddell and the Pony Express (1860)

THE DECISION TO BACK A DREAM

The United States, it has often been pointed out, is the only nation in history founded not on some notion of tribalism, religion, or the hereditary right of this or that family of rulers, but on an idea, an idea of liberty compounded of Greek and Roman concepts of government plus Enlightenment philosophy as filtered through the minds of a small but brilliant cadre of "founding fathers." This is all true enough, but we must not overlook the physical fact that underlay that idea of liberty: space.

In contrast to Europe, where all the land was claimed, carved up, and used up, the vastness of the American continent furnished sufficient space in which men and women could indeed be free. Yet the vastness of America, especially the American West, also presented formidable problems of communication, supply, and commerce. Traversing a space with few and poor roads was expensive, risky, and at times impossible. Nevertheless, if space was an obstacle, it was also an opportunity for freighters and others sufficiently enterprising to run the risks of creating transport in a wilderness.

One such man was James Brown, a freighter out of Independence, Missouri, who had made a fortune running wagons to supply troops during the U.S.-Mexican War of 1846–48 and, afterward, to supply the army garrisons patrolling the frontier. Business got to be so good that he took on William H. Russell as a partner, and when Brown succumbed in 1850 to one of the chief dangers of life on the trail—typhus—Russell took over the business and acquired a new partner, William B. Waddell. In 1854, the pair approached their chief competitor, Alexander Majors, with a proposal of merger, and in this way a charming if dandified New Englander (Russell), a tight-fisted Virginian of Scots descent (Waddell), and a Missouri plainsman (Majors) joined forces to create a freighting empire, Russell, Majors & Waddell (RM&W), that would endure until the Civil War.

In 1855 alone, the firm carried 2.5 million pounds of freight across the plains in five hundred wagons organized into twenty wagon trains. Seventeen hundred men were employed as wagon masters, drivers, stock tenders, and the like. Motive power was furnished by seventy-five hundred oxen. Alexander Majors had personally specified the design of the wagons, whose carefully seasoned wood was built into capacious boxes that flared outward to prevent five thousand pounds of cargo from shifting. The front end of each wagon was curved like a ship's prow, the rear end square to make loading and unloading easy and efficient. Majors had a general's talent for logistical organization, dividing his forces into "outfits" of twenty-six wagons each under the sovereign command of a wagon master aided by a single assistant. Each outfit also included a herder, who drove forty to fifty oxen as replacements for those actually pulling the wagons, and a night herder, who guarded the animals at rest after dark.

> "Such acres of wagons! Such pyramids of extra axletrees! Such herds of oxen! Such regiments of drivers!"
>
> —Horace Greeley, describing the Russell, Majors & Waddell Leavenworth, Kansas, terminal, in his New York *Tribune*

Freighting was labor and stock intensive, and it was slow, each wagon train proceeding at the rate of about fifteen miles per day. The business could be highly profitable, but it was always a drain on cash flow, and it was subject to any number of catastrophes, both physical and fiscal.

The year 1857 had promised to be a great one for the company. A new contract with the army called for transporting five million pounds of goods. The original five hundred wagons grew to eight hundred, and the firm was scouring the West for bullwhackers and other personnel. Then came the so-called Mormon War, in which a militant Mormon sect, the Danites, used terrorist violence to eject "gentiles" from the lands the

Danites claimed. The insurrection prompted President James Buchanan to dispatch twenty-five hundred more federal troops to insure the safe reception of the new territorial governor of Utah. Three million additional pounds of supplies had to be transported for those soldiers. Russell, Majors & Waddell paid premium prices to find the necessary oxen and drivers, but no matter. The partners had every reason to believe that their greater fortune was in the making.

What they didn't reckon on was the guerrilla tactics of the rogue Mormons, who burned three entire RM&W wagon trains. This mischance was compounded by a severe winter with a crippling snowfall. By the end of 1857, the firm was out half a million dollars, and the War Department summarily informed the partners that, because it had exhausted its appropriation, it could not pay their company. To add insult to injury, the public's perception of the Mormon War had rapidly turned 180 degrees; what had started as a universal sentiment to put these insolent bigamists in their place became admiration for a people willing to sacrifice everything to defend what they believed in. Russell, Majors & Waddell found they had hitched their wagons not only to a profitless star, but an unpopular one.

Majors and Waddell believed that only a miracle would now save them from bankruptcy. Russell believed that all he needed was a fresh opportunity. And in 1859, when Judge Joseph Holt became the United States's postmaster general, Russell was sure he had found one. The new postal chief decided to bring to the Post Office Department a new economy. Discovering that the federal government was subsidizing six western mail routes—a sea route via Panama, another via Tehuantepec, Mexico, and four overland routes, he canceled two, curtailed service between two more, and reduced the subsidy accorded the Panama sea route. Far from being alarmed at the reduction in government money, William H. Russell saw opportunity. The new postmaster's action had radically reduced competition for overland mail and freight service.

RM&W was a freighting firm, but now Russell saw coaching—the transportation of passengers and mail—as the company's way to salvation.

Now that Postmaster General Holt had fortuitously removed some competition from the field, Russell reasoned that the time was ripe for him and his partners to jump in.

The firm of John Butterfield still operated the government-subsidized "oxbow" route, which took its name from its roundabout southerly course, starting at St. Louis, going to Los Angeles, then heading north to San Francisco. This left unserved the far shorter and more direct Central Route to the West Coast via the South Pass through the Rockies. Best of all, rumors of a major gold strike were flying out of Pikes Peak country. If a gold rush came, prospectors and others would need coach and mail service, and RM&W would stand to profit from coach service between the Mississippi Valley and Denver.

Already burdened with debt, Waddell and Majors were unconvinced that the Central Route would pay off. Russell therefore decided to form a separate coaching company, teaming up with John S. Jones to create the Leavenworth and Pikes Peak Express Company. He borrowed all the money he could scrape together to build stations and scratch out roads, and to purchase fifty Concord coaches and a thousand mules to pull them—Russell well knew that mules were better suited than horses to work in the arid country the new company would serve.

Pikes Peak Express cost a thousand dollars a day to run. And the vaunted gold rush failed to materialize—at least, it failed to begin on schedule—and many discouraged prospectors deserted the brand-new city of Denver. When that happened, the embryonic firm's revenues evaporated. Staring ruin in the face, Russell decided to tap a familiar source: government subsidy. But he needed one quickly and so decided to use what little liquidity he had left to buy out a company that already had a mail contract, the John M. Hockaday stage line, which ran between Independence, Missouri, and Salt Lake City, Utah. The franchise was worth $130,000 in federal subsidy money, but Russell had to come up with a cool $144,000 to buy it, putting the operation $14,000 in the hole when it began on July 2, 1859. Russell's freighting partners, Majors and

Waddell, fearful that Pikes Peak Express would fail and that its failure would finish off RM&W as well, bought out Pikes Peak Express and renamed it the Central Overland California & Pikes Peak Express.

They had been forced into a desperate gamble. The subsidized contract Russell had acquired to carry mail between Placerville, California, and Salt Lake City was modest, and they needed to grow the company quickly beyond this. That meant knocking Butterfield out of the running, and that could only be done by providing dramatic proof that the Central Route was superior to Butterfield's oxbow.

William Russell was ready to supply the necessary drama. He had a dream, and it was a wild one.

Russell proposed to deliver mail from St. Joseph, Missouri, to Sacramento, California—a distance forty-four miles shy of an even two thousand—in ten days. The means by which he planned to accomplish this were radical. There would be no passengers on this run. For that matter, there would be no stagecoaches or wagons. Just ponies—a relay of them stretching across the continent, and a lone rider on each. He would call it the Pony Express.

Stripped down to ponies and riders with nothing but rude stations along the way, the start-up costs were relatively modest—and Waddell and Majors were desperate. They gave their visionary partner the go-ahead, and, after launching a national advertising campaign and planting stories in the nation's newspapers, Russell sent Billy Richardson, the first rider, out of St. Joseph on April 3, 1860, carrying forty-nine letters and some special-edition newspapers.

Richardson was slated to ride the first seventy-five miles or so at full gallop, until he hit the first of twenty-five "home stations" constructed along the route. There another rider would relieve him. At intermediate "relay stations"—there were 165 in all, ten to fifteen miles apart—riders would change horses. Russell had purchased five hundred horses, semi-wild "outlaw" animals, some having fetched as much as two hundred dollars. He had recruited eighty riders, who would be continuously en route, forty westbound and forty eastbound. Each of them had reportedly answered ads calling for "daring young men, orphans preferred."

They were daring, and they were young. The average age was nineteen, although one, William F. Cody—later better known as Buffalo Bill—was just fifteen when he joined up, and another boy, David Jay, became a Pony Express rider at thirteen. All were wiry, none over 135 pounds in weight, and very well paid. At a time when a common laborer earned about $20–$30 a month, Pony Express riders were paid $100 to $150 a month, in addition to their room and board.

They earned their pay. One day, Cody reached the home station at the end of his seventy-six-mile run, only to find that his relief had been killed by Indians. Exhausted as he was, Cody remounted and rode another eighty-five miles. Then he turned around and made the return trip, for a total of 322 miles.

Although a hostile climate and punishing terrain were the greatest dangers to riders, Indian attacks were common enough. Rider Bob Haslam was set upon by Paiutes and took an arrow through the arm and another through the jaw, resulting in an excruciating fracture. No matter. He rode on, making 120 miles in eight hours, ten minutes, using up thirteen horses in the process. For the riders, it was, of course, never really about the money, as good as that was. It was about adventure, about what westerners called "grit." In the nineteen months of its operation, representing 650,000 miles of travel, the Pony Express lost only one consignment of mail. Pony Express riders carried the text of Abraham Lincoln's inaugural address from St. Joseph to Sacramento not in the promised ten days, but in the incredible time of seven days, seventeen hours, and, from the very beginning, the Pony Express venture captured the nation's imagination.

> "The first trip of the Pony Express was made in ten days—an average of two hundred miles a day. But we soon began stretching our riders and making better time."
>
> —"Buffalo Bill" Cody

But it never made a dime. Mail carried by the service initially commanded the lordly sum of five dollars per half ounce, which was soon reduced to two dollars for the same weight. Yet it cost Russell, Majors & Waddell sixteen dollars to deliver a letter that, including federal subsidy, returned just three dollars in revenue. As a romantic and exciting loss leader, the Pony Express did draw business to RM&W's Central Overland Route, but hardly enough to make up the shortfall. It also did indeed dramatize the virtues of the Central Route to a Congress that was debating an Overland Mail Bill during the summer of 1860. Yet, while the Pony Express made the debate exciting, southerners in Congress managed to keep the major government mail contract in the hands of Butterfield and his southerly oxbow route.

Then the worst happened, and the end came.

On October 24, 1861, a telegraph line from the East (Omaha, Nebraska—with connections to the eastern seaboard) was joined to one from the West (at Carson City, Nevada, with connections to the West Coast). In the space of time it took to splice a few final connections, communication across the expanse of the continent was achieved in a matter of seconds rather than days. The Pony Express was out of business—the closure of the company announced just two days after the telegraph was completed—and Russell, Majors & Waddell were riding hell for leather into bankruptcy.

Russell believed he had yet one more ace up his sleeve. He traveled to Washington, D.C., late in 1860, where he met with Goddard Bailey, a man representing himself as a "dealer in government bonds." Exactly what happened next is not entirely clear. As far as can be determined, Russell sought to borrow, through Bailey, $150,000 in state securities, which he intended to use as collateral against which to raise the cash necessary to stave off the demise of his company. Bailey did deliver the bonds, whereupon Russell asked for another loan. That's when Bailey revealed that he was not actually a bond dealer at all, but a Department of the Interior clerk. He explained further that he himself had "borrowed"—a federal jury would later say embezzled—the bonds from the department's Indian Trust Fund.

It was quite a story. The thing is, on hearing it, Russell did not even flinch. Instead, he asked Bailey to "borrow" some more, until, finally, some $870,000 in securities had changed hands.

Yet so deep was the financial pit into which the freighter had slid, that even this enormous sum could not resurrect Russell, Majors & Waddell. Seeing that he would never be repaid, Bailey was carried away on a wave of despair. On December 22, 1860, he sent a letter of confession directly to President Buchanan. William H. Russell was in federal prison the next day.

RUSSELL HAD HAD A DREAM, which he shared with the nation. Much as the nation relished that dream—and stories about the Pony Express continue to be told—it was unwilling to pay for it. In an irony of history, had Russell not succumbed to the temptation of breaking the law, he and his company might have been saved after all. The outbreak of the Civil War meant that the United States could no longer subsidize the southerly Butterfield Route. The Central Route, which went through secure Union territory, was now in favor, and a million-dollar annual subsidy was in the offing. Of course, awarding a major contract to a firm tainted by criminal fraud was out of the question. The Butterfield Overland Mail got the prize.

"Nothing great was ever accomplished without enthusiasm," Ralph Waldo Emerson wrote, and yet enthusiasm alone—even in the form of vision coupled with boundless optimism—is not sufficient to achieve greatness. That the Pony Express endures in legend attests to the power of a dream. That it failed as a financial fact attests to the inadequacy of dream alone.

Count Leopold von Berchtold and His Ultimatum (1914)

THE DECISION TO START A "LITTLE WAR"

At 11:15 AM (local time) in the provincial Bosnian capital of Sarajevo, on June 28, 1914, the open-topped limousine carrying Franz

Ferdinand, archduke of Austria-Hungary, and his wife, the Grand Duchess Sophie, having made a wrong turn, came to a stop a few feet from where Gavrilo Princip happened to be standing. Bony and disheveled, his complexion ashen gray with the pallor of advanced tuberculosis, the disaffected Bosnian student reached into the pocket of his shabby greatcoat for the Browning revolver with which an agent of a Serbian subversive movement had armed him. He withdrew the weapon, leveled it point-blank at the imperial couple, and fired two or three times.

"If a general war begins," Otto von Bismarck had observed many years earlier, "it will be because of some damn fool thing in the Balkans."

He was in a position to know. In 1871, as Prussia's chancellor, Bismarck forged from a collection of petty states a unified Germany after Prussia's lightning victory over France in the Franco-Prussian War. The new empire was powered by coal from the Alsace-Lorraine, the territory France gave up as a condition of surrender. Bismarck understood that it was one thing to win territory but quite another to hold on to it, so he orchestrated all Europe as if he were a master symphonist, arranging the political isolation of France by binding Russia and Austria-Hungary to the new Germany. This led to a series of treaties and alliances among the nations of the Old World, some public and some secret so that before the first decade of the twentieth century

> **"Let us put Germany in the saddle, so to speak—it already knows how to ride."**
>
> **—Otto von Bismarck, 1867**

was over, what had begun as a clash between Germany and France turned into the division of all the major European powers into two opposing, very heavily armed camps, in some cases despite previous allegiances: Germany and Austria-Hungary on one side and France, Russia, and Britain on the other—with Italy more or less oscillating between the two.

It was a standoff, and, as the 1910s concluded, Europe appeared deceptively stable because the standoff allowed precious little movement. There was no stability—apparent or actual—in one place, however. The

Balkan Peninsula was perpetually wracked by violence culminating in the First Balkan War of 1912–13 and the Second Balkan War of 1913. The first conflict pitted the Balkan states of Bulgaria, Serbia, and Greece against Turkey and resulted in the loss of most of Turkey's European possessions. In the second, Bulgaria took on Serbia, Greece, Romania, and Turkey, the latter losing even more of its foothold in Europe. In the end, the Balkan wars not only failed to restore stability to what Winston Churchill would years later call the "soft underbelly" of Europe, they left the region smoldering with a new nationalism. Before the wars, the Balkan states had been contested over by Turkey and Austria-Hungary, the region's major powers. In the aftermath of the wars, the Balkan realms sought independence from both empires, even as they forged a pan-Slavic ethnic identity with Russia, whose Czar Nicholas II eagerly offered his empire as the defender of all who proclaimed themselves Slavs.

In the assassination of his nation's archduke, Austria-Hungary's foreign minister, Count Leopold von Berchtold, saw a shining opportunity. If he could pin the assassination directly on Serbia—recently emancipated from the Austro-Hungarian Empire and continually provoking the empire's other Slavic provinces to fight for their independence as well—he would be in a position to punish Serbia and thereby (he hoped) stave off the ongoing disintegration of Hapsburg Europe.

> **"One sees many wounded soldiers with broken noses, the result of having held their guns improperly while firing."**
>
> —Hans Freiherr von Wangenheim, the German ambassador to the Ottomans, on the incompetence of the Turkish army during the Balkan War of 1912

At his trial, Princip gave Berchtold valuable ammunition, painting his action as a grand political deed. "I do not feel like a criminal," he declared, "because I put away the one who was doing evil. Austria as it is represents evil for our people and therefore should not exist. . . . The political union of the Yugoslavs was always before my eyes, and that was my basic idea. Therefore it was necessary in the first place to free the Yugoslavs . . . from

Austria. This . . . moved me to carry out the assassination of the heir apparent, for I considered him as very dangerous for Yugoslavia."

Princip was quickly convicted. But because two decades earlier a parish priest had written in his record of Princip's baptism an incorrect birthdate—July 13, 1884, instead of June 13—Princip was officially regarded as nineteen years old when he murdered the archduke and grand duchess. At twenty, conviction for murder meant death; at nineteen, the maximum possible sentence was twenty years. Not that it much mattered. The corrosive progress of his tuberculosis doomed Gavrilo Princip to an early death, and solitary confinement in a cold, damp cell would doubtless hasten the coming of that fate.

The crime of a youth judged too young to forfeit his life would have had no further consequence if the men in power had been men of wisdom and goodwill. But Count Leopold von Berchtold, for one, was not such a man.

Princip had been coached and financed by a Serbian-based subversive band known as the Black Hand, an organization the government of Serbia both denounced and disavowed. Nevertheless, Berchtold unilaterally declared the Serbian government itself guilty of having murdered the archduke and his wife. Eager to mete out punishment to the little country and thereby crush the Bosnian nationalism that Serbia supported, Berchtold had no desire to avert a war. On the contrary, he cherished the motive to provoke one—short, sharp, cheap, and triumphant.

> "Austria-Hungary, with the bellicose frivolity of senile empires, determined to use the [assassination of Franz Ferdinand] to absorb Serbia as she had absorbed Bosnia and Herzegovina in 1909."
>
> —Barbara Tuchman,
> *The Guns of August*, 1962

Berchtold, however, failed to realize that he was a man in a dark room packed to the very ceiling with explosives. That was Europe after Bismarck: Nations great and small were bound by sheaves of interlocking treaties and covenants. To start a war with one country, even a very small and inconsequential country, was to strike a match in that dynamite-loaded room. In the Europe of 1914, there could be no such thing as a short, sharp, and local war.

As he issued a call for the mobilization of the Austro-Hungarian army, Berchtold also sent a message to the German government to confirm that the empire could count on Germany's support. On July 5, Kaiser Wilhelm II invited the Austrian ambassador to lunch in Berlin. In an expansive mood, the kaiser promised that Germany would stand shoulder to shoulder with Austria-Hungary, even if this meant war with Russia; for as Wilhelm well knew, Czar Nicholas II had bound his nation to defend the Slavic Serbs.

War with Russia could prove catastrophic, and those who were privy to the lunchtime exchange between the kaiser and the ambassador ascribed the pledge to mere impulse rather than serious diplomacy. In any case, they reasoned, Wilhelm could afford such an expansive impulse. He, like everyone else, was confident that little Serbia would comply with whatever Austria-Hungary demanded. There would never be a war.

At six o'clock on the evening of July 23, Berchtold delivered ten demands to Belgrade. For him, the most important of these was a Serbian pledge to prosecute everyone involved in the assassination. Pursuant to this, Austrian—not Serbian—officials would be in charge of the investigation and would be permitted to operate freely within Serbia, given carte blanche to ferret out in Serbia all sources of anti-Austrian sedition, subversion, agitation, and propaganda. Berchtold gave the government forty-eight hours to reply.

Serbia's premier, Nicholas Pashich, consulted the Russians. The czar, they assured him, would "do everything" to defend Serbia; nevertheless, they advised Pashich to avoid outright defiance. The Russians told him to accede to every Austrian demand that did not require total forfeiture of Serbian sovereignty and nationhood. Thus, on July 25, Pashich returned Serbia's response. He accepted nine of the ten demands unconditionally, but he balked at allowing Austrian officials to operate independently within Serbia. To permit that would put into question Serbian independence.

Berchtold deemed this single demurral a cause for war.

Britain's foreign minister, Sir Edward Grey, stepped in with an offer to mediate the crisis. Wilhelm was unavailable, however, having chosen this of all times to take a holiday. In his absence, the royal ministers flatly rejected Grey's offer. The kaiser returned to Berlin on July 27, one day before Emperor Franz Josef signed Austria-Hungary's declaration of war against Serbia. Russia responded immediately by ordering the partial mobilization of its forces near the Austrian border.

Suddenly aware that the war was real, German Chancellor Theobald von Bethmann-Hollweg fired off a nearly indignant telegram to Berchtold: "Serbia has in fact met the Austrian demands in so wide-sweeping a manner that if the Austro-Hungarian government adopted a wholly uncompromising attitude, a gradual revulsion of public opinion against it in all of Europe would have to be reckoned with."

When Berchtold did not reply, Bethmann-Hollweg sent him another telegram the next day, this time warning that Germany had no intention of being dragged into war because Austria "has ignored our advice." Even Kaiser Wilhelm woke from his state of denial, declaring that Serbia's reply to the ultimatum—agreeing to nine out of ten of its terms—"dissipates every reason for war."

Belatedly, the German leadership groped for some lever to turn off the terrible machine that had been set into motion. Yet while Bethmann-Hollweg had exhibited rationality in his admonitory telegrams to Berchtold, he presented an insulting and provocative front to Sir Edward Grey. He told Grey that if Britain pledged to stay out of the war, if it promised to remain neutral, Germany would not annex any French territory. Grey took this as blackmail and, on July 31, spurned the proposal as "infamous." At the same time, Bethmann-Hollweg put Russia on notice that Germany considered the partial mobilization of Russian troops a prelude to war. In response, the German government put its navy on a war footing in the North Sea. This moved Winston Churchill, Britain's First Sea Lord, to mobilize the British Grand Fleet.

In the meantime, Austria-Hungary's war on Serbia had already begun. On July 29, 1914, Austrian gunboats shelled Belgrade, Serbia's capital. On August 30, oblivious of Bethmann-Hollweg's warning, Czar Nicholas II elevated Russia's mobilization from partial to full. Learning of this, Helmuth von Moltke, chief of staff of the German army, picked up a telephone and instructed Field Marshal Franz Conrad von Hötzendorff, chief of staff of the Austro-Hungarian army, to "mobilize at once against Russia." It was a momentous action, indicating just how far beyond any government control events had spiraled. Moltke was a military commander, not an officer of the German civilian government. Without consulting his own government, he spoke to a military commander of another nation's army. That commander, likewise without consulting his government, summarily ordered a shift from the Austrian army's Plan B, the scenario for a local war against Serbia, to Plan R: general warfare against Serbia and Russia.

The German military was also governed by a plan, a plan that took precedence over all leaders, military and civilian. It had been drawn up at the start of the century by Count Alfred von Schlieffen and repeatedly refined and modified over the years. Yet despite all the thought that had gone into the Schlieffen Plan, it assumed only one scenario: a war against both France *and* Russia. This had the effect of committing Germany to such a war, the biggest war possible. By assuming that any European war would be a general, all-encompassing, all-out war, the Schlieffen Plan virtually ensured that any European war would instantly expand. Even more significantly, Moltke and everyone else in the German military and civilian government assumed that every other European power operated from the same set of assumptions: that war meant general war. Thus certain that the European situation was beyond compromise, Germany issued an ultimatum to Russia, demanding that it end its general mobilization. Simultaneously the German government notified the French government that it would declare war on France if it made any move to mobilize.

Russia rejected the German ultimatum outright, but the French issued nothing more than a bland reply that the republic would consult its "own interests." Acting on a set of assumptions to which it could imagine no alternative, the German government took both the Russian and French replies as a call to battle and a motive for general mobilization, which Moltke ordered on August 1, 1914.

Now the Schlieffen Plan—Germany's sole war plan—was put into execution. Always assuming a two-front war, against France and Russia, the plan also assumed that the French were a more immediate threat than the Russians. France wielded a more modern and better-led army than Russia, whose forces were bigger but poorly equipped and poorly led. The Schlieffen Plan predicted that Russia would take at least six weeks to mobilize effectively. For that reason, the plan prescribed that the majority of German forces be employed in a lightning offensive against France while a smaller portion fought a strictly defensive war to hold off Russia. The Schlieffen Plan had a strict timetable. France had to be defeated within six weeks, so that forces could be rapidly transferred from the Western Front to the Eastern Front before Russia could complete its mobilization. Once France had been neutralized, Germany would transform its defensive posture in the East to an offensive: an invasion of Russia.

Like any war plan, the Schlieffen Plan was intended as a blueprint for victory. Had it been executed faithfully—which it was not—it might have been just that. The issue of victory aside, the Schlieffen Plan ensured the inevitable, irreversible expansion of war on the most massive of scales. Tactically the plan eschewed the obvious, a direct frontal assault on France, an east-to-west march across the border. Instead, it called for a "great wheel," a wide turning movement up through Flanders Plain, northeast of French territory. From here, the German armies would swoop down on France, from the north attacking the left flank of the French army, then hooking around it from behind. Outflanked on two vulnerable sides, the enemy army would be defeated.

Five German armies were to sweep wide from the Alsace-Lorraine in a great counterclockwise wheel, driving clear to the English Channel. "Let the sleeve of the last man on the right brush the English Channel,"

Schlieffen had admonished the field commanders. Not only would the German invaders strike the French army where any army was most vulnerable, the flank and the rear, they would penetrate so deeply into France so quickly that all of the fighting would take place on French soil and not in the Franco-German border regions. Should retreat become necessary, the invaders would have plenty of France in which to maneuver and fight, so that even in retreat, France, not Germany, would be ravaged.

Tactically the plan was brilliant. Strategically it suffered from a fatal flaw. The "great wheel" required the German army to invade Belgium, whose neutrality was guaranteed by treaty with Britain. Schlieffen knew this would mean that his plan would draw in the British, even though they had tried to hold themselves aloof from a continental war; however, he believed that the regular British army was too small to make much of a difference against a massive offensive and was confident that France would be defeated before Britain could call up or conscript a larger army of citizen soldiers. Indeed, the Schlieffen Plan worked astoundingly well for the first month of war. The German armies drove deep into France, whose armies seemed all but helpless against the onslaught.

And then the realities of war on the ground, supply and communications lines stretched thin, inadequate intelligence, and general confusion began to undo the execution of the paper plan. At the end of August 1914, when he had reached the very outskirts of Paris itself, General Alexander von Kluck deviated from the plan by turning his entire First German Army to the southeast, hoping thereby to exploit an opportunity to strike the exposed left flank of what he—mistakenly, as it turned out—thought was all that remained of the French army. In making this move Kluck exposed his own forces to attack from his French foes assembled in Paris. Suddenly and unexpectedly menaced, he dug in along the Marne River and, instead of capturing the French capital, found himself fighting the First Battle of the Marne. By this single move, a month of war was multiplied into four years of slaughter along a Western Front that rapidly grew into a great scar of trenches cut jaggedly from the English Channel in the north to the border of Switzerland in the south.

—

ALL LEOPOLD VON BERCHTOLD HAD WANTED TO DO was bloody the nose of an annoying little nation that he blamed for undermining the vast Austro-Hungarian Empire—never mind that the unwieldy Hapsburg realm had been eroded by decades of corruption and a ruling class that was inept, out of touch, and decidedly uninspired. Berchtold failed to understand that, in the Europe of his day, a little war was impossible. A small-minded warmonger, he ignited a cataclysm that would, over four years, involve 65,038,810 fighting men, of whom 8,020,780 would not live to return to their homes throughout Europe, America, and beyond. Yet worse, the Great War would come to be known as the First World War, because it left Europe no more secure than Bismarck's empire-building diplomacy had in the century previous. World War I would make World War II all but inevitable.

As for Garvrilo Princip, his tuberculosis, untreated in prison, spread unchecked, necessitating amputation of one of his arms. On April 28, 1918, the twenty-three-year-old's jailers entered his cell and found their prisoner drawn up into a tight, dead ball at the corner of his palette bed. Into the wall beside that bed, he had scratched three lines of verse:

> Our ghosts will walk through Vienna
> And roam through the palace
> Frightening the lords.

PART FOUR

The Decision to Retreat

Chief Justice Roger B. Taney
and Dred Scott (1857)

THE DECISION TO DENY HUMANITY

About the year 1795—no one kept a precise record—Dred Scott was born in Southampton County, Virginia, and by virtue of his birth to slaves came into the world as the property of the Peter Blow family. In 1830, the Blows moved to St. Louis, Missouri, where they fell on times so hard they were forced to sell Dred Scott to Dr. John Emerson, a U.S. Army surgeon. Emerson's job kept him moving from one fort to another in the Illinois and Wisconsin Territories, his slave in tow. But even slaves have lives, and while he was the property of Dr. Emerson, Scott met and married Harriet Robinson about the same time that Emerson himself married Irene Sandford. The Emersons and the Scotts returned to Missouri in 1842, and when Dr. Emerson died a year later, his brother-in-law John F. A. Sandford became executor of the Emerson estate—of which Dred Scott was a portion.

Scott, financed by the Blow family, whose fortunes were now recovered and who repented of having ever owned slaves, attempted to purchase his freedom from Irene Emerson in February 1846. When she refused, the Blows backed an 1846–47 lawsuit against executor Sandford to obtain Dred Scott's freedom—which, if granted, would also win freedom for his wife. The case came to trial in 1847 in a state courthouse in St. Louis, Scott's lawyers arguing that their client was now a full citizen of Missouri, having been made free by virtue of his terms of residence in Illinois, where slavery had been banned by the Northwest Ordinance of 1785, and in Wisconsin Territory, where the provisions of the Missouri Compromise of 1820 had made slavery illegal.

The trial ended in a loss for Scott, but the presiding judge granted a second trial based on an appeal that protested the introduction of hearsay evidence. That trial came to pass in 1850, the jury deciding that both Scotts should be freed. It was now Irene Sandford Emerson's turn to appeal, and in 1852, the Missouri Supreme Court struck down the lower court ruling, even though Missouri courts had consistently ruled that slaves taken into free states were automatically free. The court blandly remarked that "Times now are not as they were when the previous decisions on this subject were made."

Having breathed free for just two years, Mr. and Mrs. Scott were returned to Irene Emerson as her chattel. The pair hired a new set of lawyers, who, this time, sued in federal court. After losing, they appealed to the United States Supreme Court, which handed down its decision in 1857.

We can only assume that the Scotts and their lawyers hoped for impartial justice from the high court. What they received was a decision all too predictably divided in the very same way that the nation itself was divided. The court's Northern justices, who opposed slavery, upheld Scott's appeal, whereas the proslavery Southerners upheld the decision of the lower court. The proslavery justices were in the majority, and the chief among them, Roger B. Taney, a venerable, wizened, and leathery native of the slaveholding state of Maryland, wrote the decision.

Chief Justice Taney began by offering a single stark reason for denying Scott's appeal. He held that neither enslaved nor free blacks were

> **"The question is simply this: Can a Negro, whose ancestors were imported into this country and sold as slaves, become a member of the political community formed and brought into existence by the Constitution of the United States, and as such become entitled to all the rights and privileges and immunities, guaranteed by that instrument to the citizen?"**
>
> —From Chief Justice Taney's opinion in *Dred Scott v. Sandford*, 1857

citizens of the United States and, therefore, they had no standing to sue in federal court.

Stunningly direct and terrible, this technicality alone would have settled the case. But Taney felt compelled to push his ruling much further. Both intellectually and morally, it is a painful experience to cut one's way through the tangled prose of the decision he wrote. His major points were these: First, the Illinois law (originally flowing from the Northwest Ordinance) banning slavery had no force on Scott once he returned to Missouri, which was a slave state. Second, and even more significantly, the law that applied in Wisconsin Territory was also without force, because, Taney ruled, the provisions of the Missouri Compromise declaring the territory free had been beyond the power of Congress to enact. Taney concluded that the authority of Congress to acquire territories and create governments within those territories was limited by, among other things, the Fifth Amendment to the Constitution, which barred passage of any law that would deprive anyone of property, including slaves freed by virtue of having been brought into a free territory. Thus the Missouri Compromise was unconstitutional.

Ever since the Constitution had come into effect in 1789 without the inclusion of definitive statements concerning slavery, the government and people of the United States struggled to avoid civil war by maintaining a precarious balance between Senate representatives of slave states

> *"Resolved,* that no allegiance is due from any man, or any class of men, to a government founded and administered in iniquity, and that the only duty the colored man woes to a Constitution under which he is declared to be an inferior and degraded being, having no rights which white men are bound to respect, is to denounce and repudiate it, and to do what he can by all proper means to bring it into contempt."
>
> —Resolution introduced by Robert Purvis to a "Negro meeting" at Israel Church, Philadelphia, April 3, 1857, in response to the *Dred Scott* decision

and those of free states. When in 1818 the Territory of Missouri petitioned Congress for admission to the Union as a slave-holding state, the balance of twenty-two slave-state senators and twenty-two free-state senators was threatened. After a long and tortured debate, the Senate hammered out the so-called Missouri Compromise, by which it was agreed that Missouri would be admitted as a slave state, but that, simultaneously, Maine would be broken off from Massachusetts to be admitted as a new free state. That took care of the immediate crisis. Looking to the future, the compromise further provided that a line would be drawn across the Louisiana Territory at a latitude of 36 degrees, 30 minutes. North of this line, slavery would be forever banned (except in the single case of Missouri) and any slaves brought into the free portion of the territory would themselves be freed.

> *"Resolved . . .* **That in the judgment of this General Assembly [of the State of Ohio], every free person born within the limits of any state of this Union is a citizen thereof, and to deny to such person the right of suing in the courts of the United States, in those cases where that right is guaranteed by the Constitution to all citizens of the United States, is a palpable and unwarrantable violation of that sacred instrument."**
>
> —Resolution of the Ohio legislature, April 17, 1857, in response to the *Dred Scott* decision

In what was certainly the ugliest irony in American history, the chief justice of the highest court in the land had found a way to use the Bill of Rights to deny freedom to a human being. That stunning fact alone was sufficient to galvanize the abolitionist movement in the United States, and if Roger Taney had intended to uphold, bolster, and protect slavery, he had instead given the opponents of slavery the gift of a mighty righteousness.

And his decision did even more to bring about the ultimate doom of what Southerners politely referred to as their "peculiar institution." The

Dred Scott case was more than a cause for moral outrage. By defining slavery as essentially an issue of property, subject to the full protection of the Fifth Amendment, Taney's decision mandated that slavery be protected by federal law in all of the states, whether or not a given state practiced or permitted slavery. Taney believed he had rescued slavery and, in so doing, had settled the tortured issue once and for all. In reality, he had merely put slavery beyond the reach of any further compromise or law. Even if the balance in the Senate should tip toward the North, that body would be forbidden by the Constitution from outlawing slavery. Abolitionists now saw that if the rights of slave holders had, by virtue of the Constitution, to be universally upheld as long as slavery itself was not unconstitutional, then the Constitution had to be changed by amendment.

Of course, that was the rub and had always been. A congressional majority was required to vote up a Constitutional amendment, which then had to be ratified by three-fourths of the states. As long as slavery remained a part of the Southern economy and way of life, this was simply impossible—at least by voluntary means. The only way the U.S. Constitution would be amended to outlaw slavery was by force. And that meant civil war. More than any other single act, the *Dred Scott* decision precipitated the War Between the States. In defense of slavery, Roger B. Taney not only sealed its doom but sealed it with fire and blood, the intensity and volume of which no one in 1857 could yet imagine.

As for Dred and Harriet Scott, they remained the property of the intractable Irene Emerson, who had remarried one Calvin C. Chaffee, from Springfield, Massachusetts, in 1850. An abolitionist, Chaffee was elected to Congress shortly after the marriage, yet, incredibly enough, did not learn until a month before Taney's 1857 decision that his wife was the owner of the most famous slave in the nation. By the time he became aware of this fact, a monumentally embarrassing turn of events for an abolitionist politician, matters had proceeded too far in the Supreme Court for him to intervene. He therefore prevailed on his wife to return Scott to the Blow family, who formally emancipated him in Missouri on

May 26, 1857. Free at last, Scott found work as a porter in St. Louis. Nine months later, he succumbed to tuberculosis on September 17, 1858. Unlike her husband, Harriet Robinson Scott lived to witness the Civil War and the universal freedom it brought. She died in 1876.

THE ABOLITIONIST MOVEMENT was visionary and idealistic, and there were many in the United States in the years before the Civil War who believed that the price of visionary idealism was too high. Roger B. Taney was one of those people. His decision in the case of Dred Scott was the antithesis of idealism: legalism. To paraphrase Saint Paul, it was the "letter" with which Taney hoped to kill "the spirit that giveth life." In this, the chief justice was very much of the same mind as the incoming president of the United States, James Buchanan, who, having been tipped off as to the drift of the Supreme Court's impending decision on Dred Scott—perhaps informed by Taney himself—is believed to have prevailed upon his fellow Pennsylvanian, Associate Justice Robert Cooper Grier, to vote with the Supreme Court's Southern majority against Scott's appeal. Like Taney, Buchanan believed a legalistic decision would end the costly idealism of abolition once and for all.

In fact, it made all but inevitable the costliest outcome of all, civil war, by which the visionary idealists purchased the Thirteenth and Fourteenth amendments required to end slavery and to bestow upon African Americans the citizenship Taney's decision had denied them. It is possible to run from what is difficult yet right, but true justice, which is almost always difficult but right—justice born of visionary idealism—cannot be denied forever.

Thomas Edison and the Fight Against Alternating Current (1893)

THE DECISION TO ATTACK WHAT

YOU DON'T UNDERSTAND

With a lifetime total of 1,093 U.S. patents to his name, covering such items as electric lighting, electric power generation, the phonograph, the first truly practical telephone transmitter and receiver, the basic technology of moviemaking, and even a process for the manufacture of artificial cement, Thomas Alva Edison must surely be counted as one of the principal creators of modern civilization. In his own long lifetime he was called the "Wizard of Menlo Park" (after the New Jersey location of his most famous laboratory-workshop) and the "modern Prometheus." It seems almost too obvious to describe him as visionary, an inventor capable of transforming the future into the present, a nearly godlike creator.

Or so it seems. There is no denying the impact of Edison on what students of civilization call our "built environment," yet the closer we look at the achievement of the modern Prometheus, the less visionary and godlike he seems.

Almost all of Edison's vast warehouse of patents were for improvements on earlier inventions—his own as well as others. They were, that is, for innovation rather than invention. The phonograph, for instance, was a development of various recording telegraph devices that Edison—and many others—were already working on or had even marketed. The technology of motion pictures, Edison's kinetoscope (a movie viewer) and his kinetograph (a movie camera), were improvements on existing devices invented by others. Even his most iconic invention, the incandescent electric lamp, was a development of an emerging electric lighting technology that had its origin in the years before Edison was born. That technology had yet to be made commercially viable, and by developing a practical incandescent lamp, Edison also created the need—and market—for an entire electric power industry, the components of which he created right along with the lamp itself. Yet even in building this industry, he turned to existing technology. Generators already existed— though Edison had to improve them. The idea of distributing and retailing energy to households and businesses also existed. Gas companies had been piping their product into homes and factories for years, for billing purposes measuring individual consumption with meters. Edison proposed changing the pipes to wires, the gaslight mantles to electric lamp fixtures (which he invented), and the gas meters to recording electric meters (which he also invented).

The source of Thomas Edison's creative impact on our world is at once less mystical and more complex than visionary wizardry. His ability to create the future was firmly based on the present. His boldest inventions were almost always analogies to existing technologies. Even his most transformative set of inventions—the electric light and the electric power systems that accompanied it—were vivid analogies to existing gas heating and lighting systems.

Creation by analogy may be less impressive than invention out of thin air, but Edison's achievements are not to be denigrated. His effect on modern life remains monumental. Nevertheless, Edison's habit of analogy—his tenacious refusal to let go of existing technologies even as he radically innovated upon them—sometimes led even the Wizard of Menlo Park into folly. When that happened, it was instructive.

Edison made all of his breakthroughs in the field of electricity with simple direct current (DC), the continuous flow of electricity in a single direction. His major patents were based on DC, and when he designed his power generating and distributing systems, he considered only this type of current. It made for a straightforward system, in which generating plants fed lines, which customers tapped to power their lights and motors. The Edison system operated at a uniform voltage level throughout. Generators would supply 110 volts, which would drop to about 100 volts at the customer's site, because of the resistance of the distributing lines. The 100-volt level worked well with Edison's incandescent lamps and was relatively safe. Contact with a live wire would produce quite a jolt, but it would seldom result in injury or death. The biggest drawback of Edison's DC system was that generating plants had to be located not more than a mile or so from all customers, so that the voltage drop-off caused by the length of the conducting wires would not be so great as to be insufficient to power lights and motors. Substantially raising the voltage level at the generators was not a practical option because Edison was unable to devise an efficient and relatively low-cost technology to allow reduction of high transmission voltage to a lower voltage for customer use.

Direct current was an inherently limited technology, but, fortunately, there was an alternative.

In 1882, Nikola Tesla, a Croatian-born Serb who had graduated from the Austrian Polytechnic School in Graz, Austria, and did advanced electrical engineering work in Prague, joined Edison's French firm, Compagnie Continentale Edison, in Paris. While he was still a student, Tesla had become aware of the limitations of DC generating systems and began searching for an alternative. By the time he joined Compagnie Continentale Edison, he had already worked out the basis of an alternating current (AC) generator. Tesla invented a dynamo armature that alternated the direction of current as it revolved. This alternating current had the advantage of dramatically decreasing voltage drop-off over long transmission distances. Whereas Edison's 110-volt DC system was practically limited to about one mile, Tesla's AC system could reliably transmit power hundreds of miles, especially after he introduced the concept of polyphase current—current generated at very high voltages, which allowed for more efficient transmission over long distances, then was stepped down at various points along the system, ultimately reaching individual customers at 110 volts.

In June 1884, Tesla left Paris for New York, armed with a letter of recommendation to Thomas Edison from Edison's most trusted assistant and co-researcher, Charles Batchelor. "I know two great men and you are one of them," Batchelor wrote. "The other is this young man." On the strength of this recommendation, Edison hired Tesla for his Edison Machine Works, ultimately assigning him the massive job of redesigning all of his company's direct current generators and motors. Tesla did as he was told, all the time also trying to interest his employer in abandoning direct current and embracing the virtues of alternating current. Edison hardly listened, dismissing Tesla's ideas out of hand as "magnificent but utterly impractical."

Edison's biographers have struggled to account for the total blindness of the modern Prometheus where AC was concerned. Many have pointed out that Edison was above all else an empirical experimenter who worked largely through dint of relentless trial and error. His most famous pronouncement on the process of invention—"Genius is 1 percent inspiration and 99 percent perspiration"—bears this out. Moreover, the largely self-educated Edison had no formal background in mathematics and physics, and engineering alternating current requires precisely such grounding in theory. It was a grounding Tesla possessed in abundance, whereas Edison did not. On a more pragmatic level, all of Edison's electrical patents up to this point were based on DC technology, and he was loath to compete against and devalue his own work by supplanting direct current devices with those suitable to alternating current.

> "It is a matter of fact that any system employing high pressure, i.e., 500 to 2,000 units [volts], jeopardizes life."
>
> —Thomas A. Edison, *A Warning,* pamphlet publicizing the dangers of alternating current, 1888

All of these were rational reasons for shunning AC. But there was more. At the bottom of it all was the fact that, to Edison, direct current was highly familiar, whereas alternating current was strange. No question that Thomas Edison was an innovator, and no question that many of his innovations radically reshaped civilization itself. Yet Edison nevertheless repeatedly gravitated toward what was familiar to him. Intellectually, economically, and even emotionally, he could not bring himself to see beyond DC technology, and he became increasingly determined to defend it, tooth and nail, against the assault by AC.

At length fed up with Edison's intransigence on the subject of AC and locked in a dispute over payment for his work on upgrading Edison's DC devices, Tesla left the Edison company to eke out a living as a manual laborer (he even dug ditches—for one of Edison's power companies!) as he continued to develop his AC polyphase systems. In 1886, Tesla found backers who financed the Tesla Electric Light & Manufacturing, but his investors almost immediately forced him out of his own company. Once again, he supported himself as a common laborer until 1888, when he managed to interest George Westinghouse in AC polyphase technology. The railroad and electric power entrepreneur backed the creation of Tesla's revolutionary system.

Thomas Edison fought back. He could neither argue nor demonstrate that DC technology was superior to AC for the simple reason that it was not. Instead, he authorized a relentless public relations campaign to disseminate the popular image of AC as too dangerous to be used by and among human beings. True, there were accidents involving high-voltage AC currents, and Edison's people made as much of them as possible, planting news stories and lobbying states for legislation to bar the technology altogether. Edison even ordered two of his employees, Arthur E. Kennelly and Harold P. Brown, to demonstrate the lethality of alternating current by using it to publicly "execute" stray cats and dogs, as well as cattle and horses that had

> **"Direct current is like a river flowing peacefully to sea, while alternating current is like a torrent rushing violently over a precipice."**
>
> —Thomas A. Edison, *A Warning*, pamphlet publicizing the dangers of alternating current, 1888

outlived their usefulness. The most spectacularly grotesque demonstration came on January 4, 1903, at Luna Park, Coney Island, when Topsy, an elephant owned by the Forepaugh Circus, was put to death by alternating current. The pachyderm was condemned because she had, over a period of three years, killed three men. The Society for the Prevention of Cruelty to Animals agreed that the "rogue" animal should be put down, but the organization vetoed the proposed method of hanging as inhumane. Seizing the opportunity, Thomas Edison proposed passing 6,600 volts of AC through her. (To ensure a fatal result, however, the elephant was fed cyanide-laced carrots just before the switch was thrown.) Some 1,500 people witnessed the electrocution live, and Edison made certain that many thousands more would see it by using one of his motion picture cameras to capture the event. Shortly after the demise of Topsy, the Edison Company released the brief documentary *Electrocuting an Elephant.*

Cats, dogs, cattle, and Topsy were not the only members of the animal kingdom to be "Westinghoused"—the Edison party's freshly coined synonym for suffering electrocution. By the time of the elephant's demise, the electric chair had been humming in some prison systems for thirteen years.

Personally Thomas Edison was an opponent of capital punishment, but in the late 1880s, he commissioned Harold P. Brown to build the first "electric chair" for the state of New York. It would, of course, be energized by alternating current. Brown presented his design to a state committee, which approved it in 1889, but then Brown found that he could not build the chair because Westinghouse refused to sell him an AC generator to power it. Backed by Edison, Brown was able to acquire the generator by purchasing it through a South American university, which, in turn, transshipped it to New York.

> **"They would have done better with an axe."**
>
> —George Westinghouse, on the execution of William Kemmler by electric chair, August 6, 1890

On August 6, 1890, William Kemmler was seated in the chair at New York's Auburn Prison. A high-voltage alternating current was passed through his body for seventeen seconds, but failed to kill him. A second attempt at higher power—2,000 volts—was applied. The effect was horrific. Kemmler caught fire, even as superficial blood vessels ruptured. It took him eight minutes to die.

EDISON TRIED, BUT KILLING AN ELEPHANT and condemned criminals failed to kill AC. In the 1890s, the Niagara Falls Commission sought proposals for harnessing the force of the falls as a source of energy to generate electricity. Edison's General Electric proposed a DC system, whereas Tesla and Westinghouse presented a design for an AC system. The commission did not hesitate to award the contract to alternating current. Construction of the facility began in 1893, and on November 16, 1896, power was transmitted for the first time from Niagara Falls to industrial customers in Buffalo.

The balance was tipped. Within a very few years, AC was replacing DC on virtually all central station power generation and distribution networks. Once alternating current became a technological fact—a feature of America's technological landscape—even Edison's companies began a costly and belated conversion from DC to AC. By this time, however, Westinghouse and others had stolen the march on Edison, who was obliged to relinquish into many other hands an enormous share of the profits from his civilization-transforming inventions. He was and would remain a rich man, but Thomas Edison never enjoyed the magnitude of wealth realized by Westinghouse and other industrialists who were far less inventive than the modern Prometheus but who were also far less deeply invested in familiar yet limited technologies.

The Wright Brothers and the Wing Warping Lawsuits (1910–14)

THE DECISION TO AVOID INNOVATION

F ew technological highlights of the modern age are more dramatic or significant than the 120-foot, 12-second controlled and powered flight of Orville Wright at about 10:35 on the morning of December 17, 1903. Concerning this momentous event, banalities abound: It was the "realization of an age-old dream of humankind," it "liberated earthbound humanity," and so on. The clichés, all of them, can be forgiven because they are perfectly justified.

The magnitude of the Wright brothers' achievement is nearly impossible to quantify. Before them, the human world was defined in terms of earth and water. After them, it also became a world of flight. Almost equally hard to capture is the magnitude of the daring, of the courage— of the audacity—required to make the first manned, powered flight. For the Wrights knew better than anyone else just what they were up against. Dayton, Ohio, bicycle makers and mechanics, they had first become seriously interested in flying when, in 1896, they read of the death of German glider experimenter Otto Lilienthal, killed in a crash. "The brief notice of his death," Wilbur Wright later explained, "aroused a passive interest which had existed from my childhood." Flight was as dangerous as it was seductive.

From 1896 on, the Wrights read everything they could find on aeronautics. It really wasn't much, but, by the very end of the nineteenth century, it was enough to convince them that human flight required just three things: wings to provide the basis of lift, a power plant to move the aircraft forward with enough velocity to create sufficient airflow over the wings to generate that lift, and a means of controlling the aircraft. They also concluded that the first two requirements had already been satisfied, at least in theory, by earlier experimenters. Wings existed, as did the internal combustion engine.

The single remaining unfulfilled requirement was control. And the Wrights concluded that it was everything: the very key to flight. Lilienthal had died and others had failed because they could not control flight. The brothers also understood the terrible fact that control could not be achieved theoretically. The only way to invent both a system and a technique for controlling flight was actually to fly. If the system worked and the technique was learned rapidly enough—in the space of seconds—the flight would succeed and the aviator would survive. If the system failed and the technique could not be mastered immediately, the aircraft would crash, and the aviator might well suffer the fate of Otto Lilienthal. As Wilbur Wright explained in a 1901 lecture, "if you are looking for perfect safety, you will do well to sit on the fence and watch the birds; but if you really wish to learn, you must mount a machine and become acquainted with its tricks by actual trial."

The pair did all they could on the ground to devise a means of control. Lilienthal had flown what was essentially a hang glider, his only means of control the shifting weight of his own suspended body. Wilbur saw this as fatal. Birds—indisputably successful fliers—used "more positive and energetic methods of regaining equilibrium than that of shifting the center of gravity." They achieved control, he concluded, not by merely shifting

> "My brother and I became seriously interested in the problem of human flight in 1899. . . . We knew that men had by common consent adopted human flight as the standard of impossibility. . . . Our own growing belief that man might nevertheless learn to fly was based on the idea that while thousands of the most dissimilar body structures, such as insects, fish, reptiles, birds and mammals, were flying every day at pleasure, it was reasonable to suppose that man might also fly."
>
> —Wilbur Wright, 1909

their body weight, but by turning the leading edge of one wingtip up and the other down.

The problem was how to imitate this complex movement with an artificial wing. Although the Wrights were diligent in their studies, the solution came with remarkable ease, almost unbidden. Wilbur Wright was working in his bicycle shop one July day in 1899 and happened to glance at the rectangular box in which an inner tube had been packed. The end tabs had been ripped off. Taking the empty box in his two hands, he twisted it. That was the solution. Build a wing that could be twisted in a controlled fashion.

Immediately, the Wrights built small model wings out of bamboo, paper, and strings. These were sufficient to prove the principle sound, and they went on to build an unmanned biplane kite with a five-foot wingspan, the warp of its wings controlled by means of strings attached to sticks held in the kite flier's hand. After flying this contraption successfully in August 1899, they set to work on a "man-carrying machine." At first, they tried to fly it like a kite—a manned kite, to be sure, but still tethered. It quickly became clear that tethering the aircraft prevented the pilot from truly controlling flight, so, beginning on October 18, 1900, they made a series of untethered glides from the top of a sand dune on the beach near Kitty Hawk, North Carolina. They now began to learn the principles of control the only way they could be learned: in flight.

There was much more work to be done. In 1901, when they returned to Kitty Hawk with a brand-new machine—which had been designed explicitly as a glider, not a kite—they were disappointed to discover that the wings they had built using calculations made by earlier aeronautical experimenters provided only one-third of the lift the numbers predicted. Through trial after trial, the craft flew, but poorly. On the train back to Dayton, Wilbur turned dolefully to Orville. "Not within a thousand years would man ever fly!" he said.

But, once back home, the brothers concluded that their mistake had been in assuming that the problem of lift had already been entirely solved by others. Clearly, the numbers were wrong. The problem had not been solved, and it was therefore up to them to solve it. To derive their own calculations, the Wrights built the world's first wind tunnel and in it tested dozens of wing shapes, carefully measuring the lift provided by each. They took the best result, scaled it up, and created the wing that would carry them aloft in 1903. By that fateful year, they had also built their own lightweight gasoline motor and had contrived a system of pulleys and cables to twist the trailing edges of the wings in opposite directions. "Wing warping," they called it, and it was the first proven means of controlling sustained, powered, human flight.

Wing warping was a breakthrough, and the Wrights improved it, ultimately combining it with a vertical rudder for greater control. Yet the system was far from perfect and, in fact, always dangerous because it was extremely difficult to master and very awkward to operate. Fortunately, a better system had already begun to emerge, appearing in embryonic form the year *before* the Wrights' first flight. In 1902, the New Zealand inventor Richard Pearse designed ailerons, small hinged tabs on each wing, which had the potential for achieving control more efficiently, reliably, and easily than warping the entire wing edge. Pearse's experimental monoplane flew about 350 yards some nine months before Kitty Hawk, but without any control at all, and the Wrights cannot be blamed for taking little or no notice of it. However, in May 1904, the year after the Wrights' first Kitty Hawk flights, Robert Esnault-Pelterie, a French aircraft experimenter, made a successful flight with an aileron-equipped aircraft. Within a short time afterward, independently of Esnault-Pelterie, the Aerial Experiment Association (AEA), which was financed by telephone inventor and aeronautical experimenter Alexander Graham Bell, created more aileron-based designs.

Throughout their work, the Wrights had been highly secretive. In part, they did not want a scoffing press to witness their failures, but, even more important, they did not want the small but growing community of aviation pioneers stealing a march on their hard-won progress. They immediately sought patent protection, drawing particular attention in their application to the concept of lateral control, which (the application stated) could be achieved by the wing warping system or by ailerons. The patent was granted in 1906, and the Wrights believed that it protected lateral control as a concept, whether it was achieved by wing warping or ailerons. Because lateral control was so basic to flight, the Wrights understood, no aircraft could be designed without it, and they therefore believed they had secured an effective monopoly on manned aviation.

On June 21, 1908, the *June Bug*, an airplane built and piloted by aviation pioneer Glenn Curtiss under the auspices of the AEA, flew more than three thousand feet. On July 4, *June Bug* flew 5,360 feet in one minute and 40 seconds, winning a prize offered by *The Scientific American*. The *June Bug* achieved control through triangular panels at its four wingtips, ailerons designed by Alexander Graham Bell. Because ailerons were mentioned in the Wrights' patent, the brothers issued a warning to Curtiss that he was infringing, and, with this, they started a patent war of lawsuits and countersuits.

The courtroom battles consumed huge amounts of money and, worse, vast tracts of time—time that the Wrights, Curtiss, and the others eventually involved in the suits could have devoted to advancing American aviation.

> **"Unnecessary delays by stipulation of counsel have already destroyed fully three-fourths of the value of our patent. The opportunities of the last two years will never return again. At the present moment almost innumerable competitors are entering the field, and for the first time are producing machines which really fly."**
>
> —Wilbur Wright, letter to Wright Company attorney Frederick Fish, May 4, 1912—his last letter before dying of typhoid fever on May 30

Repeatedly, lawyers on both sides sought an amicable settlement, but the Wright brothers always refused. In 1912, Wilbur Wright succumbed to typhoid fever, and Orville and other Wright family members bitterly blamed Curtiss, claiming that *his* refusal to back down had robbed

Wilbur of his health. Orville, in the meantime, fought on until, in 1913, the Federal Circuit Court of Appeals ordered Curtiss to cease and desist making airplanes with two ailerons that operated simultaneously in opposite directions, finding that this system was protected by the Wrights' patent.

Unwilling to accept the apparent finality of this judgment, Curtiss sought help from Henry Ford, who sent him to his own patent attorney. The Ford lawyer succeeded in winning a temporary stay of the cease and desist order, and the patent wars reopened, coming to an end only when the United States entered World War I in April 1917. Patriotic aircraft manufacturers instantly created the Manufacturers' Aircraft Association, which formed a patent pool so that all U.S. aircraft makers could concentrate on building planes for the war effort. Royalties were fixed at 1 percent and inventions and ideas were freely exchanged among the builders.

Yet this settlement had come too late to make up the time wasted in fighting the patent wars. The United States entered World War I with woefully obsolete aircraft. The Wrights themselves stubbornly refused to abandon the wing-warping system, even after it repeatedly proved fatal. On September 17, 1908, Lieutenant Thomas E. Selfridge became the first military pilot to die in a crash—though he met his death as a passenger, with Orville Wright, severely injured in the crash, at the controls. More than twenty other aviators were killed in crashes almost certainly caused by a loss of control linked to wing warping. In 1914, Grover Loening, a disciple of the Wrights working for the military, reported that the army finally "decided to change the old-style warping wings to the more modern trailing edge aileron . . . on planes used by Curtiss for six years, since 1908." Loening took all of the Wright aircraft the army owned and modified them with ailerons. Writing in 1935, he recalled that the "series of deaths that took place in Wright planes was shocking."

Yet even as the Wrights clung to wing warping, even after they were manufacturing aircraft full-time through their own company, they stubbornly defended in court their patent right to the aileron system, discouraging others from using it for fear of suffering lawsuit. Despite their legal efforts, however, by 1915 ailerons had entirely replaced wing warping, even on their own planes, and the American aircraft industry limped toward World War I. By the end of that war, Orville Wright sold his interest in the Wright Company to an investment group and retired from the aircraft business entirely, leaving behind one of the great ironies of the early history of aviation: that the Wrights, who had made the greatest breakthrough in the development of aviation, then hobbled that development before finally abandoning the field altogether.

As it turned out, there was still more irony to come. In March 2003, NASA announced the successful test of an "Active Aeroelastic Wing," which had been installed on a Navy F/A-18A supersonic jet. The flexible wing uses wing warping to maneuver the aircraft, its designers believing that this technology—a direct throwback to the Wrights—provides reduced structural weight, greater aerodynamic efficiency, and enhanced control effectiveness.

———

WING WARPING, SOME AIRCRAFT DESIGNERS now believe, is the aeronautical technology of the future. But is this a long-delayed vindication of the Wrights' stubborn adherence to their original technology? Not exactly. Wing warping works in the twenty-first century because it is controlled by advanced microprocessors—that make hundreds of control adjustments through scores of servo motors during every second of flight—and because of advanced structural materials that ensure the combination of strength and suppleness required for precise and instantaneous wing warping. Given the state of technology at the start of the twentieth century, wing warping was a breakthrough technology, but it was neither the best nor a sustainable technology. It quickly proved to be both impractical and dangerous, and the Wrights were stubbornly foolish to defend it.

It is dangerous to become possessive of innovation. When it is regarded as an achievement instead of an attitude, innovation ceases to be innovative. Its products become inert treasures to be defended at all costs rather than works in progress, to be modified, developed, improved, and, if necessary, discarded to make way for something better.

Alfred P. Sloan and Planned Obsolescence
(1920)
THE DECISION TO MANUFACTURE ARTIFICIAL DESIRE

For sheer cynicism and the power to incite consumer ire, what phrase can surpass "planned obsolescence"? No one is quite sure who coined it or exactly when, but the earliest fully documented use of the phrase in print occurred in *Ending the Depression Through Planned Obsolescence*, published in 1932 by Bernard London. It was, however, some twenty years later, in the 1950s, when postwar prosperity drove an unprecedented wave of consumerism, that the phrase became a kind of watchword. The American industrial designer Brooks Stevens used it in 1954 as the title of a speech he gave at a Minneapolis advertising conference. Widely reported, the phrase caught on—and, like wildfire, spread far beyond the bounds of Stevens's own modest, even benign definition of it: "Instilling in the buyer the desire to own something a little newer, a little better, a little sooner than is necessary."

Whereas manufacturers and retailers reveled in the growing consumerism of the 1950s, some cultural critics persisted in doing what critics do. They criticized. They pointed out that "planned obsolescence" was not benign at all, but reflected an inherently immoral capitalist philosophy of purposefully designing and manufacturing products with a limited lifespan, products that

> **"Our whole economy is based on planned obsolescence."**
>
> —**Brooks Stevens**

would wear out prematurely or that would go out of style more or less rapidly. Vance Packard, the most popular and militantly acerbic of the critics of consumerism, devoted his 1960 best-seller, *The Waste Makers*, to the concept, calling planned obsolescence "the systematic attempt of business to make us wasteful, debt-ridden, permanently discontented individuals." His analysis recognized two distinct types of planned obsolescence. "Obsolescence of function" referred to purposely designing and manufacturing products to break down or fail after a certain amount of time. Goods embodying obsolescence of function did not fail prematurely because of unforeseen or inevitable flaws in design or manufacturing or because of attempts to save costs by using inferior materials. Instead, the limited lifespan of such goods was an intentional built-in feature. The second type of planned obsolescence was "Obsolescence of desirability," which Packard also called "psychological obsolescence." In this type, the product did not wear out or fail mechanically or physically. Its obsolescence occurred only in the mind of the consumer who owned the product.

Obsolescence of desirability required a radical redefinition of industrial design. Common sense suggested that the goal of good design was to create as durable and as enduringly attractive a product as possible to provide good value for the consumer's money and thereby make the product so appealing to potential buyers that it was competitive in the marketplace. Once a good and durable design had been achieved, there would be no further role for the designer unless, as the industrial designer George Nelson wrote, he could actually "make a contribution through change." In products manufactured to embody obsolescence of desirability, however, the industrial designer is not called on to contribute to improved function, durability, or cost; therefore (as Nelson observed), "the only process available for giving the illusion of change is 'styling.'?"

Obsolescence of desirability was widely introduced into American industry and culture long before Vance Packard coined the phrase and even before the first appearance of the more general "planned obsolescence." From the time that Henry Ford introduced mass production of the

Model T in 1908 and for the next decade, demand for automobiles skyrocketed. In response, the industry tooled up and production increased dramatically. When the market showed signs of leveling off during the mid-1910s, automakers introduced installment sales in 1916. That helped stimulate flagging sales, but by the start of the 1920s, the market seemed fully mature, incapable of further significant growth.

Alfred P. Sloan Jr., analyzed the situation. A native of New Haven, Connecticut, Sloan had graduated from Massachusetts Institute of Technology in 1892 with a degree in electrical engineering. By 1899, he was president of a ball bearing factory, which merged in 1916 with United Motors Corporation, a company that, in turn, was absorbed by General Motors. Sloan became GM's vice president and then, in 1923, president. It struck him that the cars of his decade differed remarkably little from the original Model T of more than a decade earlier. The fact was that his engineers had little reason to make substantive changes. Yet without change, the consumer had no incentive for buying a new car. That, Sloan concluded, was why the automobile market had reached a plateau. He responded to the situation by instituting a manufacturing program that introduced minor—

> "Some have an idea that the reason we in this country discard things so readily is because we have so much. The facts are exactly opposite—the reason we have so much is simply because we discard things so readily. We replace the old in return for something that will serve us better."
>
> —Alfred P. Sloan Jr.

but noticeable—stylistic alterations to each year's models and major cosmetic changes every three years. He explained that, because "everyone knows the car will run," the "most important factor in the selling end of the business—perhaps the most important factor—[is] the appearance of a motor-car." By incrementally introducing cosmetic changes, making minor changes in years one and two, and major changes in year three, and the owners of year one's car would become dissatisfied with the vehicle, never mind that it still ran fine. At the very least, the dissatisfied customer would trade his "old" car for the same model of the current year; even better, however, a good salesman would have an opportunity to upsell the customer to a more expensive model—with which, of course, the buyer would become dissatisfied within three years, if not sooner, and be ripe for another sale.

In addition to establishing annual styling changes, with major changes every third year, Sloan created a rigid pricing structure for GM makes, ranging at the low end from the Chevrolet to Cadillac at the high end, with Pontiac, Oldsmobile, and Buick priced in ascending order between the two. This assured that the makes, at different price points, would not compete with each other, and yet it encouraged buyers to enter the GM "family" at a comfortable price point and stay within the family as their buying power increased over the years. Combined with planned obsolescence, this pricing structure soon catapulted GM ahead of its chief competitor, Ford, which was resistant to making stylistic changes or offering a range of makes and models. By 1927, Chevrolet dominated the low-price field, and by 1936, the year before Sloan became chairman of the board, GM held 43 percent of the automobile market in the United States. The company would retain this leadership position for more than seventy years, during which time all American automakers came to embrace the gospel of "Sloanism."

By the 1930s, GM was not only introducing annual cosmetic changes, it was also manufacturing incrementally heavier, longer, more powerful cars equipped with a variety of accessories. No longer was it necessary to move a buyer from one make to another to upsell him. Now, just keeping up with the stylistic evolution within a single make required the consumer to spend more money every year.

Planned obsolescence stimulated the automobile market even as it put GM in position to claim the lion's share of that market. Nevertheless, meeting the demands of the design cycle was not cheap. Even cosmetic redesign required much research and frequent retooling. While management funded stylistic redesign and the retooling necessary for it—because these changes were proven money-makers—it slighted innovation of the basics, such as the power train, chassis, and other mechanical systems. As a result, these failed to keep pace with the superficial developments. Sloan and his philosophical heirs failed to notice that their companies were becoming increasingly vulnerable. In the 1960s and 1970s, federal regulators began to introduce a host of safety, pollution, and energy-consumption standards, which U.S. automakers scrambled to meet—often at the expense of performance and even manufacturing quality. As American consumers began to find American-engineered cars wanting in the fundamentals, they turned to imports, which not only seemed to embody more advanced basic engineering and higher manufacturing quality, but also represented better value for money. In 1959, the German-made Volkswagen openly exploited the philosophy that had dominated the American auto industry in an advertising campaign built on such slogans as "We do not believe in planned obsolescence" and "We don't change a car for the sake of change." Indeed, a 1965 VW Beetle looked almost identical to one from 1959—a fact that was sacrilege to domestic automakers. By the 1960s and 1970s, Japanese as well as German cars were making deep inroads into American markets. Once objects of derision, the Japanese imports in particular increasingly appealed to American consumers because they were less expensive than equivalent domestic makes and were more fuel efficient, even as, in the 1970s, the United States struggled through an energy crisis. Most of all, they were more reliable mechanically, embodying better engineering as well as more stringent quality control. American industry had fallen behind.

THERE IS A PLACE FOR OBSOLESCENCE as a spur to genuine innovation, as we have seen in the last quarter century in the computer, electronics, and communications industries. True, the necessity of buying a new personal computer every two or three years sounds suspiciously like the planned obsolescence that motivates drivers to hanker after a new car at least every three years, but, typically, the innovation is genuine, often basic, and sometimes—as with the expansion of the Internet and the hardware enabling users to take advantage of it—even epoch making.

The danger comes when obsolescence ceases to be a driver of innovation and becomes an end in itself for the purposes of marketing. The danger to the consumer is obvious, but the danger to the producer is even greater. In 1980, the Chrysler Corporation, smallest of the Big Three automakers (which also included GM and Ford), was pushed to the edge of bankruptcy and had to be rescued by a government-backed loan. Chrysler CEO Lee Iacocca was instrumental in bringing the company back from the brink by introducing a new marketing philosophy, which emphasized engineering basics, reliability, and value over style. Nevertheless, in 1981, Detroit turned out just 6.2 million passenger cars, a twenty-year low for the industry, as more and more Americans passed over Chevys and Fords to buy Hondas and Toyotas. On April 25, 2007, the world press noted that, for the first time ever, Toyota sold more vehicles globally in a quarter than General Motors, and many industry experts predicted that the Japanese company would overtake GM as the world's top automaker by 2012, if not sooner. It was an obsolescence American industrialists had not planned for.

Neville Chamberlain and Adolf Hitler (1938)
THE DECISION TO APPEASE A MONSTER

For too many of us, history boils down to heroes and villains, a view that leaves out—well—most of the men and women who make history. Few figures of the recent past are more reviled than Neville Chamberlain, prime minister of the United Kingdom from May 28, 1937 to May 10, 1940, a world leader in a time of monsters; and although no monster himself, many see him as the man who enabled and empowered the biggest monster of all.

Born in Birmingham, the son of a statesman, Neville Chamberlain became a successful industrialist and in 1915 was elected lord mayor of his native city. The following year, during World War I, he joined the government of Prime Minister David Lloyd George as director-general of national service, but soon resigned out of frustration over the limited authority his position afforded him. In 1918, Chamberlain was elected to Parliament as a Conservative, then served terms as Britain's postmaster general, paymaster general of the armed forces, minister of health, chancellor of the exchequer, and finally prime minister on May 28, 1937.

The government whose reins he took up was one that desperately wished to avoid war, even as Italy's Benito Mussolini and Germany's Adolf Hitler became increasingly aggressive. Chamberlain's predecessor, Stanley Baldwin, had repeatedly resisted calls from some quarters for a program of British rearmament. The placid, even complacent front Baldwin presented clearly comforted most of the British public, which was beleaguered by the worldwide economic depression of the 1930s and, having suffered mightily in the Great War of 1914–18, did not want even to think of the possibility of a new war.

Despite Baldwin's willingness to satisfy his countrymen's state of denial, the preponderance of events, including the Italian conquest of Ethiopia, the German remilitarization of the Rhineland in violation of the Treaty of Versailles, and the German-Italian intervention in the Spanish Civil War, at last moved even him to make gestures toward strengthening the British military establishment. Winston Churchill, at the time a member of Parliament, decried these actions as too little and too meek, eloquently sounding a warning of what he later called the "gathering storm." About Churchill's alarms, Baldwin and his government outwardly demonstrated utter unconcern.

Like Baldwin, Chamberlain was a well-meaning man of peace, but his sense of the growing danger was far more acute than that of his predecessor. Reflecting a perception common in the 1930s, the principal focus of his fears was not Adolf Hitler, but the more extravagantly bellicose Mussolini. Chamberlain increased, albeit modestly, the tempo of the desultory rearmament Baldwin had begun. Aware, however, that it would take years for Britain to adequately prepare for war, Chamberlain adopted a policy he would come to call "active appeasement" to buy time. It began not with Hitler, but with Mussolini. On April 16, 1938, Chamberlain agreed to recognize Italian control over Ethiopia, despite the eloquent and moving pleas of Ethiopian emperor Haile Selassie. This accommodation, he hoped, would discourage Mussolini from making any closer ties with Hitler. To avoid provoking either Mussolini or Hitler, Chamberlain insisted on absolute British neutrality with regard to the Spanish Civil War (1936–39), in which Italy and Germany actively supported the fascist forces of Francisco Franco. Moreover, determined to demonstrate Britain's peaceful intentions, Chamberlain authorized the abandonment of the Royal Navy bases in Ireland. When Churchill—and others—protested this as both a show of weakness and a serious compromise of the nation's defenses, Chamberlain responded that it was nothing more than a symbolic gesture necessary to maintain peace.

The abandonment of the Irish naval bases began to turn some public opinion, hitherto overwhelmingly favorable, against Chamberlain. For his part, the prime minister could not publicly explain that his motive was strategic more than diplomatic. He hoped to put off war with Italy and Japan, the two nations he saw as the biggest threats to Britain, for as long as possible so that Britain might be as far along in rearmament as possible.

When, in September 1938, Adolf Hitler suddenly stepped to the fore with a demand that Czechoslovakia cede to Germany the German-speaking Sudetenland, which the German dictator defined as all ethnically German areas of Czechoslovakia contiguous with Germany and Austria, Chamberlain adjusted his strategy. He now saw Hitler as the imminent threat, and he was fearful that war with Germany would also render Britain vulnerable to simultaneous attack by Italy and Japan, which was leaning toward open alliance with the two European fascist powers. For this reason, the prime minister mounted a campaign of appeasement directed now at Hitler. Three times in September 1938, he traveled to

Germany, his tightly rolled umbrella in one hand, his trademark bowler hat in the other, determined to forestall war by any means necessary.

The two great democracies of Europe, Britain and France, were bound by the Treaty of Versailles and other agreements to guarantee the sovereignty and integrity of Czechoslovakia. As September drew to a close, French Prime Minister Édouard Daladier learned that Chamberlain intended to abrogate these obligations by giving Hitler the Sudetenland in a conference scheduled for the end of the month. Aware that France was in the grip of a malaise both pacifist and defeatist—and that it could not be successfully rallied to war—Daladier appealed for support to the great democracy across the Atlantic, the United States. But President Franklin D. Roosevelt was himself conscious of the fact that his countrymen had no desire to enter another "European war," and he responded on September 26 with nothing stronger than a tepid reminder to the leaders of Britain, France, Germany, and Italy that, by virtue of their governments having signed the Kellogg-Briand Pact of 1928, they had solemnly agreed to refrain from going to war with one another. Thus Daladier realized that he stood alone, and he realized as well that, standing alone, he was powerless. As for Chamberlain, on September 28, the eve of the conference, he broadcast a message on BBC radio, sounding more like the mayor of provincial Birmingham than the prime minister of a great nation: "How horrible, fantastic, incredible it is that we should be digging trenches and trying on gas masks here because of a quarrel in a faraway country between people of whom we know nothing." On the twenty-ninth, at London's Heston Airport, as he prepared to board his plane for Munich, he told reporters, "When I come back I hope I may be able to say, as Hotspur says in *Henry IV*, 'out of this nettle, danger, we pluck this flower, safety.'"

During September 29–30, 1938, the Munich Conference proceeded with Hitler, Mussolini, Daladier, and Chamberlain in attendance. No representative from the Soviet Union was invited, and although two Czech diplomats were called to Munich, they were not only barred from the conference chamber, but were held under Gestapo guard until the morning of

September 30, when they were abruptly summoned to hear what the four powers in attendance had decided in their enforced absence.

"Praise be to God and Mr. Chamberlain. I find no sacrilege, no bathos, in coupling those two names."

—Columnist Godfrey Winn in the *Sunday Express,* on the eve of Chamberlain's departure for Munich

They had decided that the German army was to occupy the Sudetenland by the beginning of October, and that the territory, together with its strategically critical military and industrial installations, was to be annexed to the German Reich. The Czech diplomats were assured that the sovereignty of the rest of Czechoslovakia would be guaranteed, although the nature of the guarantee and the means of its enforcement could not be specified. With that, on the same morning, Hitler and Chamberlain signed the Munich Agreement, a joint declaration pledging that Germany and Britain would "peacefully consult" whenever problems should arise between them.

Newsreel cameras rolled as Chamberlain returned to London, emerging from a fragile-looking airliner, holding aloft a mere scrap of paper. It was a signed copy of the declaration. Later in the day, addressing cheering crowds from a window of his residence at 10 Downing Street, the prime minister announced that he had secured "peace with honour." He continued: "I believe it is peace for our time. . . . And now I recommend you to go home and sleep quietly in your beds."

The Czechs, of course, saw it differently. They could not sleep quietly, having been betrayed—sold out. Most of the British people—and the French, too—regarded the scrap of paper as nothing less than an eleventh-hour miracle.

A "good man," President Roosevelt publicly pronounced Chamberlain on September 28. About this time, Mussolini spoke of him privately: "As soon as Hitler sees that old man he will know he has won the battle. Chamberlain is not aware that to present himself to Hitler in the uniform of a bourgeois pacifist and British parliamentarian is the equivalent of giving a wild beast a taste of blood." After seeing the newsreel of Chamberlain's return to Heston Airport, Munich Agreement in hand, Hitler reportedly remarked, "Well, he seemed such a nice old gentleman, I thought I would give him my autograph as a souvenir." More privately, he was allegedly cruder: "If ever that silly old man comes interfering here again with his umbrella, I'll kick him downstairs and jump on his stomach in front of the photographers."

To the House of Commons, on October 5, 1938, Winston Churchill spoke with an almost gentle resolve. "I do not begrudge our loyal, brave people . . . the natural, spontaneous outburst of joy and relief when they learned that the hard ordeal would no longer be required of them at the moment; but they should know the truth." He went on:

> They should know that there has been gross neglect and deficiency in our defences; they should know that we have sustained a defeat without a war, the consequences of which will travel far with us along our road; they should know that we have passed an awful milestone in our history, when the whole equilibrium of Europe has been deranged, and that the terrible words have for the time being been pronounced against the Western democracies: "Thou art weighed in the balance and found wanting."

Churchill saw in the fall of 1938 what few others saw then. In the hindsight of history, however, Chamberlain plainly does seem a "silly old man," his "active appeasement" a policy craven and naive, and the Munich Agreement the title page to a tragedy. Yet Neville Chamberlain had good reason to believe that Britain was ill prepared to go to war, and he had what seemed a rational hope that the Munich Agreement would buy sufficient time to rearm the nation. Chamberlain's own advice to his countrymen to "go home and sleep quietly" notwithstanding, he did not sleep, but immediately after concluding the Munich Agreement, he worked energetically to put his government on a war footing, ordering a crash program of rearmament. When, during March 10–16, 1939, Hitler broke the agreement by marching out of the Sudetenland to seize all of Czechoslovakia, Chamberlain formally repudiated active appeasement, declaring absolute the Anglo-French guarantee to defend Poland, Romania, and Greece in the event of attack, then, in April, ordering general military conscription, the first peacetime draft in the history of Britain.

Germany invaded Poland on September 1, 1939, prompting Chamberlain to ask Parliament for a declaration of war on September 3. Almost immediately after this, the prime minister had the courage and good sense to take into his War Cabinet his most vociferous critic, Winston Churchill, as first lord of the admiralty. Chamberlain was by this time keenly aware of the folly of the appeasement strategy, well intended though it had been. He resigned as prime minister in favor of Churchill on May 10, 1940. Out of a profound sense of duty, he stayed on in Churchill's coalition government as the lord president of the council until ill health forced him to step down on September 30, 1940. Within weeks afterward, a broken man, he was dead, and, in the darkest days of World War II, his passing was largely unmourned.

—

"A GOOD MAN," PRESIDENT ROOSEVELT had called Neville Chamberlain, and so he was: good and well meaning. Contrary to what many believed once the war had started, he had not hoped to purchase peace at any price—just an interval of peace so that his nation could more adequately prepare for war. His goal and his motives were not folly, but his approach was. If appeasement would have been too high a price to pay for "peace for our time," it was vastly exorbitant in exchange for the paltry interval Chamberlain hoped to secure. For appeasement—yielding to intimidation and tyranny—could not delay war, it could only invite it. Hoping to stave off the crisis of a critical illness, the misguided physician administered a drug that hastened its terrible onset.

The British Empire and Gandhi (1942)

THE DECISION TO IMPRISON A MORAL FORCE

At the outbreak of World War II, most Britons thought of India as what it had been for them since the middle of the eighteenth century: the "jewel in the crown" of the British Empire. With a population of some 318.7 million in 1940, India represented for the United Kingdom a heavy military responsibility but at the same time an enormous strategic asset. The subcontinent was rich in a variety of vital raw materials and was a potentially huge source of military manpower. Its location fronting both Africa and the Middle East was key to global warfare. To lose India, especially with the rest of British Asia either threatened by Japanese invasion or already lost to it, would mean losing the war against Japan and, perhaps, Germany as well. Holding India would have been difficult enough had the nation been a genuine partner in the British Empire, a wholehearted ally; but India was in the throes of a long struggle for independence and it could hardly be counted on to contribute to the war effort or even to remain loyal.

To characterize the situation as politically sensitive, even precarious, would be a vast understatement. Yet this did not stop Victor Hope, or Lord Linlithgow, the country's bluff, blustering British viceroy, from unilaterally declaring India to be at war with Germany on the very day World War II started in Europe. He issued the proclamation without having consulted a single Indian, including such rising leaders as Mohandas Gandhi and Jawaharlal Nehru, let alone the public.

It was an act of arrogant stupidity, which created great popular outrage, resentment, and defiance despite the fact that the majority of Indians and Indian leaders abhorred the Nazis and fascists and were therefore naturally inclined to support the Allies, including the British. But Linlithgow's high-handed proclamation effectively linked Indian support for the war effort with acquiescence in continued imperial rule.

Feeling betrayed and unwilling to be identified as puppets of the British, India's leaders—Gandhi among them—thought they were compelled to withhold support from the British Raj, as the ruling government was called. The day after the war began, Gandhi publicly pledged that he would not "embarrass" the British government. Fully understanding that the Axis powers—Germany, Italy, and Japan (which had not yet entered the war)—represented an oppressive evil far worse than Britain, Gandhi personally favored offering the British what he termed "nonviolent moral support," but he joined other leaders in demanding that Britain plead its case for Indian support by stating its postwar "goals and ideals." For the pro-independence Indian Congress, this meant nothing less than Britain's pledging that, after the war, the government would progressively lead India toward full independence. When Linlithgow refused to make such a pledge, the Indian Congress called on its provincial ministries to resign en masse in protest.

Torn between the threat of Axis triumph on the one hand and British tyranny on the other, Gandhi engaged in tortured deliberations as to what course he should take. At last, he declared it impossible for India to support a war in defense of democracy and liberty when it was precisely democracy and liberty that were being withheld from India.

The stand taken by the Hindu-dominated Indian Congress and India's most prominent Hindu leader, Gandhi, gave Muhammad Ali Jinnah, foremost among India's Muslim political leaders, an opening to garner British backing. Jinnah promised Linlithgow the support of India's Muslims, many of whom were already members of the Anglo-Indian armed forces. Even if he had wanted to reject the support, Linlithgow was now in no position to spurn Jinnah's pledge, even though, by embracing it, he promoted the dangerous division between the Hindu-dominated Indian Congress, which drifted further and further from the British, and the Muslim League. This fissure had created a divided India that was highly vulnerable to Axis subversion. If Gandhi, Nehru, and their followers opposed war itself, they opposed yet more strongly the Axis, which, after December 7, 1941, included the greatest regional threat of all, Japan. Some other pro-independence Hindus, however, seized on the war as a means of hastening independence. Chief of among these was Subhas Chandra Bose, who actively and openly worked with the Germans and the Japanese to create the Indian National Army in 1943, which collaborated in the Japanese war effort against the British.

In March 1942, some four months after Japan entered World War II, Prime Minister Winston Churchill sent Sir Stafford Cripps, a British Socialist and personal friend of Nehru, with a proposal for postwar India. The prime minister's hope was to secure India as a bulwark against the rapid expansion of Japanese control in the East. Through Cripps he therefore offered a proposal to grant full dominion status to India after the war, with the proviso that any province could vote itself out of the dominion.

Dominion was far short of independence, but, as a kind of voluntary membership in the British Empire, it could fairly be viewed as a step toward independence. Nevertheless, Gandhi saw the proviso by which any province could remove itself from the dominion as a stratagem to undermine and dismantle Indian nationhood, and he rejected the proposal. Having spurned it, he commenced in August 1942 the Bharat Chhodo Andolan, or Quit India Movement.

Starting with his efforts in South Africa's Indian community in 1893, Gandhi emerged as a champion of civil rights, human rights, tolerance, and equality despite colonial subjugation. After his return from South Africa to India in 1916, his work was directed toward achieving independence from the British Empire. He created and led a massive movement of "noncooperation": coordinated passive resistance against colonial authorities in an effort to win Indian self-determination. Gandhi developed a repertoire of peaceful protest tactics, including fasts, hunger strikes, and the patient endurance of threats, abuse, and incarceration.

In 1930, Gandhi organized the famous Salt March, in which he led seventy-eight followers 240 miles on foot from Sabarmati to the coastal village of Dandi, where he took salt from the sea in symbolic defiance of the

"It is alarming and also nauseating to see Mr. Gandhi, a seditious middle temple lawyer, now posing as a fakir of a type well known in the east, striding half-naked up the steps of the viceregal palace, while he is still organizing and conducting a defiant campaign of civil disobedience, to parley on equal terms with the representative of the king-emperor."

—Winston Churchill, commenting on Gandhi's meetings with the viceroy in 1931

coercive British Salt Tax that forced Indians to buy salt exclusively from British suppliers. He was imprisoned from May 1930 to January 1931, after which the then viceroy Lord Irwin invited Gandhi to New Delhi for a series of talks that led to a brief cessation in Gandhi's civil disobedience campaign.

By the summer of 1942, the independence movement was fully mature, and Gandhi made bold to demand that the British immediately "quit India," granting full and unconditional independence. He called on the people of India to undertake the most determined campaign of passive resistance to all British rule. On August 8, at the Gowalia Tank Maidan, a park in central Bombay (Mumbai)—later renamed the August Kranti Maidan (August Revolution Ground)—Gandhi put this in no uncertain terms, calling on fellow Indians to "do or die."

By asserting the goal of independence as an absolute demand, Gandhi hoped to summon the British government to the negotiating table without delay. Instead, within twenty-four hours of the "do or die" speech, Gandhi and virtually all of the Indian Congress leadership were rounded up and imprisoned. Indeed, in August 1942, some sixty thousand Indians were jailed, joining the twenty thousand or so who had been put behind bars earlier in the year.

Mohandas Gandhi was no stranger to prison. This latest confinement would bring to 2,089 the total number of days he spent in Anglo-Indian jails (earlier, he had been confined for 249 days in South African prisons). For him, imprisonment was the ultimate protest. Jailers and the regime that employed them could confine his body, but they could neither confine his soul nor compel his voluntary compliance and cooperation with whatever they wanted. Prison deprived him of movement, but not of freedom. Prison therefore demonstrated the final limit of the oppressor's power.

Yet the essence of prison was hardship, and, during this latest incarceration, Gandhi endured two cruel personal blows: the loss to heart attack of his personal secretary, Mahadev Desai, on whom he greatly depended, and the death of his much-loved and long-suffering wife, Kasturba, after his eighteenth month of imprisonment. A month and a half after the death of Kasturba, Gandhi himself fell critically ill with malaria.

"You are reported to have the desire to crush the 'naked fakir,' as you are said to have described me. I have been long trying to be a fakir and that, naked—a more difficult task. I therefore regard the expression as a compliment, though unintended. I approach you then as such, and ask you to trust and use me for the sake of your people and mine and through them those of the world. Your sincere friend, M. K. Gandhi."

—letter from Gandhi to Winston Churchill, July 17, 1944

On November 10, 1942, Churchill had demonstrated that even a great man can fall prey to short-sighted folly. He proclaimed that day that he had "not become the King's First Minister in order to preside at the liquidation of the British Empire" and that, rather than allow this to happen, he would "crush" Gandhi, whom he had repeatedly derided as a "naked fakir." The jailing of Gandhi and thousands of others, along with the imposition of martial law early in 1943, did suppress the Quit India Movement for the duration of the war, but it did not extinguish the call for independence.

As for Gandhi, despite personal grief and illness, he refused to be crushed. With great reluctance, British authorities released him on May 6, 1944, before the end of the war, because of his failing health. The last thing the Raj wanted was for him to die a martyr's death in prison.

To Gandhi it hardly mattered whether he was in prison or out. The "whole of India is a vast prison," he wrote in March 1945. "The Viceroy is the irresponsible superintendent of the prison with numerous jailers and warders under him. The four hundred millions of Indians are not the only prisoners. . . . A jailer is as much a prisoner as his prisoner." Gandhi did not want to defeat the British government, but to convert it to the realization that unless Britain cleansed itself morally and spiritually by freeing India, it could not truly win the war, let alone win the peace that would follow. Shortly before he was imprisoned, he explained to an American journalist the folly of attempting to coerce cooperation in a war for freedom:

> If the British wish to document their right to win the war and make the world better, they must purify themselves by surrendering power in India. Your President talks about the Four Freedoms. Do they include the freedom to be free? We are asked to fight for democracy in Germany, Italy and Japan. How can we when we haven't got it ourselves?

Britain and America, Gandhi continued, "have no right to talk of human liberty . . . unless they have washed their hands clean of the pollution."

—

IN JUNE 1942, GANDHI WROTE: "The moment we are free we are transformed into a nation prizing its liberty and defending it with all its might, and therefore helping the Allied cause." Yet Churchill and the British government lacked the faith to "quit India" during the war and instead of harvesting the powerful moral force Gandhi and the others would have provided, Britain risked thrusting India into a Japanese alliance by jailing pro-independence Indians—a total of some one hundred thousand—for the duration of the war. Weakened by war and having come to see empire more as a liability than an asset, the British finally yielded after the final defeat of Japan in 1945, giving clear indication that they intended to transfer India into the hands of the Indians. Accepting those indications as demonstrations of good faith, Gandhi called off the campaign of noncooperation, which in turn prompted the release of all political prisoners, and the process of making India a sovereign nation commenced.

Did England win the war only to lose its empire? What Gandhi understood was that a jail, no matter how vast, is no empire. As he saw it, in quitting India, the British people had relinquished a prison and thereby succeeded at long last in liberating themselves.

PART FIVE

The Decision
to Destroy

Governor Willem Kieft and the "Slaughter of the Innocents" (1643)

THE DECISION TO MURDER

The Old World came to the New in various guises and for a variety of purposes. Men from Spain called themselves conquistadors and treated the natives they encountered as a people ripe for conquest, their bodies to be subjugated with the sword, their souls with the Bible. The English arrived at first in smaller numbers than the Spanish, and their approach to the Indians was accordingly more tentative. Although they did not always conduct themselves as conquerors, the Englishmen nevertheless regarded the Indians largely with contempt and distrust. Dutch attitudes toward the Native Americans were even more ambivalent than those of the English. Their Indian policy hovered from pragmatic tolerance to belligerence to outright cruelty to timid defensiveness, and back again.

Sailing in the Dutch employ, the English mariner Henry Hudson discovered the river that bears his name in 1609. Five years later, Dutch traders built the trading post Fort Nassau on Castle Island in the Hudson, near present-day Albany, a foothold they dubbed New Netherland. The outpost was surrounded by some sixteen hundred local Indians, the Mahicans, with whom the Dutchmen concluded a trade agreement in 1618. Wisely, the Mahicans at first declined to sell any of their land to the Dutch, but they did agree to allow traders and trappers to live among them. This amicable arrangement would not have been possible with the Spanish or the English, who hungered first and last for land. The Dutch—at least initially—wanted only trade and had little interest in acquiring territory.

Fort Nassau was swept by floods in 1617, prompting its abandonment that year. In 1624, the Dutch West Indies Company, which had been founded three years earlier, built Fort Orange on dry land along the Hudson, at the site of modern Albany. Two years later, in 1626, the Dutch were caught up in their first Indian crisis, when they decided to aid the Mohawks, their trading partners, in a war that tribe had launched against the Mahicans earlier. The Dutch dispatched from Fort Orange a small force under Daniel van Kriekenbeek to fight the Mohawks. The expedition was defeated, with the loss of three men in addition to the commander. That summarily ended the Dutch commitment to the Mahican defense. The traders withdrew back into Fort Orange and quickly drew up a truce with the Mohawks. When, two years later, warriors of that tribe once again pummeled the Mahicans, the Dutch did not make bold to intervene and were soon gratified to see that the Mohawks refrained from pressing their victory to the point of annihilating the rival tribe. It became clear that what the Mohawks really wanted was to wrest from the Mahicans control of what they recognized as a profitable trade with the Dutch. For their part, the Mahicans indicated a willingness to share their trading partner, and the Mohawks and Mahicans reached an accord sometime after 1628.

With stability restored to Fort Orange and its environs, the Dutch might well have enjoyed quiet and prosperous trade with not one, but two important tribes. Yet, as their numbers grew steadily larger, the Dutch seemed unable to resist striking out against the Mohawks as well as the Mahicans with impulsive outbursts of cruelty and abuse. As late as 1660, a committee of Mohawk chiefs petitioned the magistrates of Fort Orange "to forbid the Dutch to molest the Indians as heretofore by kicking, beating, and assaulting them, in order that we may not break the old friendship which we have enjoyed for more than thirty years."

Yet the level of ill will and simmering violence on the Dutch frontier seemed downright cordial compared with what was happening in adjacent New England during this period. White-Indian warfare was chronic and bloody throughout the English settlements, whereas the rough edges notwithstanding trade proceeded at a mutually profitable pace in New Netherland until more and more colonists turned from trading to farming.

This trend resulted both from the growth of the Dutch colony (people had to be fed, so the life of a farmer became profitable) and from the depletion of the Indians' principal trade commodity, beaver, which had been hunted to near extinction along the coast.

By 1639, when Willem Kieft replaced Wouter van Twiller as director-general of New Netherland, acquisition of territory was supplanting trade as the chief focus of Dutch activity. Certainly the building of small farms and even substantial estates had become more important than maintaining friendly relations with the Indians, and Kieft did not think twice about levying exorbitant taxes on the Algonquian tribes living in the vicinity of Manhattan and Long Island. He told them that the taxes were needed to finance the cost of defending them against "hostiles." The hostility, of course, had been created mainly by the new Dutch policy toward the Indians.

In any case, the taxes were as much extorted protection money—to protect the Indians against the Dutch—as they were funding for mutual defense against any "hostile" tribes. In the atmosphere Kieft had created, Dutch-Indian relations rapidly continued to deteriorate. It was a situation that would become tragically familiar in America. Whites and Indians routinely rubbed up against each other, enmities grew, and, inevitably, some incident—often relatively minor—would explode into open warfare.

Livestock belonging to Dutch farmers often strayed onto Indian corn-fields, ravaging them. When Dutch cows ate corn on Staten Island in 1641, the local Raritan Indians retaliated, killing stock and terrorizing farmers. Governor Kieft responded by offering a cash bounty on Raritan scalps.

The atmosphere grew poisonous. In 1642, a Dutch wheelwright named Claes Rademaker was murdered by an Indian seeking vengeance for the killing of his uncle, who had been beaten to death by settlers covetous of the beaver pelts he carried. Kieft recruited a small army, which he intended to parade through the villages surrounding New Amsterdam (modern New York City) in a bit to intimidate the Indians. His effort was none too successful. The tiny band set off by night—and promptly got lost. Instead of recoiling in fear from the might of Willem Kieft, the Native American locals had a good laugh at his expense.

Historians of Dutch America give Kieft credit for creating the Council of Twelve Men in 1641, the first representative political body in New Netherland and among the first in all of the North American colonies. These historians also point out that having created the council to advise him, he habitually ignored its advice. Kieft now asked his council whether he should up the ante, escalating from a parade of benighted militiamen to full-scale war on the Indians. The council was quick to answer: "We [are] not prepared to carry on a war with the Indians until we [have] more people, like the English."

Predictably, Kieft ignored the advice and set about starting a war.

In February 1643, a band of Mohawks, still active trading partners of the Dutch and wielded by Kieft as hired thugs, traveled down the Hudson to extort on his behalf tribute money from the Wappinger Indians. Duly terrorized, the Wappingers fled downriver to Pavonia (present-day Jersey City, New Jersey, and environs) and to New Amsterdam. Failing to understand that the Mohawks worked for Kieft, they appealed to the director-general for protection.

Kieft saw his opportunity for war. He not only refused to help the Wappingers, but turned the Mohawks loose upon them. In a lightning raid, Mohawk warriors killed seventy Wappingers and enslaved others. On February 24, David Pietersz. de Vries, a Dutch "artillery master" by vocation and historical chronicler by avocation, was "sitting at table" with Kieft, who "began to state his intentions, that he had a mind to wipe the mouths of the Indians." Kieft told de Vries that the local patroons—property holders— were urging him to start the war. De Vries "answered him that there was not sufficient reason to undertake it." He reminded Kieft that in 1630, "on account of trifling with the Indians we had lost our colony in the South river at Swanendael, [along with] thirty-two men, who were murdered," and in 1640, many Dutch settlers had been killed on Staten Island after "soldiers had for some trifling thing killed some Indians." De Vries further recorded:

But it appeared that my speaking was of no avail. He had, with his co-murderers, determined to commit the murder, deeming it a Roman deed, and to do it without warning the [Dutch] inhabitants of the open lands, that each one might take care of himself against the retaliation of the Indians, for he could not kill all the Indians.

De Vries begged the director-general: "Stop this work; you wish to break the mouths of the Indians, but you will also murder our own nation."

Night came, February 25/26, 1643. Those Wappinger men who had escaped Mohawk hatchets, together with Wappinger women and children (whom even the Mohawks were reluctant to harm) cowered at Pavonia. Learning of their presence there, Kieft sent his small army across the Hudson. This time, his soldiers found their way in the dark, and Pavonia became a killing field, the screams of the men, women, and children heard clearly across the river in New Amsterdam. Locals would call this night the "Slaughter of the Innocents." De Vries bore witness:

> I remained that night at the governor's, sitting up. I went and sat in the kitchen, when, about midnight, I heard a great shrieking, and I ran to the ramparts of the fort, and looked over to Pavonia. Saw nothing but firing, and heard the shrieks of the Indians murdered in their sleep. . . . When it was day the soldiers returned to the fort, having massacred or murdered eighty Indians, and considering that they had done a deed of Roman valour, in murdering so many in their sleep; where infants were torn from their mother's breasts, and hacked to pieces in the presence of the parents, and the pieces thrown into the fire and in the water, and other sucklings were bound to small boards, and then cut, stuck, and pierced, and miserably massacred in a manner to move a heart of stone. Some were thrown into the river, and when the fathers and mothers endeavoured to save them, the soldiers would not let them come on land, but made both parents and children drown,—children from five to six years of age, and also some decrepit persons. . . . At another place, on the

same night at Corler's Hook [Corlear's Hook, part of the present-day
Lower East Side of Manhattan] on Corler's plantation, forty Indians
were in the same manner attacked in their sleep.

From Pavonia, the troops returned to New Amsterdam bearing
approximately eighty severed heads, which soldiers and citizens booted
about as footballs in the streets of the little city. Thirty prisoners, taken
alive, were tortured to death for the public amusement.

The "Slaughter of the Innocents" brought on the war Kieft had
wanted—yet not with a tribe or two, but with no fewer than eleven Indian
tribes. New Amsterdam as well as its outlying dependencies fell under
relentless attack. DeVries reported: "When now the Indians destroyed so
many farms and men in revenge for their people, I went to Governor
William Kieft, and asked him if it was not as I had said it would be, that he
would only effect the spilling of Christian blood. Who would now compensate us for our losses? But he gave no answer."

Panic stricken, Kieft called for a conference with local tribal leaders in March 1643. He offered them presents as tokens of conciliation. "But now," de Vries observed, "it might fall out that the infants upon the small boards would be remembered. They then went away grumbling with their presents. . . . A chief of the Indians came to me, and told me that he was very sad. I asked him wherefore. He said that there were many young Indian youths, who were constantly wishing for a war against us, as one had lost his father, another his mother, a third his uncle."

"Many fled from this scene [of the Pavonia massacre], and concealed themselves in the neighbouring sedge, and when it was morning, came out to beg a piece of bread, and to be permitted to warm themselves; but they were murdered in cold blood and tossed into the water. Some came by our lands in the country with their hands, some with their legs cut off, and some holding their entrails in their arms."

—from David Pietersz. de Vries's account of the Pavonia massacre

Kieft's presents notwithstanding, it was such young warriors whose will prevailed. On October 1, 1643, nine Indians came to a small fort at Pavonia, where three or four soldiers were stationed to protect a local patroon farmer. Pretending perfect friendship, the Indians gained entry onto the farm, then turned on the soldiers, killed them, then killed the farmer and his family as well, sparing from the hatchet only the farmer's stepson, whom they took captive to Tappan, up the Hudson. As for the farmer's house, it, along with all the houses of Pavonia, were put to the torch.

The flames were seen far beyond the horizon. From the Delaware Bay to the Connecticut River, tribes rose in armed wrath. From all over New Netherland, terrorized colonists fled to New Amsterdam, which lay under siege for more than a year. Only the Mohawks, still bound in profitable trade with the Dutch, refused to raise arms against Kieft's colony.

At length, Kieft hired Captain John Underhill, an Englishman who had distinguished himself in New England's Pequot War, to lead Dutch and mercenary English soldiers in a great offensive sweep through the countryside, attacking Indians and burning their villages. By 1644, no longer able to endure the war of devastation and attrition waged against them, the tribes lifted their siege of New Amsterdam and concluded a peace.

For a full decade, a sullen calm settled over the land shared by the Dutch and their Indian neighbors. The lesson of Kieft's cruel folly, it seemed, had been learned.

But then, on a day in 1655—by this time, Kieft had been replaced by Peter Stuyvesant, destined to be the last governor of New Netherland—a Dutch farmer spied a Delaware Indian woman picking peaches in his orchard. He shot her dead, and in retaliation the woman's family ambushed and killed the farmer.

Word of the violent exchange spread rapidly, inducing other bands of Delawares to strike. A number of settlers were killed in a raid on New Amsterdam, and 150 were taken captive. Stuyvesant called out the militia, which freed most of the captives and retaliated by destroying Indian villages. Thereafter, debilitating, destructive warfare became a way of life until 1664 when Stuyvesant once again employed Mohawk thugs to terrorize the Esopus Indians, at the time his colony's principal antagonists. But 1664 proved also to be the last year of Dutch rule in New Netherland. On October 4, the English took possession of the colony, which they renamed New York, and the Dutch ceased to be of consequence in the New World.

———

THE LESSON OF WILLEM KIEFT is the folly of a small man given the power of life and death. Small men are possessed of vision too limited to see beyond the labor required to fashion lives of peace and prosperity. Instead, they see only the immediate solution of dealing death to those perceived as rivals. All that is visible, both ahead and behind, is blood. Shakespeare's Macbeth understood this when he tells a suddenly conscience-stricken Lady Macbeth, "We are in blood steeped in so far that, should we wade no more, returning was as tedious as go over."

In an effort to achieve political and economical supremacy in a single night of terror, Willem Kieft doomed his colony to years of bloodshed in wars that doomed the Dutch to lose all that they had in the New World. Knowing no better than to sow the wind, he caused his people to reap the whirlwind.

Antonio López de Santa Anna and the Alamo (1836)

THE DECISION THAT MADE MARTYRS

It all started amicably enough. Before losing possession of Mexico in the Revolution of 1821, Spain had been eager to attract American colonists to part of its colony that lay north of the Rio Grande. The Spanish Crown proposed what should have been a win-win proposition: Colonists would be given cheap land and lots of it. In return, they would agree to renounce their American citizenship and swear allegiance to Spain, thereby creating a buffer community that would defend Mexico proper against Indian raids on the one hand and U.S. expansionism on the other.

This grand scheme was disrupted by Mexican independence, but the revolutionary government soon adopted a colonization policy that was strikingly similar to that of Spain. Its Colonization Law of 1824, which applied to Tejas—or Texas—the part of the newly created Mexican state of Coahuila y Tejas north of the Rio Grande, treated colonists with liberal generosity, guaranteeing them land and security as well as a four-year exemption from taxes. Similar to the Spanish plan, the Mexican law required a pledge of allegiance to Mexico.

In 1821, Moses Austin, a would-be empire builder who had created and lost a small mining empire in Virginia, then built a similar empire in Missouri, which he also soon lost, had secured a land grant in Spanish Texas along with permission to establish a plantation colony there. When he fell gravely ill before he could begin the process of populating his colony, he asked his son Stephen F. Austin to carry out his plan. Unlike his father, the younger Austin was no dreamer of empires, and he had no great desire to found a colony in Texas. But he could not refuse his father's deathbed request, and, assuming the grants Spain had promised to Moses, Stephen Austin successfully renegotiated them with newly independent Mexico, thereby becoming the foremost empresario (as the colonial grantees were called) among the dozen who soon came to Texas.

Stephen F. Austin was an honorable man, who was grateful to the Mexican government and who fully intended to honor his colony's commitments to that government. The problem was that, although he was foremost among the empresarios, he could not control them. Indeed, he soon found that he could not even control a good many of his own colonists.

That's when things became less and less amicable.

Most "Texians," as the colonists liked to call themselves, had no problem pledging their allegiance to Mexico, but, the pledge notwithstanding, they never stopped thinking of themselves as Americans—by which they meant white, Anglo-Saxon, English-speaking Protestants. Mexicans, in contrast, were Spanish-speaking Hispanics and Hispanic-Indians who were Catholics. The American colonists had few if any political differences with their Mexican hosts, but the ethnic, religious, and cultural gulf between them and the Mexicans was vast.

Revolutionary Mexico was unstable, and the men who attempted to govern it were not eager to preside over yet another group of potentially rebellious citizens. A minor uprising, the so-called Fredonian Rebellion, broke out in 1826, prompting the Mexican government to become increasingly wary of the "Texians." Mexican officials believed that rebellion on a larger scale, when it came, would not be the product of some rogue empresario or a few colonists, but would be covertly supported by the government of the United States in a bid to seize Mexico's northern borderlands. When President John Quincy Adams offered to purchase Texas for $1 million, the Mexican government did not take this as an opportunity to shed troublesome colonists, but saw it as confirmation that American land hunger was rapacious indeed. The offer was rejected, and, on April 6, 1830, Mexico barred any further American immigration into Texas.

Adams's White House successor, Andrew Jackson, raised the offer to $5 million, and after this was also turned down, he replaced Joel Poinsett, the honorable negotiator Adams had sent to Mexico, with the more morally pliable Anthony Butler. Combining bribery with fraud, Butler offered Mexico a badly needed loan with Texas posted as collateral. The deal was structured such that the loan was virtually impossible to pay back, thereby ensuring that Texas would be forfeited by default. Mexican officials nibbled, but did not bite, and the deal was never made.

Yet even as two presidents jockeyed to purchase Texas, Congress was reluctant both to provoke war with Mexico and to annex a territory populated mostly by Southern slave holders, who were sure to seek the admission of Texas to the union as a slave state. In the meantime, while the attitude toward Texas annexation grew increasingly ambivalent throughout the United States, the attitude of the Texians toward Mexico grew increasingly toxic.

Nobody is quite sure why. Some historians believe that the increase in hostility was due to the fact that the Southern Protestant colonists increasingly resented having to answer to predominantly Catholic Mexican authorities and even feared that they would lose their freedom of religion. Certainly, religion played a role in the deteriorating relations, but far from threatening to limit religious freedom, the Mexican government passed legislation in 1834 that explicitly guaranteed religious freedom, along with the liberty to express "political opinions."

Other historians see the slavery issue as the chief cause of colonial disaffection. It is true that many Texians brought slaves with them to the colony, making the slave population nearly equal to the free population. They also made no secret of the fact that they would need even more slaves as their land holdings increased. Having already abolished slavery throughout Mexico proper, the Mexican government did propose eventual emancipation for Texas; nevertheless, in 1829 Mexico yielded to Texian demands for the protection of slavery by issuing a special presidential exemption from the general abolition decree.

Still other historians have pointed to issues of trade and taxation as the causes of colonial discontent. Texians wanted to trade freely with both Mexico and the United States, whereas Mexican authorities naturally sought to create more favorable trading relations between Texas and the mother country. In response, smuggling became a major Texas industry.

No doubt, all of these causes contributed to discontent over how Mexico administered the Texas colonies, but the independence movement seems above all to have been motivated by cultural and ethnic imperatives. The fact is that the Texians considered themselves in every way superior to the Mexicans, who they believed to be the inherently lazy and corrupt slaves of their Catholic priests. The chip on the Texian shoulder was very large by 1835–36, when the Anglo population of the colony had reached thirty thousand (with almost as many slaves), whereas the number of Mexican nationals in Texas numbered a mere thirty-five hundred. Why, the Texians asked themselves, should a clearly superior majority have to continue to answer to an inferior minority? Even setting racism aside, just in terms of numbers, it was apparent to many Texians by the mid-1830s that their "country" had already in fact become American.

Considering the many motives Texians had for independence, some ugly, some rational, all compelling, a Texas revolution seemed historically inevitable. Yet not everyone wanted independence. Many, perhaps most, Texians believed that the colony should be granted a more substantial degree of autonomy or be established as a Mexican state in its own right, separate from the predominantly Mexican Coahuila below the Rio Grande. A substantial minority favored outright independence, but did so with an eye toward eventual annexation to the United States.

The people of Texas were hardly unified in their desires. A rift developed early on between the first colonists and latecomers, including a steady stream of new settlers who defied the Mexican ban on immigration. The newer settlers tended to favor independence, while the more established colonists wanted to work out a way of cooperating with the Mexican government. As Stephen Austin saw it, Texas factionalism threatened to tear the colony apart—an eventuality that would have put Texas entirely at the mercy of the Mexican overlords.

Austin kept one wary eye on Texas and the other on Mexico. As fractious as the Texians were, Mexico at this time was even less stable. The government of Anastasio Bustamante was under siege by Antonio López de Santa Anna, a man Austin recognized as nothing if not remarkable. He had been born in Xalapa, Veracruz, in 1794, the son of solid middle-class parents. In 1810, young Santa Anna joined the Royalist army as a cadet, fighting Mexican insurgents as well as unruly Indians. As a loyalist to Spain, he learned much about fighting insurgents as well as fighting *as* one. In 1813, he fought in Texas as part of a force sent against the Gutiérrez-Magee Expedition, an early Mexican-American rebellion against Spanish colonial rule. Santa Anna looked on as his commander, General Joaquín de Arredondo, crushed the rebels through a ruthless policy of swift mass executions. It was an example Santa Anna would never forget.

Between 1810 and 1821, the struggle for Mexican independence came to a stalemate, and, during this period, Santa Anna developed a reputation in his native Veracruz for magnanimity on the one hand—he built villages for those displaced by the long war—and epic dissipation on the other—he was a fierce gambler and an avid patron of whores.

He was also, politically, a well-oiled weathervane. When, in 1821, the wind abruptly changed direction from loyalty to independence, he changed direction as well, declaring allegiance to the insurgent leader Agustín de Iturbide. In service to "El Libertador," Santa Anna drove the Spanish forces from the port city of Veracruz, for which Iturbide, having proclaimed himself emperor of Mexico, promoted him to general. Two years later, in 1823, General Santa Anna conspired with other military leaders to overthrow Iturbide and declare Mexico a republic. Santa Anna rose to the governorship of Yucatán in 1824, then became a full-fledged national hero in 1829 when he repelled a Spanish attempt to retake Mexico. Against the twenty-six hundred troops of the Spanish Barradas Expedition, Santa Anna led a much smaller force, but whereas the Spanish loyalists had been decimated by yellow fever, Santa Anna's men were hale and hearty. He defeated the invaders and thereafter called himself the "Savior of the Motherland." It was a title that rang loudly and well.

Having won victory in 1829, Santa Anna emulated no less a figure than George Washington after the American Revolution. He announced his retirement to private life "unless my country needs me."

That need, he decided, came when Anastasio Bustamante, vice president of the republic, led a coup d'etat, overthrowing and killing President Vicente Guerrero. President Bustamante proved instantly unpopular, and a revolt broke out in Veracruz in 1832—with Santa Anna in command of the insurgents. It was now that Austin made his move. He approached Santa Anna with a proposal that the general extend to Texas enhanced autonomy in return for which Texas would support him in his struggle against Bustamante. Because Austin hardly controlled all of Texas, it was a bold, even presumptuous pledge, but, as it turned out, Santa Anna prevailed and gained election as president in 1833 without having to call on the Texians for help. Nevertheless, although Texas had played virtually no role in Santa Anna's ascension, Austin seized upon the defeat of Bustamante to ask Santa Anna for the next step toward enlarged autonomy for Texas: full and formal Mexican statehood independent of Coahuila. He presented a petition to that effect and awaited the president's answer.

While Austin labored to bring Texas closer to Mexican statehood, Sam Houston, veteran of Andrew Jackson's command in the War of 1812, former congressman and former governor of Tennessee, arrived in Texas. Encouraged by President Jackson, he recruited and took charge of a Texas volunteer army, then drafted a state constitution, which, even though he had yet to hear from Santa Anna, Austin took to Mexico City.

With his chief rival, Bustamante, now in exile, Santa Anna no longer saw much urgency in encouraging either greater autonomy or outright statehood for Texas. To Austin he did not even extend the courtesy of a prompt rejection. Instead, he allowed him to cool his heels in the capital city for five months before even granting him an audience. When he did finally consent to see Austin, the president was extravagantly conciliatory, promising the Texian leader that he would remedy all grievances and would do everything for Texas—short of recognizing it as a state.

If Austin was disappointed, he did not let on. He left the audience and Mexico City believing that he had at least made some progress. But Santa Anna was not finished with Stephen Austin. When Austin passed the town of Saltillo en route back to Texas, he was summarily arrested, taken back to Mexico City, and imprisoned on a charge of having written a letter urging Texas statehood. Santa Anna condemned it as sedition: a violation of Austin's original pledge of allegiance to Mexico. For two years, Austin languished in a cell, his health declining. Imprisoned without trial, he was released in 1835, also without trial, emerging from his cell embittered and broken.

Santa Anna may have believed that by locking Austin up, he had found an economical, nonviolent means of nipping Texas's political ambitions in the bud. In fact, he had blundered badly by imprisoning the most important voice of moderation among the Texians. With Austin in jail, the most aggressive pro-independence faction in Texas, the "War Dogs," multiplied in number as well as influence.

In June 1835, thirty War Dogs stormed the small garrison and customs house at Anahuac, forcing its surrender. This action did not touch off the revolution the War Dogs wanted. Worse, colonists throughout Texas both deplored and disavowed the seizure. Nevertheless—and this was the momentous thing—they also refused to surrender the Anahuac rebels to Mexican authorities.

Had he bothered to look, Santa Anna would have seen that Texas was deeply divided on the issue of remaining loyal to Mexico. Accordingly he would have enacted policies to make loyalty appear as the most attractive option on the table. Instead, he resorted to what he had learned in a military and political life lived among chronic insurgency and counterinsurgency. He cracked down.

In a single stroke, Santa Anna repudiated what he called his formerly liberal policies, not only with regard to Texas but for all Mexico, elevating himself from president to absolute dictator. Turning specifically to Texas, he threatened to extend the Mexican antislavery ban to this region. If he had done nothing else, that threat alone would likely have united all Texas in a revolution for independence. But Santa Anna did more. By the fall 1835, he began sending troops into Texas. Stephen Austin, radicalized by two years in a Mexico City prison, was now vehement in calling for outright rebellion. He called for Americans to pour into Texas from all over the nation, "each man with his rifle." For "war," he declared, "is our only recourse." On October 2, 1835, Mexican cavalry crossed the Rio Grande to demand the surrender of a cannon in the town of Gonzales. Instead of giving up the piece, locals formed themselves into a small army and forced General Martín Perfecto de Cós and his cavalrymen to retreat to San Antonio de Bejar (modern San Antonio, in Bexar County, Texas). Austin now personally assumed command of a five-hundred-man force in a siege of San Antonio during November.

Idealists believe that people will unite around any sufficiently powerful cause. More often, however, they unite not for a cause but against a common enemy. Santa Anna had made himself that common enemy. Texians were united against him, but they were not yet united in the cause of independence. Even as Austin laid siege to San Antonio, representatives of the dozen American colonies in Texas convened in an effort to decide once and for all whether to settle for less than independence or to strive far more modestly for a return to Mexico under the provisions of the liberal 1824 constitution. After much wrangling, it was decided to create a provisional government, which would be tasked with appealing to liberal, anti–Santa Anna elements in Mexico for statehood within a constitutionally governed Mexico.

Returned from the San Antonio front, Austin was hardly satisfied with this outcome. He no longer believed that *any* Mexican government could be trusted. With others, he traveled to Washington to sound out President Jackson on the likelihood of annexing Texas to the United States. As for Austin's troops, still laying siege to Cós, winter food shortages were taking a toll. When the temporary commander decided to withdraw to winter quarters at Gonzales, the fiery frontiersman Ben Milam roused the volunteers for a final assault on San Antonio. "Who will go with old Ben Milam?" became the first rallying cry of the Texas revolution.

So it was that on December 5, 1835 an army now swollen to fifty-three hundred volunteers stormed San Antonio and fought the badly outnumbered Cós in the streets. Commanding no more than eleven hundred troops, the Mexican general withdrew to barracks in a tumble-down fortress that had been converted from the town's old namesake mission. The mission's founders, Franciscan monks, had called it Mission San Antonio de Valero, but it was popularly known as the Alamo because of its proximity to a stand of cottonwoods (the cottonwood is called *alamo* in Spanish). The old mission could not shelter Cós and his men for long. The Texians trained their artillery against the Alamo's walls, lobbed a few shots, and the Mexicans gave up. The Texas men then occupied the fortress and patched it up as best they could.

As with the American Revolution, the fighting had begun before independence had been established as the objective of the struggle. Houston and Henry Smith, the man the Texians had chosen as their governor, urged a vote for independence, but were opposed by various land speculators who had amassed their holdings by bribing Mexican legislators and were therefore fearful that independence would nullify their claims. These men proposed sending a force to Matamoros, a Mexican town at the mouth of the Rio Grande known to harbor large numbers of anti–Santa Anna liberals. The speculators believed that, by seizing Matamoros, their army could join forces with the liberals to depose Santa Anna and restore the liberal federalism of the 1824 Mexican constitution. Texas would gain a degree of autonomy, and the speculators' holdings would be safe.

The men James W. Fannin Jr. led toward Matamoros fell to arguing and stopped short of their destination. They holed up instead within a fort at Goliad, by which time—January 1836—Santa Anna himself was on the march at the head of a sixty-five-hundred-man army, intent on crushing the rebellion for good.

Even as Santa Anna approached, news was coming from the Alamo that the recently installed Texas garrison there was tired, unpaid, and hungry. There was a good deal of talk of giving up and returning to the United States. For his part, Sam Houston had little interest in defending the Alamo, which he considered a remote outpost of little value. He wrote to Governor Smith on January 17, 1836, that he had "ordered the fortifications in the town of Bexar [San Antonio] to be demolished, and if you should think well of it, I will remove all the cannon and other munitions of war to Gonzales and Copano, blow up the Alamo, and abandon the place, as it will be impossible to keep up the Station with volunteers." Smith responded to Houston by refusing authorization to destroy the Alamo, arguing that the locals did not have enough horses and mules to remove cannon, ammunition, and other supplies. Houston disagreed with this assessment, countering that it was a stronger strategy to withdraw the garrison closer to San Felipe de Austin (modern Austin, Texas), which was situated in country easier to defend and more difficult to attack.

Even as Houston struggled to promote abandonment of the Alamo, Fannin was asking for permission to move out of Goliad and proceed to an attack on Matamoros, as the landowner group had wanted. Houston protested that to do this would give Santa Anna clear passage straight into the interior of Texas. He compromised by ordering the concentration of his own main forces sixty miles east of San Antonio at Gonzales, a more effective position from which to oppose Santa Anna's advance, and he sent the frontiersman Jim Bowie to San Antonio to supervise the evacuation and destruction of the Alamo as well as the removal and transportation of its artillery. In the meantime, Houston negotiated a treaty with the Cherokees of east Texas, securing their pledge to remain neutral in the approaching fight.

But Houston barely had time to breathe a sigh of relief. As soon as he arrived at the Alamo, Bowie decided to ignore his orders. With garrison commander Colonel James C. Neill, he resolved instead to make a stand rather than be "driven from the post of honor." On February 2, Bowie wrote to Smith that "the Salvation of Texas depends in great measure in keeping Bejar out of the hands of the enemy. It serves as the frontier picquet guard. . . . Col. Neill & Myself have come to the solemn resolution that we will rather die in these ditches than give it up to the enemy."

Santa Anna had his own problems. In harsh winter weather, over a landscape that offered little sustenance, he had driven his army hard. By the time he reached the outskirts of San Antonio, only about two thousand of his sixty-five hundred troops were fit for duty. Still, Neill and Bowie commanded little more than one hundred men. They appealed to Fannin for reinforcements, but he refused, reasserting

> **"Since you have chosen to elect a man with a timber toe to succeed me, you may all go to hell and I will go to Texas."**
>
> —Davey Crockett's message to the people of his Tennessee district when they failed to return him to Congress

his intention to leave Goliad for an assault on Matamoros. Colonel William B. Travis, a committed War Dog, did bring in a handful of reinforcements, as did David "Davey" Crockett, who led a dozen volunteers from Tennessee. A former Tennessee congressman, Crockett enjoyed national fame as a frontiersman and the publisher of a phenomenally popular almanac, which, in addition to making weather predictions, listing tables of tides, and setting out the phases of the moon, regaled its readers with tall tales of the exploits of—who else?—Davey Crockett.

By February 11, 1836, Neill had left the Alamo, turning over command of about 150 men to Bowie and Travis. They were keenly aware that Santa Anna was on his way and that his forces were vastly superior, but they did not believe that even he would try to march an army through a barren South Texas winter. They assumed that the attack would not come before spring, by which time ample reinforcements would surely have arrived. They counted on the strength of Travis's many letters appealing to patriots for aid. Carried out of the Alamo by messengers, the letters were regularly published in the nation's newspapers.

But they assumed wrong.

Santa Anna had no regard for the welfare of his men and thought nothing of marching them, properly clothed or not, with or without adequate rations, as far as necessary and whenever necessary. He and his much-reduced army entered San Antonio on February 23. As for the anticipated influx of patriots, it did not happen.

As word of Santa Anna's arrival spread, women, children, and few old men sought refuge with the Alamo garrison. In the meantime, Travis, who suffered from chronic illness, became critically ill after he was injured while placing a heavy cannon. Helpless, he was confined to a cot. On March 1, thirty-two (some sources say twenty-five) new reinforcements arrived—against Houston's explicit orders—from the Gonzales militia. By most modern counts, this brought the Alamo garrison to 187.

On March 2, delegates met at a place they had christened Washington-on-the-Brazos to approve the Texas Declaration of Independence. Now the Alamo defenders had an unambiguous cause, and, four days later, before dawn, Santa Anna unleashed his artillery against the walls of the former mission.

Mexican artillerists were chronically plagued by a faulty recipe for gunpowder—it would bring disaster during the 1846–48 U.S.-Mexican War—and, after five days of bombardment, Santa Anna had failed to kill a single Texian within the Alamo, even as the grapeshot and rifle fire of the garrison had exacted a heavy toll among the attackers. Grapeshot consisted of small iron balls—typically nine—put together between iron plates. Fired from a cannon, this projectile would break apart, the balls separating from the plates in a lethal expanding cluster for about a thousand yards, cutting down whoever was in the way. But the ancient, crumbling, patched, and battered walls of the Alamo could not stand up indefinitely even to the Mexicans' feeble powder. On March 6, seeing a sufficiently wide breach in the mission wall, Santa Anna raised a bloodred flag. It signaled that no quarter was to be given to the defenders.

> Commandancy of the Alamo
> Bejar, Fby. 24th, 1836
> To the People of Texas & all Americans in the world Fellow Citizens &
>   Compatriots
> I am besieged by a thousand or more of the Mexicans under Santa Anna.
> I have sustained a continual bombardment & cannonade for 24 hours &
> have not lost a man. The enemy has demanded a surrender at discretion,
> otherwise the garrison are to be put to the sword if the fort is taken. I
> have answered the demand with a cannon shot, and our flag still waves
> proudly from the walls. I shall never surrender nor retreat.
>   Then, I call on you in the name of Liberty, of patriotism, & of every-
> thing dear to the American character, to come to our aid with all dispatch.
> The enemy is receiving reinforcements daily & will no doubt increase to
> three or four thousand in four or five days. If this call is neglected, I am
> determined to sustain myself as long as possible & die like a soldier who
> never forgets what is due to his own honor & that of his country.
> **Victory or Death**
> ‗‗‗‗‗‗‗‗‗‗
>
> William Barret Travis
> Lt. Col. comdt.

P. S. The Lord is on our side—When the enemy appeared in sight we had not three bushels of corn—We have since found in deserted houses 80 or 90 bushels & got into the walls 20 or 30 head of Beeves—

Travis

Santa Anna divided his forces into four columns plus a force held in reserve for security and pursuit. Beginning at about 5 AM, General Cós led the first column of three hundred to four hundred men to the northwest corner of the Alamo. The second column (380 men under Colonel Francisco Duque), the third (four hundred soldiers commanded by Colonel José María Romero), and the fourth (one hundred light infantrymen under Colonel Juan Morales) soon followed, advancing toward other sides of the Alamo. All had to move across some three hundred yards of open field leading up to the mission walls. This exposed the men to murderous gunfire, but it also forced the defenders to spread themselves thinly in an effort to cover all directions. As the men of his principal columns advanced, Santa Anna deployed 350 cavalrymen under Brigadier General Joaquín Ramírez y Sesma to patrol the surrounding countryside in order to cut off any escape and to intercept any last-minute reinforcements.

The Texians managed to drive back one of the columns, but the one led by Cós rapidly pushed their way through the badly breached north wall. Among the first defenders to fall was Travis, reportedly killed by a shot to the head. As the Cós column continued to pour into the fortress, the other three columns battered at the Alamo elsewhere along its walls. Within an hour and a half, it was all over. Almost all of the Texians lay dead, and, according to some accounts, Bowie, unable to rise from his cot, was bayoneted where he lay. The handful of garrison men who did survive, including Crockett, were allegedly rounded up and executed in summary fashion.

Santa Anna spared fifteen women and children (some sources report as many as twenty) in addition to two slaves, Bowie's Sam and

Travis's Joe. All of those prisoners were quickly released, but Santa Anna took time to tell one of the women, Susannah Dickerson, to carry the word of the terrible punishment that had been meted out at the Alamo. He was convinced that her account would discourage any further rebellion.

Immediately after the fall of the Alamo, Houston ordered Fannin to destroy the fortress at Goliad and retreat. Fannin obeyed, but was delayed—and the delay proved fatal. A fourteen-hundred-man force under General José de Urrea surrounded Fannin's retreating troops, who held out for two days before surrendering on March 20. Less than a week later, Santa Anna, still believing it most effective to drown the rebellion in blood, ordered Urrea to execute all of his prisoners.

What happened in the immediate aftermath of the Alamo and the "Goliad Massacre" suggested that Santa Anna was right. Defeat at the Alamo and Goliad triggered the so-called "Runaway Scrape" in which thousands of Texians fled east to the United States border. As for the Texas provisional government, it also decamped—except for Sam Houston, who turned flight into a strategic retreat. Houston had not wanted the Alamo held, but now that it had been lost, he set about exploiting the gift of mass martyrdom. The fall of the Alamo furnished the Texas revolution with a pantheon of dead heroes as well as a stirring battle cry, "Remember the Alamo!" Armed with these, Houston raised and trained an army of 740 determined men and, on April 21, 1836, surprised Santa Anna at the Battle of San Jacinto. In the space of eighteen minutes, Santa Anna and his fourteen hundred soldiers had been totally routed. Houston's soldiers pursued, inflicting on the Mexicans all of the brutality Santa Anna had directed against the Alamo defenders and Fannin's command. The battle and pursuit ended with more than 630 Mexicans killed and Santa Anna taken prisoner. Hauled before Houston, who was nursing a wounded leg, Santa Anna anticipated summary execution. Instead, Houston offered him his life in exchange for his signature on the hastily drafted Treaty of Velasco, by which the

Mexican dictator agreed to evacuate all of his troops from Texas and to recognize the territory as an independent republic. Texas had won its revolution, and Santa Anna had lost Texas.

———

ANTONIO LÓPEZ DE SANTA ANNA was a leader remarkable in nineteenth-century Mexican politics: a survivor. Beginning life as a Spanish loyalist, he easily switched allegiance to those fighting for Mexican independence, rising to the presidency of the new republic and converting that office into a dictatorship. Defeated by Houston, he nevertheless managed to survive the war with Texas and lived to be defeated a decade later by General Winfield Scott in the U.S.-Mexican War of 1846–48.

Santa Anna was no fool, but his estimate of his fellow man was informed by his own nature as a survivor, at once pliable and hollow. He could not conceive of the power of genuine conviction, a force that could not only withstand the exercise of terror, but that could, in fact, build moral momentum upon it. In return for his blind brutality, Santa Anna gained not a brutal triumph but an ignominious defeat.

Patriotism and Poison Gas (1914–18)

THE DECISION TO INVENT A WEAPON OF

MASS DESTRUCTION

Announcement of the award of a Nobel Prize often commands publicity, but rarely controversy. Yet when the Nobel Committee announced Fritz Haber as the winner of the 1918 Nobel for chemistry, many scientists protested, some even refusing to accept awards made to them. The 1918 prize was announced on November 13, 1919, precisely one year and two days after the armistice that had ended the Great War, a cataclysm to which Haber had contributed the most effective chemical weapons: poison gas.

Haber's defenders—there were more than a few—argued that his Nobel was not for his work on weapons of mass terror, but for his work with fellow chemist Carl Bosch during 1894–1911, developing the "Haber (or Haber-Bosch) process," by which ammonia was "fixed"—produced—from hydrogen and atmospheric nitrogen. In terms of both science and humanity, the Haber process was an extraordinary achievement. As a scientific milestone, it marked the successful creation of a method of obtaining ammonia—and, from it, a host of nitrogen-based products, including fertilizer, explosives, and animal feedstocks—without resorting to the use of natural deposits. In the past, producers of nitrate fertilizers had to import costly sodium nitrate (caliche) from Chile. Haber's process now made available cheap nitrogen-based fertilizer, which averted food shortages and even mass starvation throughout parts of the world. It was a profound service to humanity. (At least it was at the time. In the long term, nitrogenous fertilizer runoff proved to be a major source of ocean pollution, and environmental scientists are now calling for alternative fertilizer strategies.)

Yet, in addition to being a scientist and humanitarian, Fritz Haber was a patriot. And it was his understanding of patriotic duty that led him to obscene acts of folly.

Shortly after Germany entered World War I in the summer of 1914, Haber volunteered his services as a military scientist. He was given the rank of sergeant-major in the artillery, but was soon promoted to captain by Kaiser Wilhelm II himself. The Haber process had already enabled Germany to synthesize not just nitrogen-based fertilizer, but also all the nitrogen-based explosives it needed, thereby ensuring the nation a steady supply of gunpowder and high explosives. With the war under way, Haber was given the task of developing poison gases and supervising their manufacture as well as their battlefield use.

Contrary to enduring popular belief fostered by Allied propaganda, Germany was not the first of the combatant nations to use poison gas in battle. The French employed it in the very first month of the war, August 1914, lobbing at the Germans 26-mm grenades filled with tear gas. German forces retaliated in October 1914 with artillery shells packed with an irritating agent. But it was Germany's Haber who first recognized the tactical value of deploying large amounts of gas—and not just tear gas or other irritants, but deadly poisons.

Trench warfare on the Western Front was stalemated. As a "morale weapon"—a weapon of mass terror—gas, Haber understood, could not in itself win the war, but it could be used to drive the enemy out of the trenches, disrupting their positions sufficiently to open a breach that would break the stalemate. Haber advised using the gas in overwhelming quantity as the prelude to a major offensive. The generals listened, but they did not take the advice of a mere captain, and gas was not used in sufficient quantity to achieve the major breakthrough Haber had envisioned. Instead, initial, tentative gas attacks succeeded only in triggering Allied retaliation, which touched off an arms race between the Germans and the Allies, each side striving to produce the deadliest agent. Instead of ending the war in quick German victory, poison gas added yet another horrific dimension to a protracted struggle.

Chlorine was the earliest World War I gas weapon Haber (and others) developed. It caused temporary blindness, burning of the lungs and throat, uncontrollable coughing, asphyxiation, and death. Haber went on to develop phosgene during the second year of the war. It was an especially cruel weapon because, unlike the pungent chlorine, phosgene smelled of new-mown hay, tempting many a homesick farm

> "A scientist belongs to his country in times of war and to all mankind in times of peace."
>
> —Fritz Haber

boy–turned–soldier to sniff the air, then breathe deeply—only to find himself drowning in his own dissolving tissues as the phosgene turned to hydrochloric acid in the lungs. Haber's next compound, chlorpicrin, was designed expressly to defeat gas masks. Chlorpicrin penetrated many of the neutralizing agents used in masks, including charcoal filters. Although it was not especially deadly in itself, chlorpicrin induced nausea and vomiting, which prompted victims to tear off their masks, thereby exposing them to the more lethal gases that were fired simultaneously with the substance.

By the end of 1916, improvements in gas masks had made them generally effective even against chlorpicrin, and Haber therefore introduced a new substance, dichlorodiethyl sulfide, better known as mustard gas. In low concentrations, it was barely noticeable except as an agreeable scent of lilacs in bloom, but at higher concentrations, it caused first- and second-degree burns on whatever organ it contacted: skin, eyes, or the membranes of throat, nose, or lungs. In relatively small doses, it caused disability. Soldiers who took in a substantial amount of mustard gas suffered an agonizing death as they strangled on their own disintegrating tissues. Mustard gas was not really a gas at all, but a finely atomized liquid, which settled onto everything, collecting and concentrating in dugouts, trenches, and shell holes. Hours, even days after a mustard gas attack, the battlefield remained contaminated, so that a soldier seeking refuge from machine gun fire in a shell crater might find himself wallowing in a pool of burning liquid.

Haber understood that mustard gas was a powerful, even repellent weapon, and he counseled the generals to use it—on a massive scale— only if they believed the war could be won within no more than a year. Beyond this span, he warned, the Allies would surely retaliate with a new and equally terrible chemical weapon of their own. Once again, the generals failed to heed Haber. They used the gas, but the war dragged on, and, as the chemist had predicted, the Allies answered with new and more effective gas

> "If you want to win the war, then please, wage chemical warfare with conviction."
>
> —Fritz Haber

weapons of their own. Worse, by this time, the Allies possessed superior manufacturing capacity and better methods of turning out gas weapons and were soon using more gas than the Germans.

It never occurred to Haber to call a halt to the ever-escalating race to produce increasingly lethal poison gases. He was frequently at the front, supervising the use of the weapon, observing its terrible effects with an eye toward making them even more terrible. Early in the war, Haber's wife, the beautiful Clara Immerwahr, a chemist herself, had pleaded with her husband to break off his war work. As a loyal German, he told her, he could not. At the end of April 1915, he returned to Berlin from Flanders, where he had directed on April 22 the war's first massive poison gas attack. On May 2, Clara took her husband's service pistol in hand, walked out into the garden of the couple's home, pressed the muzzle of the gun into her chest, over her heart, and pulled the trigger. She died in the arms of her son, who had come rushing out when he heard the weapon's report.

The very next day, Fritz Haber, German patriot, left for the Russian front, to direct the first gas attack there. He continued to develop chemical weapons and supervise their use through the end of the war.

By all accounts, Germany's surrender in 1918 shattered Haber as the suicide of his wife had apparently failed to. He was left, according to a friend, "about 75 percent dead." Yet he remained morally unchastened, his patriotism undimmed. He embarked on an effort to create a chemical process to separate gold from seawater, believing that this might rescue his country from the economic collapse to which the ruinous reparations called for in the Treaty of Versailles. Haber raised sufficient funds to build an experimental ship, but the process he developed obtained amounts of gold that were far too small to be cost effective, and, in 1928, Haber abandoned the gold-from-seawater project. He turned next to representing Germany as a kind of goodwill ambassador to Argentina, the United States, and Japan. Presumably his mission was to promote peace—"We believe that in the long run every nation will best serve other nations as well as itself by learning to understand their thoughts and feelings," he said—yet the most enduring creation of his goodwill efforts, the German-Japan Institute, helped pave the way for the creation of the Rome-Berlin-Tokyo "axis," the unholy alliance at the heart of World War II.

That was a war Fritz Haber would not live to see. The chemist considered himself first and foremost a German, but to Adolf Hitler and his Nazis, he was a Jew, and when Hitler became Germany's chancellor in 1932, he announced his plan to dismiss all Jews working at the Kaiser Wilhelm Institute, the nation's premier scientific research laboratory. Haber's war record would not save him. Though he had even converted from Judaism in an effort to win acceptance from the new regime, he saw that his case was hopeless and preemptively resigned as director of the institute before he could be dismissed. He moved to Cambridge, England, briefly and pondered accepting a professional post in Rehovot, Palestine British Mandate (modern Israel), but, before he finalized his decision, he died of a heart attack on January 29, 1934, in a hotel in Basel, en route to a convalescent retreat in Switzerland. He was sixty-five.

After Haber's death, his second wife, Charlotte, settled in England with their two children. The son from the chemist's first marriage, Hermann Haber, whose arms had cradled the head of his dying mother, immigrated to the United States during World War II—and committed suicide there in 1946. Other Haber relatives also died in the new world war, victims of Zyklon B, a poison gas Haber had developed as a powerful pesticide, but which Hitler's SS used in the extermination camps of the Third Reich.

FRITZ HABER NEVER CLAIMED TO BE AN APOSTLE of "pure science." He believed, rather, that science must serve humanity and country. It was an intensely moral position. Yet Haber made a terrible mistake in assuming that humanity and country were essentially one and the same, as if the cause of one's government was, like the cause of humanity, naturally and always good. This confusion of values led him to create some of the most inhumane weapons the world has ever known.

Roberto Goizueta and the "New Coke" (1985)

THE DECISION TO REFORMULATE SUCCESS

BusinessWeek and other journals of commerce agree: Coca-Cola is the world's most recognizable brand. With 2006 revenues of $23 billion and a market value (as of March 17, 2006) of $101 billion, the company ranked eighty-ninth that year among the Fortune 500. Its eponymous flagship product is sold in more than two hundred countries, which means that you are more likely to see the resurrected Elvis or get hold of Bigfoot's real-life toenail than ever land in a place that doesn't have a Coke to sell you.

Remarkably enough this modern marketing phenomenon started out with an act of sheer folly, when Atlanta tycoon Asa Griggs Candler, having bought the Coca-Cola formula from its inventor, pharmacist John Stith Pemberton of Covington, Georgia, for $2,300 in 1887. Then having transformed it through astute merchandising into a nationally successful soda fountain drink, Candler sold the bottling rights to Benjamin Thomas and Joseph Whitehead for $1 in 1899.

Candler believed the chief market for the drink would always be the drugstore soda fountain. Of course, it truly flooded the world only after it had flowed out of the fountain and into bottles. Coca-Cola emerged as the realization of the alchemist's ancient dream, for most of the twentieth century turning ordinary water into gold. Over the many years of the product's success, the company devoted great effort to innovating sophisticated marketing operations, building ever-greater revenues as Coke penetrated more and more markets, but ever and always the product—whose formula was top secret—was left alone. You don't tamper with success.

But in 1984, company executives started to worry. For much of its career, Coca-Cola's closest competitor had been Pepsi-Cola. "Closest," however, was a relative term, since Pepsi's second-place showing was always comfortably distant. By 1984, however, it seemed to be catching up—fast. It became clear that Coca-Cola's market share was actually slipping, its lead over Pepsi reduced to a frightening 5 percent, maybe slightly less. Coca-Cola poured on the ad money, but Pepsi had taken a leaf from the playbook that had served auto rental company Avis so well. As Avis had played up its number-two position behind industry giant Hertz—"We're Number 2. We try harder."—so Pepsi launched its "Pepsi Challenge," challenging loyal consumers of the number one product to try number two. Not only did the challenge campaign stimulate sales of Pepsi, it seemed that, in blind taste tests, a majority of drinkers actually preferred Pepsi to Coke.

By this time, Roberto Goizueta had been Coca-Cola chairman for four years. When he took over the top spot in 1981, he told his company's employees that he intended to keep no sacred cows. Everything, he said, was up for change. It was an approach typical of the dynamic Goizueta. Born into a prosperous family in Havana, Cuba, and educated in the United States—he earned a degree in chemical engineering from Yale in 1948—Goizueta returned to his native land in 1953 to help run his family's sugar refining business, then went to work for the Coca-Cola bottler in Cuba, soon becoming chief technical director of five Cuban bottling plants. When Fidel Castro took over the country in 1959, nationalizing all private industry, Goizueta, vacationing in Miami, decided not to return. He defected to the United States, carrying with him total assets of $40 cash and a hundred shares of Coca-Cola stock.

The refugee found work with Coca-Cola in Miami, then became company chemist for the Caribbean region. In 1964, he was transferred to Coca-Cola's Atlanta headquarters and, at age thirty-five, was promoted to vice president of technical research and development—the youngest person ever to hold the position. Rising to the helm of legal and external affairs in 1975, he precipitously jumped to company president four years later after the resignation of J. Lucian Smith. He became chairman in March 1981 on the retirement of J. Paul Austin.

Most sacred among Coca-Cola's sacred cows was the commandment that no other product produced by the company would ever be called "Coca-Cola." True to his everything's-up-for-change policy, Goizueta oversaw the introduction in 1982 of Diet Coke. Unlike the company's existing one-calorie diet cola, called Tab, which was essentially Coca-Cola with saccharin and cyclamates (the latter was banned by the FDA in 1970), Diet Coke was completely reformulated so that it would taste good with its zero-calorie aspartame sweetener. Corporate traditionalists were fearful of committing the sacrilege of diluting the company's flagship brand name, but Goizueta was instantly vindicated as sales of Diet Coke quickly outstripped those of Tab, propelling the new beverage to the position of third most popular soft drink in America.

Yet the spike in company revenues concealed a hidden cost of Goizueta's innovation. To begin with, Diet Coke competed with regular Coke, encroaching on some of its sales as calorie-conscious consumers discovered they could consume their favorite soft drink guilt free. More insidiously, however, the sugarless Diet Coke actually tasted sweeter than regular Coca-Cola and therefore contributed to a shift in consumer preference for sweeter-tasting soft drinks, whether sugarless or sugared. Throughout their long history of competition, one of the defining differences between number-one Coca-Cola and number-two Pepsi-Cola was that Pepsi always tasted sweeter. The grand slam Goizueta hit with Diet Coke suddenly seemed to have batted in the other team's runner, increasing demand for the competitor's sweeter drink.

Goizueta pored over the data and concluded that Coca-Cola had actually started losing ground to Pepsi in the 1970s. He commissioned a top-secret initiative, dubbed "Project Kansas," directed by marketing vice president Sergio Zyman and Coca-Cola USA president Brian Dyson to formulate, test, and perfect a new, sweeter flavor for Coca-Cola. It was a radical step. Some in the company believed it necessary and overdue, while others condemned it as a lapse in confidence on a par with a loss of religious faith.

Zyman and Dyson's marketing team ventured into the field, testing an array of new sample tastes. On balance, the results seemed unambiguous. A new formula with high fructose corn syrup consistently beat not only regular Coke, but Pepsi as well. A substantial majority of test participants reported that they would buy the newly formulated drink if it were Coca-Cola—although they conceded that it would take "some getting used to." Yet there was also a nagging additional result. Ten to 12 percent of tasters reported feeling "angry" and "alienated"—those were the adjectives they used—at the mere thought of a reformulated Coca-Cola. How would they act on these feelings? They might well stop drinking Coke, period.

It was a disturbing finding, but it was nevertheless countered by the fact that anywhere from 88 to 90 percent of tasters felt positive about a new formula. Yet the significance of the minority went beyond their numbers. The angry 10 to 12 percent were so angry that their very presence in focus groups (in which discussions were held after each test) actually skewed results toward the negative. In other words, after the tests, the disaffected minority forced some of the more complacent majority to change from a positive to a negative response.

Even this notwithstanding, Goizueta and his senior management team were persuaded that they should proceed with the rollout of a new formula in 1985, the centennial year of the invention of Coca-Cola. Management briefly toyed with taking an intermediate position, adding the new flavor to the company's line as a new beverage, but they concluded that this would simply join Diet Coke as another competitor for original Coca-Cola, further eroding the flagship's market. Goizueta decided to play

> **"[It's] smoother, uh, uh, yet, uh, rounder yet, uh, bolder . . . it has a more harmonious flavor."**
>
> —Roberto Goizueta's response to a reporter's request that he describe the new taste of New Coke, April 23, 1985

all-or-nothing, and he deliberately highlighted the reformulation by labeling Coca-Cola as "New." For this reason, the product was universally known as "the New Coke."

On April 19, 1985, Coca-Cola executives alerted the media to expect "a major announcement" on April 23 concerning "a change in Coke." Pepsi management responded to this tipping of the hand by declaring a companywide holiday on the twenty-third and taking out a full-page *New York Times* ad declaring victory in the "cola wars." The ad and various other media efforts created a climate of skepticism prior to the April 23 launch of the New Coke. Pepsi even furnished reporters with questions to ask at the news conference Coca-Cola held at New York City's Lincoln Center. Armed with those questions, many of the reporters were openly if vaguely hostile, and Goizueta, apparently rattled, was uncharacteristically tentative in his responses to questions about just why and how the New Coke was an improvement over the original.

Despite the disappointing press conference, Coca-Cola stock rose and the American public took careful note of the change. Moreover, the initial consumer response was gratifying, as Coca-Cola sales rose 8 percent over the short term, and surveys indicated that most consumers liked the new, sweeter flavor. Before long, however, came a gathering backlash.

Directly reflecting the earlier prelaunch taste test results, a vocal minority emerged and began speaking up, not merely criticizing the New Coke, but actually ridiculing it. When ads for New Coke lit up the scoreboard at the Houston Astrodome, they were greeted by raucous boos from the crowd. In Atlanta, company switchboard operators fielded thousands of angry phone calls, and the company's public affairs department plowed through tens of thousands of irate letters. Calls also flooded the company hotline, 1-800-GET-COKE, coming in such volume and with such vehemence that Coca-Cola hired a psychiatrist to monitor them. He reported that many callers sounded genuinely grieved, as if they were talking about a death in the family. Indeed, there *was* grief within Goizueta's own family. The chairman's aged father publicly questioned his son's wisdom in changing the Coca-Cola formula. But perhaps the capping damnation came from the Goizueta family's archnemesis, Fidel Castro, who, although he was always anti-American, had remained pro-Coke. He loved the soft drink and now denounced the New Coke as but the latest evidence of capitalist decadence in the United States.

Back in the United States, the debut of New Coke triggered an activist movement in the form of the Seattle-based Old Cola Drinkers of America, which appealed to the company either to bring back the original formula or sell it to someone else. The organization even filed a class action lawsuit against the Coca-Cola Company, which was dismissed before it came to trial by a judge who commented on the side that he was a Pepsi drinker himself.

Contrary to popular mythology, the New Coke brought neither an instant decline in sales of Coke nor an instant increase in sales of Pepsi. Nevertheless, Coca-Cola executives began to see a bleak future as public skepticism, ridicule, and outright hostility showed no signs of letting up and even exhibited indications of intensifying. They recognized the remarkable fact that consumers did not dislike the taste of the New Coke; rather, they mourned—and were angered by—the killing of the "old" Coke. It was an act perceived as a yet another betrayal by Big Business.

In addition to facing consumer protest—including public demonstrations, boycotts, and the ceremonial emptying of New Coke bottles into the streets of some cities in the South—Coca-Cola faced a revolt among its bottlers, some of whom were engaged in ongoing litigation with the company. It did not take Roberto Goizueta long to recognize, acknowledge, and act to rectify his error. On July 10—just three months after the launch of New Coke—the company announced the return of the original formula. At least one television network, ABC, interrupted regular programming to broadcast the bulletin of the announcement, and one U.S. senator, David Pryor, Democrat of Arkansas, noted it on the floor of the Senate as "a meaningful moment in U.S. history."

The company continued to sell New Coke alongside what it now called "Coca-Cola Classic," and although Pepsi briefly stole the lead from Coca-Cola, by the end of 1985 Coke Classic was outselling New Coke as well as Pepsi. Since then, it has never relinquished its number one position, and in 2002, New Coke was discontinued entirely.

IT IS TEMPTING TO CONCLUDE THAT THE LESSON of the New Coke fiasco is—simply—to leave well enough alone. But that is not the lesson. Goizueta and his management team did not arbitrarily decide to fix what wasn't broke. They attempted to respond proactively and intelligently to a demonstrated change in the market for their company's flagship product. Their mistake, as Keough put it, was a failure to appreciate and understand that "all the time and money and skill poured into consumer research . . . could not measure or reveal the deep and abiding emotional attachment to original Coca-Cola felt by so many people."

The folly of the New Coke was in trying to reformulate success exclusively in terms of flavor chemistry and market analysis while allowing the emotional and spiritual meaning of the product to evaporate. Any item of merchandise has both features and benefits. Features are facts embodied in the product's specifications. Benefits are the feelings the product evokes in the consumer. In the end, the decision to part with hard-earned cash in exchange for a product is motivated more by a perception of benefits to be enjoyed than by a list of features, more by feelings than by molecules.

> **"Have you tried it?"**
> **"Yes."**
> **"Did you like it?"**
> **"Yes, but I'll be damned if I'll let Coca-Cola know that."**
>
> —Coke president and chief operating officer Donald Keough, reporting a conversation he overheard at his country club outside Atlanta

PART SIX

The Decision to Drift

James Buchanan and Secession (1860)

THE DECISION NOT TO DECIDE

Governing the American democracy has always relied on the faith that, somehow, the wisest, best, and brightest would arise from the people to gain election to the nation's highest offices. This has not always occurred, but there was reason to hope it would in the case of James Buchanan, fifteenth president of the United States.

Born in 1791—the last president born in the century of the founding fathers—James Buchanan was the son of Irish immigrants who had made good in Pennsylvania. Having grown prosperous, they sent their son to excellent schools, including Dickinson College, from which the young man went on to study law. After service in the War of 1812—in a regiment that saw no combat—Buchanan earned a reputation for legal brilliance in his Lancaster, Pennsylvania, law practice and amassed a considerable fortune. While practicing law, he served in the state legislature from 1814 to 1819, and courted the beautiful Ann Caroline Coleman, who, under pressure from her family (who disapproved of Buchanan) and believing her suitor was secretly seeing another woman, broke off the engagement. Just days afterward, she died, and her family, vaguely blaming him for her death, barred Buchanan from her funeral. The young lawyer swore that he would never marry, and he never did. To date, he remains the nation's only bachelor president.

After Coleman's death, Buchanan threw himself into work, gaining election to the U.S. House of Representatives in 1820 and serving in Congress from 1821 to 1831. He had run as a Federalist, but abandoned that moribund party to enter the orbit of Andrew Jackson and become one of the architects of the emerging Democratic Party. In 1832, Jackson named Buchanan envoy to Russia, a post in which he triumphed by negotiating a much-desired but hitherto elusive trade treaty. In large part on the strength of his distinguished diplomatic career, he won a U.S. Senate seat, serving from 1834 to 1845.

Throughout his career as a legislator, Buchanan always thought and acted as a lawyer. In his own time, this was seen as a strength. In the eye of history, it has emerged as his cardinal weakness. During his long Senate tenure, slavery was in the forefront of American politics. Personally and morally, Buchanan abhorred the institution, yet as a lawyer he believed that the Constitution upheld the right of slave ownership. This led him to regard abolitionists as meddlers in the law and therefore as a greater threat to the Union than slavery. In lawyerlike fashion, holding the Constitution before all else as a legal compact—essentially a contract— he held that all Americans were legally obligated to protect slavery, personal morality notwithstanding.

> "I believe [slavery] to be a great political and a great moral evil. I thank God, my lot has been cast in a State where it does not exist. But, while I entertain these opinions, I know it is an evil at present without a remedy . . . one of those moral evils, from which it is impossible for us to escape, without the introduction of evils infinitely greater."
>
> —James Buchanan, 1826

Buchanan's ambition reached beyond the Senate, and in 1844 he hoped to gain the Democratic nomination for the presidency. It went instead to James K. Polk, who subsequently named Buchanan his secretary of state. The 1848 election ushered Whig candidate and Mexican War hero Zachary Taylor into the White House, and Buchanan, out of office, returned to his Pennsylvania home to lay out a strategy for capturing the 1852 Democratic nomination. That year, however, he found himself locked in a struggle with Senator Stephen A. Douglas of Illinois and both ended up losing the nomination to a compromise candidate, nonentity Franklin Pierce.

Pierce appointed Buchanan minister to England, which meant that Buchanan was effectively out of domestic politics during the turbulent and tortured period that saw the bitter violence created by the controversial Kansas-Nebraska Act of 1854. In effect, Buchanan's overseas appointment allowed him to remain innocent of all action during the early prelude to civil war.

But not entirely innocent.

From abroad, warily courting Southern favor, Buchanan tried to cobble together a scheme to acquire Cuba by purchase or conquest for the purpose of expanding U.S. plantation agriculture and, therefore, expanding slavery as well. The plan outraged abolitionists, but did win Buchanan solid support among Southerners, putting him in position in 1856 to make another run for the presidential nomination.

Fellow Democrats Pierce and Douglas were both tainted by their identification with the unpopular Kansas-Nebraska Act and therefore had no support in the North. Uncontaminated, Buchanan had a modicum of Northern support as well as solid backing in the South. Moreover, he had a distinguished background as a brilliant lawyer and as a successful diplomat-statesman. He was a professional politician, suave, conservative, and a trifle boring—all of which made him irresistibly attractive in an era of intense social idealists and angry firebrands. He was, in fact, a kind of political and moral neuter—"doughface," was the term current in his day—a Northerner who was nevertheless sympathetic and accepting to the South.

Buchanan easily secured the Democratic nomination, earning the right to face the nominee of the newly formed Republican Party, the western explorer known as the "Pathfinder," California Senator John C. Frémont. Frémont was as dashing as Buchanan was dull, and therein lay his liability. For, politically, he had virtually no record. Many saw him as all flair and no substance, except for his strong antislavery stance. Millard Fillmore, the lackluster figure who had served out the term of the short-lived Zachary Taylor from 1850 to 1853, ran on the so-called Know-Nothing ticket, a third party that stood for little but stood against immigrants and Catholics.

Events swirled about the campaign as the nation hurtled toward civil war. In truth, none of the candidates demonstrated that they were equal to the gathering crisis, and all three remained more or less aloof from the fray, letting underlings and associates do the campaigning for them. All that was clear to voters was that Frémont believed it incumbent on the federal government to bar slavery from all territories of the United States, whereas Buchanan held that each state and territory should decide for itself the fate of slavery within its own borders. As for the Know-Nothings, they avoided the major national issues altogether and instead spread a rumor that Frémont was Catholic. That, along with popular fears of his "black Republicanism"—destined to bring universal abolition and eleva-tion of "Negroes" to equality with whites—gave Buchanan a narrow victory, a plurality rather than a clear majority in the three-way race.

Be careful what you wish for, goes the old saying. *You just may get it.* Buchanan had long hungered after the presidency, but, just before he began his campaign in 1856, he wrote: "I had hoped for the nomination in 1844, again in 1848, and even in 1852, but now I would hesitate to take it. Before many years the abolitionists will bring war upon this land. It may come during the next presidential term."

The statement reveals all that was wrong with James Buchanan as a leader in time of crisis. To begin with, he persisted in blaming national disunity on the opponents of slavery rather than on slavery itself. More important, he spoke of the war that might come "during the next presiden-tial term" and not of his intention, much less his plans, to prevent it. It was as if he saw his role as president to be nothing more than just another passive victim of the coming conflict. It was characteristic of him that he served ice cream—some twelve hundred gallons of it—at his inauguration, while barely touching on the slavery issue in his inaugural address, except to point out that he and the federal government had little to do with it, because slavery was a matter for the states and territories to decide for themselves.

There was one passage in the speech that was hardly noticed at first but, within days, assumed great significance. The Supreme Court, at the time deliberating the case of Dred Scott—a slave suing for his freedom on the basis of having lived in free states and territories—covertly informed the president-elect that it was about to decide against Scott and therefore in favor of the Southern position on slavery. Accordingly, without actually revealing the decision, Buchanan inserted in his address a reference to its coming and asked "all good citizens" to obey the ruling—whatever it might be.

Why did the Court tip its hand to Buchanan? Because he had already demonstrated his interest—and his sympathies—in the decision by prevailing upon one of the Northern justices to side with Chief Justice Taney and the court's Southerners against Scott's plea.

The *Dred Scott* decision came just two days after Buchanan assumed office. As a lawyer, Buchanan believed—or perhaps he hoped—that the decision, which effectively upheld the federal government's legal obligation to protect slavery, would mean an end to abolition because active abolition would be rendered, in effect, against the law. This, he believed—or hoped—would avert war, at least during the span of his administration.

Just two days into his presidency, however, James Buchanan had a rude awakening. No sooner did Chief Justice Taney hand down his decision than abolitionists, far from being cowed, rose up in anger and redoubled righteousness. If anything, the *Dred Scott* decision galvanized the abolition movement, prompting these activists to declare themselves on the side of God's law—and if the laws of the United States as presently constituted were not in harmony with the laws of God, the burden of wrong was on the people of the United States and their clear moral duty was to change the nation's laws. If that meant fighting a war to force such change, so be it. For their part, the proslavery Southerners were equally vehement in embracing what they took as their vindication by the highest court in the land.

By legally certifying protection of slavery under the Constitution, the *Dred Scott* decision placed the slavery issue beyond compromise. Either the Constitution would stand as it was and, with it, slavery. Or the Constitution would have to be amended to outlaw slavery and slavery would fall. There were many in the North who would not permit the former, and there were many in the South who would not allow the latter. The *Dred Scott* decision, therefore, made civil war all but inevitable.

The new president did what he thought was most expedient to evade inevitability, appointing moderates—"doughfaces," like himself—to his cabinet and to other posts. But it was to no avail. Thanks to the Kansas-Nebraska Act, enacted three years before Buchanan took office, Kansas was the scene of a bloody guerrilla war. The law left to Kansans themselves the decision to seek admission to the Union as a slave or a free state. The problem was that the population of Kansas was divided between vehement pro-slavery people and equally vehement "free-soilers." In 1855, "border ruffians" crossed into Kansas from Missouri to vote up a pro-slavery territorial government, then returned to Missouri. Free-soilers protested that the resulting government was illegitimate, having been created by Missourians, and they formed their own free-soil government. Buchanan intervened by voicing his support for the pro-slavery Lecompton Constitution, even though it was supported by a clear minority of legitimate Kansas residents. The territorial governor Buchanan himself had appointed urged the president to reject the Lecompton document but, eager to retain the support of pro-slavery Democrats, Buchanan sent a message to Congress calling for acceptance of Kansas as a slave state.

It was, Buchanan believed, the easy way out, the way that would avoid all-out war. But Senator Stephen Douglas challenged the presidential endorsement and forced a compromise, which sent the Lecompton Constitution back to Kansas for another vote. In this revote, Kansans overwhelmingly rejected slavery, thereby paving the way for the admission of Kansas as a free state.

For Buchanan, it was the worst possible outcome. The admission of Kansas as a free state outraged the South, pushing it toward war, and it simultaneously shattered the integrity of the president's administration.

On the one hand, Buchanan looked like a meddler, interfering in the will of the people; on the other, he simply appeared inept and spineless. His popularity, not great to begin with, plummeted, as evidenced in midterm elections that gave Republicans control of the U.S. House of Representatives.

No sooner had the Kansas crisis come upon Buchanan and the nation than John Brown, most militant among abolitionists, raided and seized the federal arsenal at Harpers Ferry, Virginia (present West Virginia) on October 16, 1859, as the opening battle in what he envisioned as a slave rebellion that would sweep the entire South. Buchanan authorized armed suppression of the seizure, and on October 18, Colonel Robert E. Lee led a company of U.S. Marines (the nearest force available) in retaking the arsenal. Brown was tried by the state of Virginia and convicted of treason and inciting a servile rebellion. His execution on December 2, 1859, elevated him to martyrdom in the eyes of many abolitionists, who saw that slavery would have to be defeated by whatever means were necessary. Southerners understood as well. The North, they were now convinced, would stop at nothing, war included.

Even with the nation in the last extremity of moral and political crisis, Buchanan could not find within himself the capacity to lead. In his last State of the Union address on December 3, 1860, he claimed that it would be "easy . . . for the American people to settle the slavery question forever and to restore peace and harmony to this distracted country. . . . All that is necessary, . . . and all for which the slave States have ever contended, is to be let alone and permitted to manage their domestic institutions in their own way. As sovereign States, they, and they alone, are responsible before God and the world for slavery existing among them. For this the people of the North are not more responsible and have no more right to interfere than with similar institutions in Russia or in Brazil."

Today, this statement seems outrageous, a negation of nationhood. Yet, in 1860, many, Democrats and Republicans alike, agreed with it. What they could not agree on was the fate of the territories, which were under federal jurisdiction. Referring to the *Dred Scott* decision, Southerners claimed the right to take their slaves into the territories, whereas Republicans denied that they had such a right. The president remained silent on the issue.

By 1860, James Buchanan was intent only on running out the clock of his presidency in the hope that civil war would not erupt before he left office. He had pledged in his inaugural address to serve a single term only. Now, as that term approached its end, not a single voice was raised to ask that he reconsider. Absenting himself from candidacy, his party split, the Northern Democrats nominating Stephen Douglas, the Southern wing nominating John C. Breckinridge, Buchanan's Kentuckian vice president. The split paved the way for Republican Abraham Lincoln's plurality victory, which prompted South Carolina to secede from the Union on December 20, 1860. Within the next six weeks, a half dozen more Southern states followed suit.

> **"The fact is that our Union rests upon public opinion and can never be cemented by the blood of its citizens shed in civil war. If it cannot live in the affections of the people, it must one day perish. Congress possesses many means of preserving it by conciliation, but the sword was not placed in their hand to preserve it by force."**
>
> —James Buchanan, final State of the Union address, December 3, 1860

War had not begun on his watch, but the United States was surely dissolving, and James Buchanan did nothing. His inaction was sufficiently eloquent to embolden the seceded states to style themselves the Confederate States of America. At this, all the Southerners in the Buchanan cabinet resigned, as did Secretary of State Lewis Cass, a former Michigan Territory governor and military man intent on demonstrating his disgust with the president's inertia.

Although Buchanan did refuse to give up Fort Sumter in South Carolina's Charleston Harbor—a stand that would occasion the first shots of the war, though not until Lincoln assumed office—he persisted in claiming inability, both legal and practical, to do anything to prevent secession. After he left the White House, Buchanan would tell anyone who would listen that his policy of forbearance had staved off civil war. Doubtless this was the case, but his failure to act had also given the Confederacy ample time to arm itself and to create a provisional government. While an enemy nation brought itself to birth on the border of the Union, the president of the United States did nothing.

"THE IMPORTANT FACT TO REMEMBER," Harry S. Truman wrote in the first volume of his *Memoirs*, published in 1955, two years after he left the White House, "is that the President is the only person in the executive branch who has final authority, and if he does not exercise it, we may be in trouble. If he exercises his authority wisely, that is good for the country. If he does not exercise it wisely, that is too bad, but it is better than not exercising it at all." Elsewhere, in a piece that was not published until after his death in 1972, Truman observed: "Presidents have to make decisions if they're going to get anywhere, and those presidents who couldn't make decisions are the ones who caused all the trouble."

James Buchanan made the unspoken assumption that refraining from decisive action would prevent others from taking adverse action. Truman would have seen this for what it was: a most destructive folly. Bad decisions surely create problems, but the far worse failure of leadership is making no decision, right or wrong, good or bad. The absence of decision is the absence of direction, which is by definition disaster.

If James Buchanan's failure to act enabled the disintegration of the nation, his conduct did succeed in bringing together American historians, who have been united in their judgment that he was the worst of all America's presidents, a consensus challenged only after some 140 years by the two terms of George W. Bush.

George Gordon Meade and Ulysses S. Grant at the Battle of the Crater (1864)

THE DECISION TO AVOID RISK

The American Civil War was the violent culmination of a struggle over slavery, an issue that the founding of the United States in the late eighteenth century had left unresolved. Slavery and Union were momentous causes, and yet the people of the North and the South had embarked on civil war if not casually, at least with a sense that the fighting would be short and sharp. Northerners believed the "rebels" would be quickly and easily whipped, whereas Southerners believed that their rebellion against the North would have the same effect as the original thirteen colonies' rebellion against England: the larger, richer, and more populous "nation" would inevitably lose its will to fight and therefore let the smaller, poorer, less populous but more determined "nation" win its independence. Both sides, of course, were wrong, and they were stunned by the cost of a war neither was willing to let go of.

Powerful as it was, the North could not seem to gain traction against the South. President Abraham Lincoln went through one commanding general after another in search of a military leader with both the skill and sheer grit to push the Union's campaign to victory. Three years passed and nearly a million men had been killed or wounded on both sides before the U.S. president found Ulysses S. Grant, an adept tactician who was also willing to accept and exploit the terrible calculus of the struggle at hand: the ineluctable fact that the North had more men and money than the South and could therefore afford to spend more of both. Even in victory, the resources of the Confederacy, in cash as well as manpower, steadily wasted away and could not be replenished. Even in defeat, the Union could find still more money and still more men.

In the spring of 1864, Grant began his grand Overland Campaign targeting the Confederate capital of Richmond, Virginia. The campaign was a purgatory of blood. The Battle of the Wilderness (May 5–7, 1864) cost Grant 17,666 killed or wounded out of 101,895 men engaged. The Battle of Spotsylvania Court House, which came next (May 7–20), produced nearly 11,000 Union casualties. It was later followed by Cold Harbor (May 31–June 12), with the loss of another 12,000 men. None of these battles could be counted as Union victories, yet with each battle he lost, Grant retreated not an inch, but instead sidestepped his adversary, General Robert E. Lee, and continued to advance southward, just as if he had won. For his part, Lee lost ground and lost men with each tactical victory he achieved.

Having pushed closer and closer to the Confederate capital, Grant suddenly turned toward a different objective. He had not been spending his soldiers' blood in a war

> **"I propose to fight it out on this line if it takes all summer."**
>
> —Ulysses S. Grant, at Spotsylvania, Virginia, May 11, 1864

of attrition alone, trading Lee man for man. For the past terrible month and more, he had also fought a war of maneuver, executing one turning movement after another against Lee's right flank, forcing Lee to stretch his lines thinner and thinner, ultimately deceiving him into concentrating around Grant's obvious objective, Richmond. The Union commander even feinted toward that city before suddenly crossing the James River and marching toward Petersburg instead.

Grant's greatness as a strategist lay partly in his refusal to harbor illusions of glorious conquest. The long, tragic line of failed Union commanders who preceded him had all been bent on capturing this or that territory and taking one city or another, but Grant understood that winning the war was not a matter of capturing any place—not even Richmond—but killing the enemy army. Kill that army, and the war would be over and the places won. Although the politicians of the North pressed him to take Richmond, Grant saw that Petersburg was the more important prize at this point. Big for a Southern city of the time, it had a population of some eighteen thousand and lay just twenty-two miles south of

Richmond. It was a city of factories and warehouses located on the Appomattox River and at the junction of the major southeastern rail lines and roads. Petersburg was critical to the supply of Richmond, and was even more critical to the supply of Lee's Army of Northern Virginia, the principal force of the Confederacy. Grant knew that if he took Petersburg, Richmond would weaken and fall, and, far more important, Lee's army would starve for want of food as well as bullets. To capture Petersburg was to kill the Army of Northern Virginia.

For most of the war, Petersburg was a very formidable objective. Confederate engineers had used soldiers and slaves to dig elaborate trench fortifications to defend it. Given the manpower, Lee could have held off an assault indefinitely, inflicting horrific casualties on any attacker. But, in the spring of 1864, Lee's army was dissolving and, even worse, he had been duped by Grant's long, bloody, turning advance and had therefore deployed most of his meager resources to cover Richmond. Petersburg was more vulnerable now than it had ever been.

The principal constituent of Grant's forces in Virginia was the Army of the Potomac, which, as it arrived at the outskirts of Petersburg on June 15, 1864, was a battered and depleted force, having lost during the Overland Campaign 50,000 of its number killed or wounded: 41 percent of its original strength. Robert E. Lee's Army of Northern Virginia had lost fewer men during this period—32,000 killed or wounded—but because that army was much smaller, its losses represented 46 percent of its original strength, virtually none of which could be replenished. Between April 1861 and April 1865, the span of the Civil War, roughly 1.15 million Union and Confederate soldiers were killed or wounded in seventy-six major battles. As of June 1864, nine of those major battles had yet to be fought, and the more than 150,000 men who would be killed or wounded in them were still living and whole.

Take Petersburg, and Richmond would fall. Take Petersburg, and the Army of Northern Virginia would starve. With the Confederate capital captured and the Confederacy's principal army neutralized or killed, the Civil War would be over and at least some portion of 150,000 men would be saved.

Of course, General Grant could have no idea of just how many lives a victory at Petersburg would save, but he knew that victory would shorten the war. Presumably Major General George Gordon Meade knew this as well.

Whereas Ulysses S. Grant was general in chief of the Union armies, Meade was commanding general of the Army of the Potomac. On paper that was clear enough, but in practice Meade was in a most uncomfortable and ambiguous position. Grant was general in chief of the Union armies, but since the principal Union army in this theater *was* the Army of the Potomac, Meade was never quite certain just how much command authority he really had. This ambiguity of position doubtless magnified Meade's gravest flaw as a commander. Although a competent and skilled West Point man, Meade was conventional and cautious. In the summer of 1863, he had led the Army of the Potomac to what was arguably the most important victory of the Civil War: Gettysburg. Yet his failure to pursue Lee's defeated Army of Northern Virginia back into the Confederacy after that battle was one of the war's costliest missed opportunities. Immediately after Gettysburg, Meade had believed his army was just too tired to press the advantage it had won. Now in June 1864, it was even more exhausted—some would say bled nearly white.

As Grant saw the situation, although the Army of the Potomac was depleted and tired, Petersburg was so vulnerable now that it was ripe for the plucking, and he could therefore allow the Army of the James, a much smaller force than the Army of the Potomac, to do most of the heavy lifting necessary to take the town. That army's command had just been given to Benjamin Franklin Butler, a portly, crude exemplar of what people in the Civil War era called a "political general," a man of few or no military qualifications who is nevertheless given high command because of his political pull. Eager to give the Army of the Potomac a rest, it was to this poor excuse for a general and his Army of the James that Grant issued orders to take Petersburg. He would soon regret the decision.

Butler planted his small army at Bermuda Hundred, between Richmond and Petersburg at the confluence of the Appomattox and James

Rivers. To him, this seemed like an ideal place from which to attack Petersburg from both the north and the east; however, it also put his back against the two rivers, which meant that he had left his army with no room to maneuver, rendering it vulnerable to entrapment. Because he dithered instead of making a coordinated simultaneous thrust against Petersburg from both directions available to him, Confederate general P. G. T. Beauregard was able to send no more than a few thousand soldiers to pinch off the space between the two rivers, thereby bagging most of Butler's small army in a neat little sack. The Union commander had not been defeated in battle, but he was effectively neutralized nonetheless.

Seeing that Butler had gotten himself in a hopeless situation, Grant decided to order the Army of the Potomac to cross the James. He would take Petersburg himself. He "borrowed" from Butler the one corps of his army that had not been trapped. This unit, XVIII Corps, was commanded by William "Baldy" Smith, who, in contrast to Butler, was a well-trained West Pointer. Years before the war, however, he had contracted malaria while serving in Florida and never fully recovered, struggling continually with bouts of depression and fatigue.

By June 15, 1864, when he and XVIII Corps were called on to attack Petersburg, Baldy Smith was frankly sick and dog tired. A tired commander is typically a timid commander, and although Smith's assault on Petersburg began promisingly enough, its energy flagged in apparent reflection of the commander's. Like Butler, Smith dithered and delayed, allowing Robert E. Lee all the time he needed to transfer his men from Richmond to Petersburg. The Union momentum was lost and could not be regained. Several more attacks were mounted, but were all repulsed at the now reinforced fortifications around Petersburg. All of the Army of the Potomac's generals were exhausted, as were the men they commanded. Grant finally sent a message to General Meade: "Now we will rest the men, and use the spade for their protection until a new vein can be struck." Instead of attacking, the Army of the Potomac would dig trenches of its own and settle in for siege.

No Civil War soldier—or commander—relished siege duty, which typically brought an agony of boredom punctuated by the short, sharp terror of snipers' bullets and artillery bombardment. The question on everyone's mind was, *Could anything be done to bring it all to a quicker end?*

One who actually answered this question was Lieutenant Colonel Henry Pleasants, who commanded a regiment in large part consisting of Pennsylvania coal miners. Before the war, Pleasants himself had been a coal mining engineer in Pennsylvania. By the time the regiment found itself at Petersburg only about a hundred of the miners who had originally joined it were still alive and fit for duty. They were rough men, Irish immigrants mostly, many of them Molly Maguires, veterans of bare-knuckle labor wars against the hired thugs of the mining companies. Three years of combat against the Confederates had only hardened them even more. Pleasants was better educated than his men, but just as tough. He by no means hated combat, but he could not endure siege warfare. Being on the move, marching, maneuvering, thrusting forward, even falling back were infinitely preferable to the prospect of hours and days and weeks of peering over a parapet, dodging snipers, enduring bombardment and boredom, passing the time, waiting for one side or the other to break, ever so slightly, so that movement could begin again.

On June 19, having participated the day before in a failed attack on the Petersburg entrenchments, Lieutenant Colonel Pleasants contemplated the fresh red clay of the newly dug trenches in his sector. He mounted the firing step of his own trench and peeked over the parapet. It occurred to him that the line he occupied was no more than 130 yards from the nearest Confederate position, a redoubt—or earthen fort—dubbed Elliott's Salient. Gazing now at this enemy strongpoint, Pleasants pictured to himself what would happen if the salient—which, he could see, was held by just a few men—could be overcome or destroyed completely.

A wide breach would be opened in the Confederate line, that's what would happen. If a Union force charged through that gap, it could flank, or even get entirely around, the enemy line. In short, kick open this door, and Petersburg lay beyond, exposed.

Flushed with insight, Pleasants turned from the trench wall and sprinted most of the quarter mile to the tent of his commanding officer, Brigadier General Robert Potter, commanding the Second Division, of which his own 48th Pennsylvania Regiment was a part. Catching his breath, he blurted out: "We could blow that damned fort out of existence if we could run a mine shaft under it."

As it turned out, Robert Potter was just the man best prepared to receive these words. Before the war, Potter had been a lawyer, and he knew nothing about mining, but earlier that very day, he had also gazed over the trench, pondering Elliott's Salient, and the thought had occurred to him: Dig a mine—the military term for *tunnel*—under the redoubt, plant explosives, detonate them, then charge through the gap blasted into the Confederate line. Now here was Henry Pleasants, an experienced mining engineer, giving words to his very own thoughts.

Potter fired off a memorandum to the commander of IX Corps—of which Second Division was a part—Ambrose Burnside. When Burnside failed to reply, Potter asked Pleasants to turn his idea into a detailed proposal. In response, Pleasants made a hazardous personal reconnaissance of the ground in front of the Union lines—the divisional staff officer who accompanied him on this mission took a sniper's bullet in the face during this foray—then talked it over with other engineers and some of his own miners. On June 24, he returned to Potter with a plan, which Potter in turn transmitted to Major General John G. Parke, Burnside's chief of staff, who in turn conveyed it to Burnside.

This time, the IX Corps commander instantly grasped the significance of what was being proposed. He summoned Potter and Pleasants to his tent and asked a few questions, mostly about ventilation. Had Burnside been a trained military engineer, like Robert E. Lee for instance, he would almost certainly have rejected the proposal out-of-hand over this very issue. In all history, no military tunnel had ever exceeded four hundred feet in length, because beyond this distance the air goes bad. Normal atmospheric pressure is not sufficient to sustain adequate oxygen levels, and the buildup of carbon dioxide quickly turns lethal. To construct a tunnel more than four hundred feet long was almost certain to create deadly conditions. Pleasants calculated that *his* tunnel would have to be just over five hundred feet, but, as a mining engineer, he knew of a method of ventilation that used a small furnace to draw fresh air into the shaft. He assured Burnside that he could make this work, even in a tunnel of more than five hundred feet.

That was all Burnside needed to hear. He, too, was desperate to find an alternative to a long siege. As IX Corps commander, he was subordinate to Army of the Potomac commander Meade. There had been a time, however, when their situations were reversed. Burnside had once commanded the Army of the Potomac, and Meade, a corps commander, took orders from him. But then Burnside led his army into slaughter at the Battle of Fredericksburg (December 11–15, 1862) and had been demoted to subordinate command as a result. If he could preside over a war-winning breakthrough here at Petersburg, he would be redeemed.

Burnside took the idea to Meade, who, without the slightest hint of enthusiasm, turned the matter over to Major James C. Duane, his chief engineer. As Meade well knew, Burnside and Duane had a history. Before he served under Meade, Duane had

"A few miner's picks, which I am informed could be made by any blacksmith from the ordinary ones; a few hand-barrows, easily constructed; one or two mathematical instruments, . . . and our ordinary intrenching tools, are all that are required. The men themselves . . . are quite desirous, seemingly, of trying it. If there is a prospect of our remaining here a few days longer I would like to undertake it. . . . I think, perhaps, we might do something, and in no event could we lose more men than we do every time we feel the enemy.

—From Robert Potter's memorandum of June 24, 1864, to Major General John G. Parke, Burnside's chief of staff been Burnside's engineer, and it was Duane's failure to make a timely delivery of pontoons that led to a delay the Army of the Potomac experienced in crossing the Rappahannock River—a delay that contributed to the disaster over which Burnside presided at Fredericksburg. Never one to point a finger, Burnside did not blame Duane for Fredericksburg—on the contrary, he always accepted sole responsibility for the defeat on that dark day—but this generosity of spirit failed to earn Duane's gratitude or loyalty. On the contrary, it seemed only to increase his contempt for Burnside, and he now turned a coldly disparaging eye on "Burnside's mine." As the author of a West Point manual on military tunneling, Duane pronounced the project impossible. It was an opinion he would stubbornly maintain even after the tunnel had actually been dug.

Meade had the gaunt, ascetic features of a Protestant preacher, and a chilliness that matched his demeanor. In his postwar memoirs, Grant wrote that Meade was "brave and conscientious," yet also cautious, dull, and quarrelsome, "of a temper that would get beyond his control . . . and make him speak to officers of high rank in the most offensive manner." To most of those who served under him, Meade seemed unimaginative, mean-spirited, and ready to pounce, whether the enemy wore a uniform of gray or of blue. To be sure, he regarded not a few subordinates with contempt, but of no officer was he more contemptuous of than Ambrose Burnside, to whom he himself had once been subordinate and over whom he now wielded command. Yet even in his contempt there was a vein of the old envy and resentment Meade had felt over Burnside's rapid elevation, earlier in the war, above him. In this regard, Meade's disdain easily matched Major Duane's low opinion of Burnside and his pack of ignorant Pennsylvania coal miners.

> "I don't know any thin old gentleman with a hooked nose and cold blue eye, who, when he is wrathy, exercises less of Christian charity than my well-beloved Chief."
>
> —Description of George Gordon Meade by one of his staff officers

Meade listened to his chief engineer, but after consulting with

General Grant, he decided to let the project proceed, not because he thought it would succeed, but because he believed the work would keep the men busy during the long siege. Besides, if it failed—and he fully believed it would fail—it would only serve to make Burnside look all the worse, as if that were even possible.

Having been given tepid approval, Burnside told Potter to proceed with the mine. The work was personally supervised by Henry Pleasants, whose men in the space of three weeks managed to move eighteen thousand cubic feet of earth without being discovered by the Confederates. They braved random musket fire, cave-in, and suffocation, and they even survived the utter indifference of Meade and his chief engineer, who denied them basic surveying equipment and even the most primitive of mining tools. The men had to scrounge the shoring timbers they desperately needed from scrap lumber hauled from as far as six miles away, and they cobbled together their only digging tools—improvised picks and shovels—from hickory sticks and cracker barrels. They worked by candlelight in a shaft four and a half feet high, four feet wide at the floor, and tapering to two feet at the ceiling. Above them was the deadly heat of a dry Virginia summer and the incessant pounding of enemy artillery.

Burnside's progress reports to Meade were met with little or no response. Nevertheless, Burnside himself took heart as he saw the steady advance of the tunnel. While the digging was under way, Burnside turned his attention to planning the assault. Once there was a breach in the Confederate defenses, troops would need to mount an immediate well-executed attack designed to take advantage of the enemy's surprise, demoralization, and confusion. Burnside chose two African-American brigades for special training. These troops would be the first to fight and would form the advance guard of the Union invasion of Petersburg.

He did not choose them out of any political or moral motive— although the issue of "colored troops" was a highly politicized one. From the beginning of the war, African-American leaders such as former slave and abolitionist activist Frederick Douglass, along with a cadre of white abolitionists, had struggled to persuade the Union army to accept black volunteers. Proponents were met with a strident chorus of racist objection. Nonetheless, black brigades were finally formed. They were, however, strictly segregated units: black troops led by white officers. (By war's end, 178,985 blacks would fill out the ranks of the Union Army, amounting to about 10 percent of total enlistment.)

All of the African-American soldiers were volunteers, and all of them knew that surrender would not be an option. If captured, death was certain. The Confederate congress, outraged by the deployment of "slave" soldiers against them, had ordered the South's armies to take no black prisoners. They were to be shot at once, together with any white officers indecent enough to lead them. Nevertheless, they hungered for combat. But, most of the time, they were assigned to labor details, doing the kind of grunt work behind the lines that many of them had done as slaves. So it was with the black brigades at Petersburg. They had served in the rear— and *this* was precisely why Burnside chose them as his shock troops.

Unlike the white troops, weary from more than a month of continuous combat, exhausted and battered to the point of having become gunshy—shell-shocked, as a later generation would term it—the African-American brigades were not only fresh but even thrilling for a fight. Thus, while the miners inched their way toward them under the Confederate lines, Burnside had his officers and noncommissioned officers train the black brigades in the intricately choreographed movements necessary for the assault. Burnside's plan was to mass the two brigades and move them forward as soon as the powder in the mine had been detonated. When (in Burnside's words) "the leading regiments of the two brigades" had passed "through the gap in the enemy's line" created by the explosion and were headed for the high ground behind Elliott's Salient known as Cemetery Hill, a portion of the attacking force would peel off on either side of the main thrust and assume positions perpendicular to the principal attack so as to sweep the defenders from the Confederate trenches on either side. These movements were essential because of the way Elliott's Salient was positioned. If all went well, it would be blown up, but the portions of the Confederate trench remaining intact would be angled toward the point of Union attack through the breach created by the blast. Because of this, the enemy would be able to concentrate its fire directly on the attackers—unless the peeling-off maneuver neutralized the defenders first.

Not only were the movements Burnside planned important to the attack, they were quite intricate, especially under combat conditions. Yet, intricate does not mean unfeasible. Burnside used the time required for the completion of the mine to thoroughly train and drill the two brigades.

On July 17, the tunnel had reached its final length of 510.8 feet. Sergeant Henry Reese, the noncom in charge of the digging crews, reported to Pleasants that the men were hearing "digging noises." Pleasants immediately descended into the shaft to investigate personally. He was concerned that the Confederates were digging a countermine, an enemy shaft sent out to intercept the attackers' tunnel. The countermine would be packed with explosives and detonated, causing the attackers' mine to collapse, burying everyone inside.

Once he was underground, Pleasants ordered his men to silence their picks. In the depths of the narrow tunnel illuminated only by flickering candlelight, he strained to hear. There it was: the muffled cadence of enemy implements. He continued to listen, then finally turned to his men, declaring the sounds to be nothing more than evidence of routine construction along the Confederate lines. He instructed his miners to dig side "galleries," narrow shafts branching in wide arcs to the right and left of the main tunnel and passing directly under Elliott's Salient. The explosives would be packed into them.

By 6 PM on July 23, the galleries were completed and the mine was ready to be loaded. Major Duane, still an opponent of the plan, shorted Pleasants on the amount of blasting powder allocated, issuing four tons instead of the six Pleasants had ordered. He also failed to ensure that Pleasants received the state-of-the-art waterproof "safety fuse" the mining engineer had specified. Instead, he furnished ordinary blasting fuse scraps in short, ten-foot lengths that had to be spliced together. These handicaps notwithstanding, the miners and their commander made do. While some set about the tedious work of splicing, others loaded the extremely explosive twenty-five-pound powder kegs into burlap sacks and hauled them, sack by sack, through the length of the mine.

On July 28, Pleasants reported to Potter and Burnside that the mine was "ready to be sprung" or detonated. Burnside could hardly contain his excitement as he reported the success to Meade on the night of July 29. The dour commander listened without emotion and without comment until Burnside told him that two brigades of the United States Colored Troops of General Edward Ferrero's Fourth Division had been selected and specially trained to lead the assault. Following the blast, Ferrero's troops would be the first to go in.

Meade objected.

Taken aback, Burnside stammered out his rationale for having selected the black units, how they, in contrast to his white troops, were fresh and eager, and how he had spent weeks training them. Meade listened and at length agreed to consult General Grant that afternoon. The next day, about 11 AM, Meade came to Burnside's headquarters and told him that General Grant agreed that the "colored division" must not be allowed to participate in the vanguard of the advance.

After the battle, Grant testified to a congressional committee that "General Burnside wanted to put his colored division in front, and I believe if he had done so it would have been a success. Still I agreed with General Meade in his objection to that plan. General Meade said that if we put the colored troops in front, (we had only that one division), and it should prove a failure, it would then be said, and very properly, that we were shoving those people ahead to get killed because we did not care anything about them. But that could not be said if we put white troops in front."

The "colored troops" wanted nothing more intensely than to make the attack. They had been trained to do it. They knew the risks, but they also clearly saw the moral force of black men fighting against those who would deny them their freedom and humanity. This, however, was precisely what

Grant and Meade, the two leading commanders in a war to restore union and end slavery, were somehow unable to see.

Burnside was stunned. After weeks of tunneling, during which a highly motivated assault force had been specially trained, Meade, just fifteen hours before the scheduled attack, had ordered him to hold back the carefully prepared black units. Meade ordered him to select instead two white brigades, raw, untrained, exhausted, and gun-shy, for the initial assault.

It was as if something simply broke inside the commander of IX Corps. Ambrose Burnside trudged back to his headquarters, wearily summoned all of his brigade commanders, and, instead of even trying to make a rational command decision, simply ordered his generals to draw straws. One of two short straws fell to James H. Ledlie, by universal consent (both among his contemporaries and in the opinion of later historians) the worst general in the Union army. He was a "political general" even less competent than Butler, a man Grant later described as "inefficient," by which he meant utterly unable to achieve anything. According to Grant, he was also possessed of a "disqualification less common among soldiers," by which he meant cowardice.

Thanks to Meade—and with Grant's consent—two entirely untrained and battle-weary brigades, one of which was headed by a cowardly incompetent, were ordered to make what should have been one of the most consequential attacks of the Civil War. Had it worked, Petersburg would have fallen and the war might well have ended within weeks, but tragically mishandled, the assault on the Petersburg line failed.

It started out very promisingly when the Pleasants mine was successfully "sprung"—detonated—at 4:44 on the morning of July 30. The unprepared white troops, waiting in the Northern trenches, were stunned to paralysis by the blast that tore through the enemy fortifications, sending artillery, horses, and men—or pieces of them—high into the air amid a thick cloud of red earthen dust. Seeing and hearing the blast, many of the Union troops cowered, seeking cover, or even pushing to the rear of their own lines—anything other than moving forward, charging to attack.

Officers used the flats of their sabers to herd them back to the front of the trenches. Pleasants personally wielded his saber so liberally, smacking the backs of so many unwilling bluecoats, that he badly blistered his hand. But even those troops who did not bolt were so stunned by what they saw and heard that no one moved forward for at least fifteen minutes. This was just the first of what would prove to be many tragic delays and missteps. Burnside, doubtless despairing over the last-minute substitution of raw units for trained ones, had failed to order his own parapets to be dismantled. As a result, his men had to first surmount the Union trenches before they could charge Confederate lines. Desperate troops thrust their bayonets between logs in the walls of the trenches, then clambered up those improvised stairs. Once over the top, they became entangled in an array of defensive obstacles that Burnside had neglected to remove.

As his men stumbled through smoke and dust toward the Confederate lines, General Ledlie, true to form, shrank back. Pleading a phantom wound, he retreated to the brigade surgeon's "bombproof"—his shelter—and cadged from the doctor a bottle of medicinal rum. During most of the battle, he hid in the comforting darkness of the dugout taking pulls from the bottle as his leaderless troops pressed on.

Many of those who witnessed the blast—the instantaneous creation of the "Crater" from which the battle drew its name—would later invoke the shade of Dante to describe the aftermath. It was a landscape wrenched inside out, littered with fragments of human remains and, even more horrible, with the buried bodies of still-living soldiers. Many Yanks, running toward their objective, stopped in their tracks at the sight of hands clawing the air just above the earth. Attackers paused to dig out their desperate enemies. Such yielding to the instinct of humanity added to the already fatal delay of the assault, which became hopelessly fragmented and piecemeal.

Because they had not been trained in how to exploit the breach created by the detonation of the mine, the first Union troops launched an attack that guaranteed self-destruction. Throwing themselves headlong into the blasted gap, they did not carefully skirt the crater or attempt to suppress defensive fire from the undamaged portions of the Confederate trenches, as the black troops had been trained to do. Instead, many streamed down into the crater, which initially provided cover from enemy fire, but which soon proved to be a deadly snare. They had transformed themselves into fish in the proverbial barrel, trapped in the bottom of the pit. Poised on the edges of the crater, the Confederate riflemen shot the Yankees as they struggled up the sides.

Roused from stunned lethargy, Burnside scrambled to reinforce his failing first wave. He sent (among others) the two African-American brigades that should have constituted the vanguard. By this time, however, the attack had been sapped of momentum. Advancing Union soldiers piled up against one another, unable to move through or around the crater. Those few who advanced were immediately beaten back. They sought cover in abandoned portions of the Confederate trenches, which soon became more crowded than the crater. As for the Confederates, they turned their particular wrath against the incoming blacks, firing at them point-blank, skewering them with bayonets, or clubbing them with musket stocks. Black soldiers who did manage to advance beyond the first line of Confederate trenches

Little did these men anticipate what they would see upon arriving at [the Crater] . . . [It was] an enormous hole in the ground . . . filled with dust, great blocks of clay, guns, broken carriages, projecting timbers, and men buried in various ways— some up to their necks, others to their waists, some with only their feet and legs protruding from the earth. One of these near me was pulled out . . . [he] said that he was asleep when the explosion took place, and only awoke to find himself wriggling up in the air; then a few seconds afterward he felt himself descending, and soon lost consciousness. The whole scene . . . struck every one dumb with astonishment.

—Major William H. Powell, one of General Ledlie's staff officers

were routed. In panic, they ran back into the masses of their white comrades hunkered down in the trenches. These became so tightly packed with simultaneously advancing and retreating Union troops that many soldiers were unable to move their arms—either to fire, surrender, or plead for mercy.

The danger of being crushed and suffocated became as great as the danger of being shot. All the while, withering musket fire poured on the jammed trenches and the crater. By nine o'clock in the morning, soldiers waded ankle-deep in blood. By ten o'clock, most of the surviving Union troops had left the trenches and collected in the teeming crater, only to be overtaken by advancing Confederate soldiers who now fired their muskets and lobbed mortar rounds directly into it. Huddled bluecoats frantically attempted to pack earth along the rim of the crater, but rebel artillery simply blasted through. Someone shouted: *"Put in the dead men!"* and soldiers began building a breastwork of corpses, rolling the bodies up the slope of the pit. It was reported that a fog—first a wispy mist, then a dense vapor—rose from the crater. This was the evaporating sweat and condensing respiration of so many bodies huddled so desperately together.

Every battle has a "tipping point," the hour or moment in which the contest is decided. At the crater, the tipping point came well before noon. Until then, there had been a possibility that the assault might succeed after all. Despite Meade's catastrophic eleventh-hour decision to send unprepared troops into battle—an act of folly based in part on unsoldierly scruples, envy, contempt, and absence of vision, and in part on a strangely twisted racism—the attack still might have succeeded. For all their blunders, Union forces still came within three hundred feet of the last knot of Confederate defenders. Had they breached this position, the way to Petersburg would have been cleared. But valiant defenders managed to reinforce the vulnerable spot and held it until reinforcements arrived for a fatal Confederate counterattack.

By early afternoon, as most of the demoralized attackers writhed in the crater, unable to climb out, the whites among them grew fearful of being captured in company with "colored troops." They began shooting and bayoneting their black compatriots. In the meantime, from the rim of the crater, the Confederates continued firing their muskets or picked up the bayonet-tipped weapons of the fallen and hurled them, harpoon-fashion, into the writhing mass of Union troops. They even gathered spent cannonballs and shell fragments to rain down on the helpless Federals.

The battle ended late in the afternoon in an anticlimax as muted as the opening blast had been apocalyptic. In the thick of hand-to-hand combat, a Confederate officer, face-to-face with a Union colonel, barked at him: "Why in the hell don't you fellows surrender?"

"Why the hell don't you let us?" the colonel replied.

And it was over.

———

As CIVIL WAR BATTLES GO, the Battle of the Crater was modest, with a total of some 5,600 killed, wounded, or captured on both sides. Of course, these figures are deceptive. The Union victory that Meade and Grant threw away, however, might have saved some 150,000 casualties.

The tragedy of the Battle of the Crater was the result of the top commanders' inability to appreciate the force of moral hope, even as they yielded to the perceived hazard of moral liability. By allowing the black troops to serve as the vanguard of the assault, Meade and Grant might have handed them an opportunity to win their freedom and, in the process, to win a battle that might have ended the war. In the process, all or some of these black men might have lost their lives, whether in success or failure, victory or defeat. But, fearful of public opinion, the white leaders were unwilling to allow black soldiers to post their lives as collateral against what could have been a military, moral, and spiritual triumph. It was this fatal lapse of faith, of hope, and of moral courage that made the Battle of the Crater what Ulysses S. Grant himself called it, "the saddest affair I have witnessed in the war."

Rasputin and the Russian Royals (1916)

THE DECISION TO BELIEVE IN MIRACLES

At the start of the twentieth century, Russia was an empire straddling Europe and Asia and even touching on the Middle East. Of its estimated 146 million people, the great majority were unspeakably poor, doomed to lives of great privation relieved only by their brief duration. At the summit of this vast misery were Nicholas II and his wife, Alexandra, czar and czarina—absolute emperor and empress—of "all the Russias." The people were taught to call them "papa" and "mama," but, in reality, they knew little of the Russian people and had contact with only a small circle of aristocrats and court officials.

Nicholas and Alexandra were certainly the richest couple in Europe and quite probably the entire world. Rulers by birth, wealthy beyond measure, they might as well have occupied a different planet from the people they ruled. They did not, in fact, seem of their world or even of their century. In one of the splendid uniforms he so loved to wear and in one of her magnificently bejeweled gowns, the czar and czarina not only looked every inch the regal pair, they seemed to have emerged from a fairytale realm that had nothing whatever to do with early twentieth-century Russia. For this very reason, they can almost be forgiven for having regarded as a miracle of God their introduction to one Grigory Yefimovich Novykh, a peasant from Siberia, surely the most remote region of their empire. For under no ordinary earthly circumstances imaginable could the orbit of the royal couple have otherwise intersected with that of a man born so far away into filth and poverty, barely literate and of degenerate reputation.

Compounded of legend and rumor with few indisputable facts, Novykh's biography must be called a story rather than a history. He was born in 1872—perhaps—near Tyumen, Siberia, and did go to school for a time, but did not learn to read and write until late in life. Almost nothing is known about his childhood, except that family members and other locals believed he had certain supernatural powers, especially an uncanny faculty for identifying thieves and swindlers. Very early in life, he seems to have become notorious for his sexual prowess, prodigal sexual exploits, intractable perversion, and open licentiousness. The descriptions of his behavior vary, but none of them are wholesome.

Traditionally it is believed that his outrageous behavior earned him the surname by which he became known to the world, *Rasputin*, usually translated as "debauched one." But even the meaning and origin of this, one of history's most infamous of names, is shrouded in mystery, controversy, and doubt. No native Russian speaker even recognizes "rasputin" as a word, but it is a not uncommon Russian surname. The Russian language does have the adjective "rasputny," meaning "licentious," but the noun equivalent that would be used to describe a person as licentious—a "licentious one"—is "rasputnik," not "rasputin." Still, it is possible that someone sometime branded Novykh with a name that at least suggested debauchery or licentiousness. Yet why would Novykh himself embrace the name? Some recent writers have suggested that "rasputin" is actually rooted in a word for "way" or "road," which, to Novykh, may have had an agreeable mystical or symbolic ring. Still others hold that Rasputin was a local place name, signifying the place where two rivers meet, believed to be an apt description of Novykh's birthplace. Whatever the name means or does not mean, there is even dispute over whether Rasputin was born Novykh and then later adopted (or accepted) the name Rasputin, or whether, in fact, he was born Rasputin and tried, after a religious conversion, to change his name to Novykh, which suggests "novice," in the sense of one who aspires to the priesthood. Try as he might, some say, Rasputin could not make the name stick, and so he was always known—and known to history—as Rasputin.

It is generally agreed that, when he was about eighteen, Rasputin spent three months in the Verkhoturye Monastery. It is not settled, however, whether this was a voluntary sojourn motivated by a religious conversion, or something forced on him as penance for an act of theft. Even among many of those who believe he entered the monastery involuntarily, there is a consensus that, once there, he suffered a religious conversion. Certainly he himself reported one, which either included or led to a mystical vision of the Mother of God. Either at the monastery or shortly after he left it, Rasputin came into contact with the Khlysty (Flagellants). This fanatical sect was banned both by the Russian Orthodox Church and by czarist law. Khlysty faithful would literally whip themselves into a state of religious ecstasy. It is not clear whether Khlysty doctrine actually specified orgiastic sadosexual practices to attain a holy state of mind or whether it was Rasputin who perverted inherently sadistic Khlysty practices into a doctrine he called "holy passionlessness"—a purified state of bliss attained through the sexual exhaustion that followed prolonged and unbridled debauchery.

Although often called a monk, Rasputin never took religious orders. It is known that he visited someone called Makariy, a self-professed holy man who lived a hermetic existence near the monastery, and became his protégé or acolyte. Yet Rasputin did not immediately embark on a religious life. Instead, now nineteen years old, he returned to his village and married Praskovia Fyodorovna Dubrovina. Some sources claim he fathered four children with her; others hold that only three of his four children were hers.

In 1901, a dozen years after marrying Dubrovina, Rasputin embarked on a period of religious wandering, traveling as far as Mount Athos, Greece, and Jerusalem. He lived during this peripatetic period as a holy mendicant, financed not by wealthy patrons but by donations coaxed from the poor. His appearance was singular. Tall, gaunt, and angular, he grew a long, perpetually matted beard and possessed piercing, staring eyes. Many believed him endowed with intense holy powers and acclaimed him a Russian Orthodox *starets*—a man of God and quasi-prophet, who could foretell the future and who, by prayer and a laying on of hands, could heal the sick.

When Rasputin's wanderings took him to St. Petersburg in 1903, his reputation for augury and healing accompanied him. Moreover, like

Nicholas and Alexandra, he, too, appeared to have stepped out of the pages of a book—not a volume of fairy tales, to be sure, but a scripture of ancient prophets, of wandering, otherworldly men with unkempt beard and flowing garments threadbare, ragged, and stained with the holy soil of pilgrimage. Rasputin's lore and looks were sufficient to commend him to Theophan, inspector of the religious Academy of St. Petersburg, and to Hermogen, bishop of Saratov, both of whom greeted him warmly as a man unquestionably of God.

Not far from the academy was the Hermitage, which included the Winter Palace of Czar Nicholas II. Tall, trim, and handsome, his beard cut in the striking "imperial" style first popularized by Napoléon III and as meticulously coifed as Rasputin's was wildly unkempt, Nicholas was a hollow man who devoted his energies to creating the appearance of mastery far more than to the actual business of government. Dull rather than bright, he was in fact no less intelligent, wise, or skilled than any other of Europe's monarchs. Yet, unlike those others at the dawn of the twentieth century, he was no mere figurehead. Even after consenting to a measure of constitutional government in 1905, he ruled virtually without constraint. Much like his fellow kings and emperors, he was clearly unsuited to govern, but in contrast to them, his rule was very real—indeed, absolute.

Or, rather, it was subject to one mistress: the will of the czarina. For all his authority, titular and actual, Nicholas was a henpecked husband and delighted in making no secret of the fact. What the beautiful Alexandra wanted, the beautiful Alexandra invariably got.

In 1905, Russia was swept by the first of the three revolutions that would, within little more than a decade, bring about the end of the reign of the Romanovs, the last of the czars. Nicholas handled the 1905 uprising by promising reform on the one hand while covertly authorizing right-wing legions of "Black Hundreds" to terrorize those who agitated for the rights of peasants, workers, and Jews. The Black Hundreds were arch-conservatives, fanatically czarist, and always and above all, anti-Semitic. What Nicholas did not do was seriously address any of the underlying issues that had motivated the revolt. Instead, he, Alexandra, and others in their court wiled away much of their time in any number of stylish pursuits, including yachting, horseback riding, hunting, and playing at spiritualism, mysticism, and the occult.

Some historians believe that Rasputin presented himself to the royal family as a healer, traveling from Siberia to St. Petersburg in 1905 when he heard reports that the czarevich, the czar's son and heir, Alexei, had lapsed into a life-threatening hemophiliac crisis following a fall from a horse. A genetically transmitted disorder, hemophilia was known as the "royal disease," since it was found in the royal houses of Spain, Prussia, and elsewhere. It is more likely, however, that Rasputin was already in the city and was introduced to the royal family for no other reason than that someone in czar's circle deemed him a most diverting specimen of occult spirituality. Yet while Rasputin, disheveled holy man and incorrigible fornicator, may have been introduced to Nicholas and Alexandra as a source of amusement, it is definitely known that a desperate Alexandra prevailed on her husband to summon him back to the palace in 1908 when Alexei suffered another, even more alarming episode of uncontrolled internal bleeding. At this time, Nicholas did not think highly of Rasputin and was especially wary of his connection with the Khlysty, a sect banned by his own decree. Yet, as always, he could refuse Alexandra nothing, especially now with their son hovering near death.

Rasputin answered the summons, visited with the boy, prayed for him, and also advised the czarina to keep the physicians away from Alexei and to allow him to rest. The czarevich's condition rapidly improved. Rationalist skeptics attributed the boy's recovery to coincidence, or to the power of suggestion, or to the sound and beneficial advice to stop the doctors from prodding and poking the boy and from administering to him various medications of dubious or even harmful effect, including the newly developed analgesic aspirin (an anticoagulant, aspirin was surely the very last thing the young hemophiliac needed). Some suggested that Rasputin possessed powerful skill as a hypnotist and relieved the boy through some form of hypnosis. Alexandra, however, believed she had found in Rasputin a worker of holy miracles. For his part, Rasputin had no doubt of what *he* had found. It was opportunity.

When he left the palace, he warned the grateful czarina and her husband that not only was the future survival of Alexei dependent upon him but also that of the Romanov dynasty itself. What had most likely begun as a casual relationship between Rasputin and the royal family—a mere diversion, a recreational excursion into mysticism—rapidly evolved into a matter of life and death. Rasputin was repeatedly summoned whenever Alexei suffered a hemophiliac crisis and, over the next decade, he became a fixture of the court, exercising an increasingly powerful influence not only over the royal family but over all affairs of government and state.

Throughout it all, Nicholas had episodes of doubt concerning the wisdom of Rasputin's counsel, but he always yielded to Alexandra, whose faith, linked to the well-being of her delicate son, never wavered. The more the czar's ministers tried to wean him from Rasputin's influence, the more Nicholas resisted and rejected his ministers' warnings. Although he himself ordered one covert investigation of Rasputin after another, Nicholas almost invariably rejected any negative findings.

And the findings of each investigation were unquestionably negative—indeed, scandalous. Before the czar and czarina, Rasputin played the part of the holy man, monkish, humble, and pure. Away from the palace, he behaved very differently, not only indulging his orgiastic sexual appetite, but presenting it as part and parcel of

> **"Dear friend,**
> **Again I say a terrible storm cloud hangs over Russia. Disaster, grief, murky darkness and no light. A whole ocean of tears, there is no counting them, and so much blood. . . . We all drown in blood. The disaster is great, the misery infinite."**
>
> **—Rasputin to Nicholas II, July 1914**

his religious doctrine, preaching that sex with him was a purifying and healing experience. Many women proved ready to be purified and healed.

For years, Nicholas closed his eyes and ears to the reports, often responding to them by sending the accusers into exile to various outposts of the empire. In 1911, however, P. A. Stolypin, the prime minister himself, presented Nicholas with a report that graphically detailed Rasputin's drunken debauchery. Stolypin had names, places, and dates. Nicholas could no longer turn a blind eye. Steeling himself at long last, the czar expelled Rasputin from the palace. Alexandra pleaded; Nicholas this time did his best to resist, but, within months, she succeeded in restoring Rasputin to court. Nicholas found it impossible to hold out against his wife for long. Besides, retaining at court a man who, whatever else he did, seemed undeniably able to help his son, allowed Nicholas to rationalize his own passive reliance on faith, which became increasingly intense and unthinking as political discontent in Russia grew ever more critical. To all questions concerning the deepening crisis of government, Nicholas would answer simply, "God will provide."

"I feel cruel worrying you, my sweet, patient Angel—but all my trust lies in our Friend [Rasputin], who only thinks of you, Baby [Alexei] & Russia— And guided by Him we shall get through this heavy time. It will be hard fighting, but a Man of God's is near to guide your boat safely through the reef . . . Be Peter the Great, Ivan the Terrible, Emperor Paul—crush them all under you . . . be the Master, & all will bow down to you."

—Czarina Alexandra to Czar Nicholas II, October 31, 1916

Yet Nicholas never wholly capitulated to Rasputin, whose influence operated mainly through Alexandra. In August 1914, the czar took Russia into the Great War—World War I—and, after months of combat in which his poorly led, poorly trained, and poorly equipped armies suffered one catastrophic defeat after another, Nicholas decided in September 1915 to assume personal command of all forces. If the czar was unsuited to govern, he was even less capable of leading a military enterprise. Inevitably the defeats multiplied. Worse, on leaving for the front, Nicholas entrusted the internal governance of Russia to Alexandra, who turned exclusively to Rasputin as her sovereign advisor.

Rasputin seems to have had no particular political agenda other than maintaining himself in a comfortably powerful position at court. Accordingly his advice to Alexandra typically concerned the appointment of pliable church officials and cabinet ministers who were sympathetic to him. Just how destructive his influence was is difficult to gauge, since Russia had long been on a ruinous course in any case and the tempo of self-destruction was now greatly accelerated by the devastation of the world war. Since he sponsored cabinet members and other high officials solely on the basis of how they felt about him, we can assume they were men of little or no political or administrative ability. Far more important, however, than anything Rasputin actually moved Alexandra to do was the perception his presence created—both in court and among a growing segment of the public—that Russia's destiny had been relinquished into the hands of a besotted, perverted swindler and madman.

Desperate to save themselves and czarist rule, a number of highly placed royals and courtiers conspired to assassinate Rasputin. All failed until, on the night of December 29/30, 1916 (December 16/17 by the old Julian calendar then in use throughout Russia), Prince Felix Yusupov (husband of Nicholas's niece) invited Rasputin to his home for a "gramophone party." Unknown to Rasputin, Yusupov had joined with Vladimir Mitrofanovich Purishkevich (a member of the Duma, the legislative body formed in 1905) and Grand Duke Dmitry Pavlovich (Nicholas's cousin) in a determined plot to kill him.

The three conspirators made the mistake of thinking it would be easy. Yusupov plied his guest with poison wine and cakes. With gustatory relish as unappeasable as his sexual appetite, Rasputin drank and ate enough to kill any number of men, yet he suffered no ill effect. Seeing this, Yusupov took a more direct approach, drawing a fine English Webley revolver and shooting him at point-blank range. Rasputin's knees buckled, and he dropped to the floor—only to rise again and run out into the courtyard of the prince's grand residence. There Purishkevich was waiting. He too shot Rasputin, after which all three assassins stood over him in the courtyard. Discovering to their horror that he was still alive, they kicked him mercilessly, then bound him with a rope, dragged him to the frozen Neva River, which flows through St. Petersburg, found a hole in the ice, and slipped him through. Thus Rasputin died by the combined effects of poisoning, gunshot, battery, and drowning.

He died hard, and he died for nothing. Whatever damage he had done to Russia and to the continuation of Romanov rule had already been done and was irreversible. Within a matter of weeks following the assassination of Rasputin, Nicholas II was forced to abdicate as a new revolution engulfed the empire. There was talk of packing Nicholas, Alexandra, their daughters, and their son off to exile in England, but they were sent instead to western Siberia—Rasputin's country—and on the night of July 16/17, 1918, in the cellar of a house in which they had been held prisoner since April 1918, they were gunned down by their Bolshevik guards.

FOR ALL THE LURID HISTORY AND MYTHOLOGY surrounding him, Grigory Yefimovich Novykh—Rasputin—did not himself bring about the overthrow of Romanov Russia, but he did provide a flesh-and-blood metaphor for everything that was wrong with the national stewardship of Nicholas II.

Nicholas, in turn, remains an enduring example of the folly of leadership by faith, whether at the start of the twentieth century or the dawn of the twenty-first. Asked *What will you do about the future of Russia?* the czar of all the Russias answered "God will provide." Asked if he had consulted his father—former president George H. W. Bush—before invading Iraq in 2003, the president of the United States replied, "You know he is the wrong father to appeal to in terms of strength. There is a higher father that I appeal to." Both answers are instructive, but neither suggests an adequate basis for making the rational decisions demanded by government.

Ford Motor Company and the Edsel (1957)

THE DECISION TO DESIGN BY THE NUMBERS

In May 1958, Vice President Richard Milhous Nixon's "goodwill" visit to Peru turned nasty when demonstrators hurled eggs and rotten tomatoes at him as he drove by in an Edsel convertible. He later quipped: "They were throwing eggs at the car, not me." In the Ho Chi Minh Museum in Hanoi, the defeat of the United States in the Vietnam War is depicted symbolically in a monumental artwork featuring as its centerpiece a real-life Edsel.

The most you can expect from any automobile is movement from point A to point B. The Edsel, however, manages to carry us across barriers of culture and politics. Produced for just three short years, this car endures as a universal symbol of catastrophic misjudgment.

It should never have been so. Few products of modern industrial civilization more thoroughly embodied the old maxim "Look before you leap" than the Ford Edsel. Although the car was introduced in 1957, its origins can be traced to September 28, 1948, when company president Henry Ford II instructed his forward product-planning committee to start researching production of a new medium-priced car. Henry Ford II and his top executives wanted desperately to capture as much of industry front-runner General Motors' huge market share as possible. They speculated that GM's extremely wide range of vehicles, from the entry-level Chevrolet and Pontiac, through the mid-priced Buick and Oldsmobile, and up to the premium-priced Cadillac, was the secret of the company's market success. Unfortunately the Korean War (1950–53) forced Ford to put planning for its own medium-priced contender on hold because the "national emergency" President Truman had declared made both the market for large consumer goods and the availability of raw materials uncertain and also held the possibility that, as in World War II, the government might commandeer heavy industries for war production.

An extensive 1952 market study commissioned by the company confirmed the sense of the president as well as Board Chairman Ernest Breech that a market gap existed between the bottom-priced Ford and the Mercury, which verged on the premium range of the top-end Lincoln. Additional money and effort were devoted to further market studies, which suggested that the new car should be aimed at the "young executive," and early in 1954, a special task force began planning a midpriced car to be sold through Lincoln-Mercury dealers. On July 7, 1954, the resulting new car program was transferred to the stylists.

This handoff was supremely significant. It was not company engineers who took the lead, but, from the beginning, once management had decided on a need for the car, the project became one of styling rather than technical substance. It was a move hardly peculiar to Ford. Since the 1920s, when GM's helmsman Alfred P. Sloan Jr. introduced the concept (if not the phrase) "planned obsolescence," the American auto industry had begun emphasizing visual appearance at the expense of engineering fundamentals. The early planning of Ford's new car took place in a time of unprecedented sales for U.S. automakers. A record 7,169,908 new cars were sold in 1955, as the postwar generation rushed to acquire the means of mobility in an increasingly suburban America and to parlay their new conveyances into symbols of success. The new American lifestyle needed personal transportation, but families also craved emblems of their affluence. More than ever, style was selling cars.

On December 6, 1954, Ford's planning committee presented its new car program to the Ford administrative committee and, little more than a month later, on January 10, 1955, the planning committee moved on to make its presentation to the executive committee. The executives deliberated at a stately pace, finally voting on April 15 to add a new line of midpriced cars. But they added a new wrinkle. The original proposal had been to sell the new offering through the company's existing network of Lincoln-Mercury dealers. Executive committee member Lewis D. Crusoe emphatically took the position that a whole new Ford division should be created to produce the new line and that the cars should be sold through their own dedicated dealer network. This proposal directly emulated the GM model of different divisions and dealers for each of its major lines. Success is an apt object for imitation, but start-up costs would be formidable. Nevertheless, Henry Ford II and Ernest Breech agreed with Crusoe, and the Ford Motor Company was restructured into three divisions: one for Ford, another for Mercury-Lincoln, and a division for the as-yet unnamed mid-priced car.

Before receiving a name, the car-in-progress was referred to as the "E-car"—for "experimental"—and was assigned on April 18, 1955, to the new "Special Products Division," which was put under the leadership of its own president, Dick Krafve. As he saw it, his first major job was to find a name for the E-car. He wanted a name that would thrill potential buyers without scaring them away. It had to be different from the existing Ford, Lincoln, and Mercury marques, yet bear a family resemblance to them. The Ford Thunderbird, first produced in 1955, was enjoying excellent sales, a fact executives attributed in significant measure to its name, which had been the product of extensive and expensive scientific market research. The same approach was applied to the E-car. Marketing employees conducted polls in New York City, Chicago, and two small Michigan towns, soliciting ideas and asking respondents to say what came to mind when various names were mentioned to them. At the end of this exhaustive process, marketers had "narrowed" the range of candidate names to more than two thousand. Foote, Cone & Belding, chosen as the ad agency for the new division, conducted research of its own by running a contest for its employees. That produced another eight thousand suggestions, later "reduced" to six thousand candidate names.

Polling and the contest having yielded a bewildering and therefore essentially useless plethora of possibilities, Ford's own head of market research decided to take a new tack. He put in a call to the woman many considered the most prominent American poet of the day, Marianne Moore, and informally commissioned her to present a list of names that would evoke what he called "some visceral feeling of elegance, fleetness, advanced features and design." Even among literary critics and fellow poets, Moore was considered an eccentric. Her

> **"May I submit UTOPIAN TURTLETOP? Do not trouble to answer unless you like it."**
>
> —Letter to the Ford marketing department from Marianne Moore, December 8, 1955

suggestions more than lived up to that reputation. Among them were Resilient Bullet, Andante con Moto, Pastelogram, Mongoose Civique, Ford Silver Sword, Varsity Stroke, Utopian Turtletop, Thundercrest (and the variant, Thundercrester), and Intelligent Whale. A late entry was Turcontinga, which combined the name of a South American bird, the cotinga, with turquoise, a popular car color in the 1950s.

The executives, we can only imagine, shook their heads.

Time was running out. Back in August 1955, the E-car stylists had unveiled their first full-size clay mock-up for Henry Ford II and the planning committee. The onlookers had burst into applause—something that was virtually unprecedented in the company. By the end of September of that year, a new manufacturing plant was dedicated in Mahwah, New Jersey, followed the next month by another in Louisville, Kentucky. On August 7, 1956, five regional sales offices were established specifically to market the E-car, and just a week later, on August 15, the car's basic sheet-metal styling was approved. On October 15, company executives selected twenty-four district sales managers.

But still the E-car was without a name. Before a single car was manufactured, the Ford Motor Company had spent $400 million on development—a preproduction figure unprecedented in the auto industry. With the clock ticking, however, this investment in painstaking method suddenly yielded to sheer frustration. In November, the Ford Executive

Committee met. Exasperated with the name game, company chairman Ernest Breech sputtered: "Why don't we just call it Edsel?"

Since he was chairman of the board, the question was largely rhetorical. In point of fact, Edsel Bryant Ford, the only son of company founder Henry Ford I, had died in 1943 and so was unavailable to voice an opinion, but his three sons, William Clay, Benson, and company president Henry Ford II, were very much alive. All three objected to the name. Yet it was adopted nevertheless.

Whereas the entire new car project had been founded in an unparalleled avalanche of market research, the twelve months of work that had been devoted to finding the right name were simply thrown to the four winds. The name of Henry Ford's dead son meant absolutely nothing to the car-buying public. Worse, it didn't even sound like a real person's name—a John, Bill, or even a Henry—and when Ford marketers, in a last-ditch bid to scrap the choice, asked focus groups to give their associations with the name, responses ranged from "pretzel" to "weasel." In considerable disgust, the Special Product Division's public relations director, C. Gayle Warnock, fired off a memo notable for its blunt brevity: "We have just lost 200,000 sales."

It was to no avail. On November 19, 1956, the name of the new car—Edsel—was publicly announced, and the Special Products Division was renamed the Edsel Division of Ford Motor Company. With the make named, it only remained to christen the models: Pacer, Citation, Corsair, and Ranger for the sedans; Roundup, Villager, and Bermuda for the wagons.

Armed at last with a name, Ford cranked up the publicity, announcing on January 11, 1957, that Edsel's design would be radically different from anything else produced by the company. Days after this announcement, Edsel division management set a 1958 sales goal of two hundred thousand cars—by coincidence, precisely the number of sales the division's PR director predicted would be lost on account of the name. No matter. On January 21, the division's chief, Richard Krafve, upped the ante by predicting that the Edsel would "surpass the originally announced first-year sales goal of 200,000 units."

Early in February, Ford released the names and features of the Edsel models and announced the locations of five assembly plants where the car would be manufactured, adding that a sixth plant, on the West Coast, would be coming later. Most of all, publicity and advertising touted the styling of the Edsel—even while the company kept this feature under tight wraps, publishing in ads "artistically" blurry or dark photographs that barely hinted at the car's looks. Everything was intended to tease and entice.

This initial ad campaign began after two years' worth of deliberate, carefully placed leaks to the print media. It was a masterfully orchestrated public relations effort that prompted both *Time* and *Life* to publish periodic mentions of "Ford's mystery car," which, the magazines reported, would be the first totally new car to emerge from Detroit in two decades.

The fact was that, while the most visible styling features were indeed new, the Edsel was essentially compounded of major components from the Ford and Mercury lines. Ranger, Pacer, Roundup, Villager, and Bermuda models were built on an existing Ford chassis, whereas Corsairs and Citations sat atop a Mercury chassis. Moreover, even though new plants were announced and some even built, Edsels were turned out entirely in existing Ford and Mercury plants. During the first year of production, every sixty-first car that came down a Ford or Mercury assembly line was designated an Edsel. This meant that line workers had to dip into different parts bins to complete every sixty-first chassis that passed them. Not surprisingly the result was frequent errors in assembling the Edsels. The company found itself facing a quality-control crisis.

As for the major element—styling—it, too, was the product of intensive research, at least initially. Designers decided that the most dramatic styling statement any automobile could make was at the front end. Accordingly, they photographed the front ends of every new car manufactured in America. The Edsel front end was to be designed in stunning contrast to the prevailing look, and a strong vertical theme was proposed to set the Edsel apart. The front end was to include concealed air scoops below the bumpers, giving the car a truly dreamlike and genuinely futuristic look, which was, indeed, very different from the run of the Detroit mill.

Too different, as it turned out. Engineers objected to the amount of retooling that would be required to accommodate cooling and ventilation in the new design. Production managers therefore objected to the increase in production costs. Marketers and executives feared that an overly radical style would scare off the public. In the end, Edsel design was the product of multiple compromises dictated by various committees, and while the car's vertically oriented grille was distinctive, few consumers thought it attractive.

It was, in fact, the Edsel feature most people old enough to have actually seen an Edsel remember most vividly. A gaping ovoid, the grille was variously likened to a horse collar, a toilet seat, and an "Oldsmobile sucking a lemon." More than one psychoanalyst spoke of the design in vaginal terms.

As for the rest of the Edsel, the PR and ad campaigns notwithstanding, it looked pretty much like any other automobile of the late 1950s. Where mechanical and build quality were concerned, the Edsel was markedly inferior to other cars of its price class. Premonitions of disaster came early. The company planned to release seventy-five preproduction Edsels to automotive journalists, who would drive the cars from Ford headquarters in Dearborn, Michigan, to their local Edsel dealers and then report on the experience. To ensure that the seventy-five cars were

> "For years, the Edsel was the brunt of cheap jokes on television, in the magazines and even as part of some off-color jokes; but out of those ashes, people who own an Edsel have seen interest in the vehicle and its values rise like the Phoenix. Today Edsel owners are very proud of their cars and some have even been financially rewarded."
>
> —Automotive historian Phil Skinner, commenting in 2007 that an Edsel, priced between $2,500 and $3,800 in 1957, may now trade to collectors for more than $100,000

in tip-top shape, Ford technicians tested and drove them for two months to iron out any kinks. And there *were* kinks—so many that, at the conclusion of the test period, only sixty-eight of the cars could be delivered because seven had to be completely cannibalized for spare parts to repair the other sixty-eight. The average cost for repairs that had to be made before each car could be turned over to a journalist was a whopping $10,000—significantly more than double the price of a showroom-new top-model Edsel with all the accessories.

Despite disappointments and difficulties, the Edsel division soldiered bravely on, introducing the car to the public on September 4, 1957, and sponsoring on October 13 an hour-long special "Edsel Show" starring Frank Sinatra, Bing Crosby, Louis Armstrong, and Rosemary Clooney, bumping from its regular Sunday night broadcast on CBS nothing less than the top-rated *Ed Sullivan Show.* To maintain the TV-generated buzz, Edsel took over sponsorship of the popular western series *Wagon Train* beginning on October 23. Via a closed-circuit television broadcast from Dearborn on November 21, the nation's Edsel dealers were addressed by Henry Ford II, who proclaimed to them, "Gentleman, the Edsel is here to stay!"

Alas, it was not.

Conceived in a boom time for auto sales, the car was launched in the midst of an economic recession that hit Detroit especially hard. All automakers in 1957 saw sales dip to between 75 and 50 percent of 1956 sales. Instead of selling two hundred thousand cars in 1957, only sixty-three thousand Edsels moved off dealers' lots. Ford compounded the effect of the recession, undercutting sales of the midpriced Edsel by introducing another midpriced car, the Ford Fairlane, just one year before. The Fairlane was a good-looking and solid if unspectacular vehicle. It sold for less than the Edsel and was almost universally perceived as the better value. The Fairlane was an honest car, whereas, for all the hype, consumers could see nothing special about the Edsel.

That the Edsel was ultimately ordinary was not the only thing buyers didn't like about it. No one seemed to appreciate the bizarre front end, of course, but there were also other annoying oddities. For instance, push buttons for the automatic transmission were mounted on the steering wheel hub, where the horn was "supposed" to be. This ergonomic disaster resulted in many drivers shifting gears when they wanted to honk the horn. Another strange design decision was embodied in the taillights of the 1958 Edsel station wagons. Shaped like boomerangs, they were positioned such that they created a real problem when the turn signals were operated. From a distance, the left turn signal looked like an arrow pointing right, and the right looked like an arrow pointing left.

And, of course, there were the quality issues. With its V-8 engine, the Edsel was actually a fast and nimble car—when it ran. Manufacturing problems created many mechanical failures and earned a scathing review from the influential *Consumer Reports*.

In 1959, Robert McNamara, who had been brought into the Ford Motor Company after World War II to turn the ailing company around and who, in 1961, would leave Ford to become secretary of defense in the cabinet of John F. Kennedy, sought to cut Edsel's losses by ditching the separate Edsel division and consolidating the line into a single Mercury, Edsel, Lincoln "M-E-L") Division. It was McNamara who, in a bid to save on production costs, had advocated putting the Edsel on Ford and Mercury chassis, and now he pushed for a redesign that would bring the car even closer to a Ford. By 1960, the final year of its production, the Edsel would be nothing more than a Ford decked out in Edsel trim.

The year 1959 saw Edsel sales stalled below forty-five thousand. McNamara responded with a philosophy of not throwing good money after bad. He slashed the extravagant Edsel ad budget, whittling it close to zero by 1960, the year he persuaded Henry Ford II to drop the doomed car altogether. Only 2,846 Edsels were sold in the automobile's third and final year.

———

AT THE HEART OF THE EDSEL FIASCO was corporate arrogance, an assumption that a manufacturer has complete control over the fate of his product. In the instance of the Edsel, the arrogance took several forms. First, all planning was done on the basis of a best-case scenario. The naïve assumption was that the current boom in the marketplace would continue indefinitely. Starting from this assumption, Ford management went on to substitute the techniques and trappings of market research for a genuine endeavor to delve creatively into the marketplace, try to understand it, then create to satisfy it. Moreover, despite the amount of time and cash devoted to market research, top management ultimately disregarded most of it and instead acted out of a combination of exasperation and executive fiat.

Arrogance also contributed to an attitude that thwarted any effort at follow-through. The car was conceived as a radical innovation, but it was executed fraudulently as a mere imitation of currently available vehicles, differing from them only in superficial elements of design. The creators of the Edsel worshipped at the altar of styling, turning their backs on genuine innovation and sound engineering. Far more attention was devoted to creating predelivery hype than to building a great car. The hype certainly piqued public interest—some three million potential buyers walked into Edsel showrooms in 1957—but hype alone could not motivate actual sales. As delivered, the Edsel was certainly flawed—though, on balance, it was no worse than most cars of its day. The hype, however, had created such a lofty degree of expectation, that the actual car was perceived as that ultimate automotive joke: a lemon.

Sell the sizzle, not the steak, runs the ad man's aphorism. With the Edsel, Ford's folly was thinking consumers could be coaxed into buying the sizzle *without* the steak.

John F. Kennedy and the Bay of Pigs (1961)

THE DECISION TO RELINQUISH CONTROL

When John F. Kennedy opposed Richard M. Nixon in the presidential race of 1960, he really ran against the administration of Dwight D. Eisenhower—Nixon was his two-term vice president—presenting himself as the young, vigorous, and inspiring alternative to the golf-playing retired general whose consistent goal had been the complacent perpetuation of the status quo.

Kennedy played on a popular perception that, whereas Democrat Harry S. Truman had been unrelenting in the "containment" of Communist expansion worldwide, Eisenhower's policy was more isolationist. In particular, candidate Kennedy cited the case of Cuba. Since the end of the Spanish-American War in 1898, Cuba had been for all practical purposes an American client-state, dominated by U.S. multinational corporate interests and by the American government itself.

In 1952, Rubén Fulgencio Batista y Zaldivar, a faithful supporter if not an outright puppet of the United States, assumed the presidency of Cuba and ruled virtually as a dictator, creating a government that was both corrupt and repressive—yet, as always, most friendly to the United States, just ninety miles away. Under Fidel Castro and other leaders, a revolutionary movement crystallized, and in 1959 Castro led a successful rebellion against Batista, becoming Cuba's new premier. The Eisenhower administration, which had been embarrassed by the exuberant corruption of Batista, at first looked on hopefully, and for his part Castro signaled his desire for cordial relations with the United States. But, in a rapid about-face beginning in 1960, Castro abruptly aligned himself and his government with the Soviet Union. Imposing Marxist rule on his island nation, he summarily nationalized and seized U.S. oil refineries, sugar mills, and electric utilities in Cuba. Eisenhower responded by breaking diplomatic relations, but, Kennedy charged, he did almost nothing for the masses of Cuban exiles who had fled to the United States and burned to retake their nation as "freedom fighters."

Neither Ike nor candidate Nixon responded by revealing what they both well knew: that as early as 1959, just after Castro took power, the U.S. Central Intelligence Agency (CIA) had begun began planning an invasion of Cuba to be landed near Guantánamo Bay, the U.S. naval and marine base in the southern portion of the island, specifically at a place called the Bay of Pigs (in Spanish, Bahía de Cochinos). Vice President Nixon, not President Eisenhower, was closest to those planning the operations and who actively encouraged the project.

To his dying day, the perpetually suspicious Nixon believed that Democrats on the CIA staff had informed candidate Kennedy of the top secret plans and that JFK deliberately used the issue of the Cuban "freedom fighters" in the campaign, knowing that Nixon was obliged to guard the secret and could not therefore defend himself. No one ever seriously disputed assertions that Nixon was motivated by a strong streak of paranoia. Looked at objectively, it is highly unlikely that Kennedy had any knowledge of the CIA plans

> "Now, with regard to Cuba, let me make one thing clear. There isn't any question but that we will defend our rights there. There isn't any question but that we will defend Guantanamo if it's attacked. There also isn't any question but that the free people of Cuba . . . are going to be supported and that they will attain their freedom.
>
> No, Cuba is not lost, and I don't think this kind of defeatist talk by Senator Kennedy helps the situation one bit."
>
> —Richard M. Nixon, during the 1960 Kennedy-Nixon presidential campaign debates, responding to Kennedy's assertion that the Eisenhower administration "lost" Cuba

under way during the closing years of the Eisenhower administration. Certainly, JFK seemed taken aback when he was briefed on the plan shortly after he was elected. Then, after he took office, he was informed that the plan had been expanded. Originally it had been conceived as an insurgent operation involving the establishment of a guerrilla base in the Cuban highlands. The new plan, CIA director Allen Dulles told Kennedy, was much more ambitious. Under the direction of Richard Bissell, the CIA administrator who had created and now ran the U-2 spy plane program, the Bay of Pigs operation would be an invasion by a brigade-size force—nearly fifteen hundred men—who would be landed amphibiously and who would march on Havana. Dulles and Bissell assured Kennedy that the CIA had ample intelligence indicating that Castro's hold on the island was very weak and that even this modest invasion of Cuba *by* Cubans would be sufficient to incite a full revolt resulting in a coup d'etat followed by the installation, once again, of a friendly capitalist regime.

The new president was wary and reluctant. In his inaugural address, he had trumpeted his bold plan for an Alliance for Progress, an ambitious reincarnation of FDR's Good Neighbor Policy aimed at giving non-Marxist Latin American leaders the political and economic support they needed to stabilize their governments and bring about genuine reform throughout the hemisphere. Although the CIA—and therefore the U.S.—connection to the planned invasion was to be kept secret, Kennedy feared that it would inevitably get out and, when it did, would quite justifiably raise familiar protests against Yankee imperialism that in turn would surely derail the Alliance for Progress. Even more urgently, Kennedy feared that a U.S.-backed action against Cuba would incite the Soviet Union's Nikita Khrushchev to make an aggressive move elsewhere in the world, perhaps in Europe against West Berlin or in Asia against Laos.

On the other hand, Kennedy felt himself trapped by his own campaign rhetoric. His criticism of Ike for tolerating the presence of an unfriendly Communist regime just ninety miles from America's own shores had been unrelenting. Besides, Dulles was supremely confident of success in Cuba, and he had compiled a reputation for brilliance in the direction of covert actions, beginning with his leadership of OSS (Office of Strategic Services) ops in Europe during World War II and then throughout the early Cold War. As a spymaster, his credentials were overwhelmingly impressive. As for Bissell, he was Dulles's handpicked man and he had already proven himself by creating an invaluable intelligence asset with the U-2—something the Soviets did not have and apparently lacked the technology to create—and he possessed the distinction of having mentored one of JFK's most trusted inner-circle intimates, his national security advisor, McGeorge Bundy. Bissell had been Bundy's economics professor at Yale.

Despite lingering misgivings, Kennedy gave Dulles and Bissell the green light for the invasion on condition that no American fingerprints would be left on the operation and on the further strict understanding that, under no circumstances, would he commit any U.S. military forces to the effort. Dulles and Bissell agreed, although they must both have assumed that, in the event of demonstrated need, Kennedy would never leave the "freedom fighters" in the lurch, but would send in the military. Certainly the Cuban exiles were led to believe that the CIA, which had trained, supplied, and backed them, had in turn the full support of the American army, navy, and air force.

The invasion stepped off on April 15, 1961, with the bombing of Cuba by what appeared to be disaffected pilots of the Cuban air force. Three Cuban military bases were attacked, as were airfields at Camp Libertad and San Antonio de los Baños, and the Antonio Maceo Airport at Santiago de Cuba. Casualties were seven Cubans killed at Libertad and forty-seven elsewhere.

Two of the World War II–vintage B-26 medium bombers involved in the attack flew to Miami, the pilots claiming to be defectors from the Cuban air force. Reporters crowded and quizzed them, quickly piercing their paper-thin cover story. Their aircraft were quickly identified as CIA property and the pilots' own CIA connection soon surfaced. The cover

Dulles and Bissell had promised Kennedy was blown even before the landing phase of the invasion—the invasion proper—had begun.

Worse, from a tactical point of view, the damage inflicted by the bombing was inconsequential. Most of the assigned targets had, in fact, been missed, and almost all of Castro's small—but quite loyal— air force survived. Disaster accompanied the major phase of the invasion, which commenced at 2 AM on April 17. Two battalions waded ashore at the Bay of Pigs, only to find themselves bogged down in a swampy marsh. Despite all of the work that had gone into the plan since 1959, no one, it seemed, had bothered to reconnoiter the landing ground.

> **"They fought like tigers, but their fight was doomed before the first man hit the beach."**
>
> —Grayston Lynch, CIA officer commanding La Brigada 2506 in the Bay of Pigs invasion

For its part, Castro's military was quick to react. The Cuban air force strafed the landing parties—which, bogged down as they were, made easy targets—and it bombed the four converted freighters that supported the landings, sinking one of them, the *Mariposa*, which served as the command and control vessel and carried the bulk of the invaders' crucial communications equipment. Another of the four ships, the *Houston*, was forced onto the beach and had to be abandoned. The loss of those vessels disrupted the coordination as well as the logistics of the invading forces. In a single stroke, the "freedom fighters" were cut off and could not withdraw from their beachhead.

While Castro's air force and members of his army engaged those who had landed, the battle in the air resumed on April 18. Cuban air force pilots shot down ten of the dozen aircraft flown by the invaders. Denied close air support, the fighters on the ground were pinned to their landing beaches. Over the next seventy-two hours, Castro's troops pounded away at the isolated forces with artillery and tank fire. While the barrage was under way, pro-Castro ground units enveloped the invaders. One hundred fourteen "freedom fighters" were killed in combat, a few broke through and fled into the hills, but the vast majority—more than twelve hundred—of the fifteen hundred men deployed surrendered. During 1962–65, the release of many of these POWs would be obtained when private donors ponied up what amounted to a ransom of $53 million in badly needed food and medicines delivered to Cuba. Thirty-six prisoners died in captivity, and a few were held for as long as twenty years.

True to the warning he had given Dulles and Bissell, President Kennedy categorically refused to send military forces to aid the invasion. Bissell and others submitted hurried plans to the president asking for navy and air force support, arguing that the diplomatic cat had already been let out of the bag when the B-26 pilots were unmasked: Cuba and the world knew that America was behind the Bay of Pigs. Unwilling to escalate the failed insurgency into a pretext for retaliatory aggression by the Soviets, Kennedy remained steadfast in his refusal to support the invaders. To many, it looked like a betrayal worse than any weakness Kennedy had alleged on the part of Ike Eisenhower. It exposed the new president to barbed questions about his competence, his commitment, and even his courage. These had a bitterly personal dimension, since Kennedy carried into office the heavy family baggage his father, Joseph P. Kennedy Sr., had bequeathed to him. As U.S. ambassador to the Court of St. James's—America's ambassador to Great Britain—the senior Kennedy, during the years leading up to World War II, had voiced strong approval of Prime Minister Neville Chamberlain's now-infamous appeasement policy. As a result, Ambassador Kennedy was indelibly branded as an appeaser and a defeatist, a man willing to make a bargain with the devil rather than stand up for the principles of liberty and democracy. Pointing to the disaster of the Bay of Pigs and to JFK's craven failure to stand behind the "freedom fighters," some claimed an instance of "like father, like son." The younger Kennedy, it seemed, was as willing to sell out Cuba in 1961 as the elder Kennedy had been willing to back Chamberlain's sell-out of Czechoslovakia in 1938.

The president tried to put the fiasco into the best possible light, as in his April 20, 1961, address to the American Association of Newspaper Editors:

It is not the first time that Communist tanks have rolled over gallant men and women fighting to redeem the independence of their homeland. Nor is it by any means the final episode in the eternal struggle of liberty against tyranny, anywhere on the face of the globe, including Cuba itself.

Mr. Castro has said that these were mercenaries. According to press reports, the final message to be relayed from the refugee forces on the beach came from the rebel commander when asked if he wished to be evacuated. His answer was: "I will never leave this country." That is not the reply of a mercenary. He has gone now to join in the mountains countless other guerrilla fighters, who are equally determined that the dedication of those who gave their lives shall not be forgotten, and that Cuba must not be abandoned to the Communists. And we do not intend to abandon it either!

One thing he consistently refused to do was shift blame to the CIA, which had painted a wildly inaccurate picture of Castro's political standing and military capability. He believed that the nation would not be served by questioning the competence of this agency. Instead, to a reporter's question concerning CIA failures, Kennedy famously responded with "an old saying that victory has a hundred fathers and defeat is an orphan. I am the responsible officer of this government." Later, however, and in private, he summoned Dulles and Bissell to the Oval Office. He told them that they were to wait for the passage of a plausibly decent interval of time and then, separately, they would have to resign. "In a parliamentary system," he explained to them, "I would resign. In our system the President can't and doesn't. So you . . . must go."

THERE ARE UNMITIGATED AS WELL AS MITIGATED disasters. The Bay of Pigs invasion falls into the latter category. Its abject failure was an international embarrassment as well as a threat to the effectiveness and credibility of the young administration of JFK, but, thanks to the president's refusal to escalate the CIA's tactical miscalculation into a world-altering strategic fiasco, the damage was contained and neither a larger war nor European or Asian crisis ensued.

Still, it was bad enough. The Bay of Pigs was not the brainchild of John F. Kennedy, but it was allowed by him. Feeling trapped by his earlier pugnacious pronouncements and overriding his own doubts and better judgment, he assented to a scheme in which he had no authorship and from which he withheld the fullest measure of support. He relinquished control at the outset, reasserting it only after considerable damage had been done. That made the outcome better than it might have been, but, still, it was bad enough.

The Bay of Pigs was a foolish mistake, but the fact that Kennedy realized, accepted, and understood the nature of his folly in making this mistake provided a measure of redemption. After the Bay of Pigs, the president was determined never again to relinquish control. It was this determination, in October of the following year, that allowed him to steer the nation through another, far more perilous Cuban crisis when it was discovered that the Soviet Union had planted nuclear missiles on Castro's island. Everyone wanted to take control of the Cuban Missile Crisis—Castro, Khrushchev, and the leadership of the U.S. military as well—but, this time, the president stood firm, secured the best advice he could, and made decisions that were firm, cautious, and wise, decisions that very likely spared the world from thermonuclear war.

Tonkin Gulf, Persian Gulf (1964, 2003)

THE DECISION FOR BLIND FAITH

*T*he specter of Vietnam. The phrase became a mantra of American politics after April 30, 1975, when U.S. Navy and Marine helicopters plucked the last evacuees from the roof of the American embassy in a fallen Saigon. Depending on the measure used to mark the beginning of the war, it had been raging for one or two decades by the time the United States withdrew, surrendered, or came to its senses—back then, the precise description of what happened was largely a function of the speaker's politics. As the years went by, however, it became increasingly difficult to find any number of rational people who thought of America's involvement in the Vietnam War as something other than a tragic misjudgment and a strategic quagmire. Thus, when President George H. W. Bush decided, in 1990–91, to go to war against Iraq, he had to overcome "the specter of Vietnam" by persuading the American public and lawmakers that his objective, driving Saddam Hussein's invading armies out of Kuwait, was strictly limited and would not lead America into another quagmire. The limited mission accomplished in 1991, the specter resurfaced in 2003 when President George W. Bush decided to invade Iraq again, this time to remove the Hussein regime once and for all and replace it with "freedom" and "democracy." Because the volume of doubt was far greater in 2003 than it had been in 1990–91, the president was at greater pains to pry his proposed war out from under the specter of Vietnam, and he and members of his administration repeatedly disclaimed any similarity between the conflicts.

Five years into the Iraq War, President Bush addressed a Kansas City, Missouri, convention of Veterans of Foreign Wars (VFW) on August 22, 2007. "One unmistakable legacy of Vietnam," he declared, "is that the price of America's withdrawal was paid by millions of innocent citizens whose agonies would add to our vocabulary new terms like 'boat people,' 'reeducation camps' and 'killing fields.'" In the bizarre calculus of a conflict that a majority of Americans now considered unwinnable— perhaps a quagmire even more hopeless than Vietnam—the president chose now not to evade but to embrace the specter of Vietnam to defend the choice he had made to take his nation to war.

Of course, evoking Vietnam was no real defense of the choice to go to war. Over the course of the second Iraq War, President Bush had repeatedly asserted that America was better off for having invaded Iraq. But during his Missouri speech, the proposition he offered was that *Iraqis* would be a lot worse off if, having invaded Iraq, America should suddenly leave it, just as the *Vietnamese* and neighboring peoples suffered when the United States pulled out of Vietnam. Had he taken his comparison further, pursuing the similarities between the decision to go to war in Vietnam and the decision to go to war in Iraq, the president would probably have received little or no applause, even from a conservative VFW audience in Kansas City.

Both Vietnam and Iraq were wars of choice rather than necessity, and both were shrouded in misinformation: faulty information, distorted information, and (certainly in the case of Vietnam, and many allege in Iraq as well) outright fabrication. The major phase of America's commitment to the Vietnam War was launched by the Tonkin Gulf Resolution in much the same way as the Bush administration's war in Iraq relied on persuading Americans—the public and their political leaders—that Saddam Hussein possessed vast stockpiles of "weapons of mass destruction" and surely intended to use them.

In contrast to so much of the legislation Congress enacts, the resolution that gave the president virtually unlimited power to make war was as stark in its simplicity as it was sweeping in its effect:

Tonkin Gulf Resolution, August 7, 1964

Resolved by the Senate and House of Representatives of the United States of America in Congress assembled, That the Congress approves and supports the determination of the President, as Commander in Chief, to take all necessary measures to repel any armed attack against the forces of the United States and to prevent further aggression.

Sec. 2. The United States regards as vital to its national interest and to world peace the maintenance of international peace and security in southeast Asia. Consonant with the Constitution of the United States and the Charter of the United Nations and in accordance with its obligations under the Southeast Asia Collective Defense Treaty, the United States is, therefore, prepared, as the President determines, to take all necessary steps, including the use of armed force, to assist any member or protocol state of the Southeast Asia Collective Defense Treaty requesting assistance in defense of its freedom.

Sec. 3. This resolution shall expire when the President shall determine that the peace and security of the area is reasonably assured by international conditions created by action of the United Nations or otherwise, except that it may be terminated earlier by concurrent resolution of the Congress.

Yet there is a critical difference between the decisions to begin the major phase of the Vietnam War and invade Saddam Hussein's Iraq. However one feels about the course those wars took, America's role in both was born in folly, folly compounded by faulty intelligence at the very least, and fabricated information at the very worst, combined with an attitude of nearly messianic geopolitical arrogance pervading the highest levels of government. The difference between the decisions was in the quality of the folly. Whereas the choice to make a major commitment to the Vietnam War had a long and complicated history, reaching back through the administrations of Presidents Kennedy, Eisenhower, and Truman, the choice to invade Iraq originated within the closed ideological circle of a single administration. With Vietnam, the lethal governmental illusions evolved over time; with Iraq, they sprang full-blown from the fused brows of the president and vice president.

This means that before we can speak of the Tonkin Gulf Resolution, momentous as it was, or compare and contrast it to the Persian Gulf wars, we must look backward to an era decades before Lyndon B. Johnson (LBJ) occupied the Oval Office.

After France surrendered to Germany in June 1940 during World War II, Germany's ally Japan elected to allow French colonial officials to remain nominally in control of their French Indochina colony, which included Vietnam. After France was liberated by the Allies in 1945, Japan seized control of Vietnam, ejecting the French government that had, often through sheer brutality, kept indigenous nationalist groups in check. The largest and most powerful of these groups was the Viet Minh, which under the leadership of Soviet-trained Ho Chi Minh launched a guerrilla war against Japanese occupation forces. Aided by the U.S. Office of Strategic Services (OSS) military teams, Viet Minh took control of Vietnam's north. When World War II ended, Ho Chi Minh refused to relinquish to returning French colonialists the power he had accumulated, and a chronic state of guerrilla war developed.

By temperament and personal conviction, President Harry S. Truman was an anti-imperialist, for whom colonialism was simply wrong. Nevertheless, Truman was convinced that an independent Vietnam would become a Communist Vietnam, and when the Communists emerged victorious in China in 1949 after a long civil war, Truman held his nose and endorsed French rule in Vietnam. On February 7, 1950, the U.S. government formally recognized Vietnam as constituted by the French under their puppet, the emperor Bao Dai.

Allied victory in World War II, Truman understood all too clearly, had not brought peace to the planet, but merely ushered in a new war, the Cold War, a global struggle that demanded an entirely new political and military strategy, which the president's administration called "containment." Truman was determined to block or contain the aggressive expansion of Communism wherever and whenever it occurred. The French understood that the so-called Truman Doctrine made a non-Communist Vietnam as important to the United States as it was to France, and within two weeks of American recognition of the Bao Dai government, France threatened to withdraw from Vietnam and leave the nation to Ho Chi Minh if Truman did not send economic and military aid. Immediately some $75 million was appropriated. About four months later, on June 25, 1950, Communist forces from North Korea invaded South Korea, touching off the Korean War, and President Truman stepped up aid to the

French in Vietnam. Then on August 3, 1950, the first contingent of U.S. military advisors, the U.S. Military Assistance Advisory Group (MAAG), landed in Saigon to work with the French forces.

By 1952, the United States was financing one-third of the French military effort in Vietnam. Despite American logistical support, the French lost the pivotal battle of Dien Bien Phu during March 13–May 7, 1954, to Communist forces. Dwight D. Eisenhower, who had become president in January 1953, held a news conference on April 7, 1954, during the battle. Ike offered a rationale for committing the United States to fighting Communism in Vietnam. "You have a row of dominoes set up," he explained, "you knock over the first one, and what will happen to the last one is the certainty that it will go over very quickly." This awkward sentence, spoken in the heat of a press conference, was transformed by journalists into the so-called "domino theory," which presented to the American public a simple metaphor that justified U.S. commitment to a far-off and obscure country more persuasively than any abstract political discussion could have. For the next two decades, the "domino theory" would be invoked as the rationale for ever-deepening involvement in Vietnam.

On October 24, 1954, President Eisenhower pledged support to Bao Dai's new prime minister, Ngo Dinh Diem, and even pondered sending direct American military aid to prop him up. Yet as much as Ike feared relinquishing Vietnam to the Communists, the president's hand was stayed by the failure of the French, who, demoralized by the defeat at Dien Bien Phu, refused either to train or employ indigenous troops and absolutely refused to commit to an independent democratic Vietnam. In the end, Ike sent no troops.

The fall of Dien Bien Phu was followed by additional Viet Minh victories, which convinced the French in July 1955 to conclude with the Viet Minh the Geneva Accord, calling a cease-fire and dividing Vietnam along the seventeenth parallel, much as Korea had been divided along the thirty-eighth parallel. While Ho Chi Minh set up a Communist government in the North, the United States worked with French and South

Vietnamese authorities to build an ostensibly "democratic" South Vietnamese government as well as a military to defend it. Gradually the French withdrew altogether, leaving the country—and its problems— to the South Vietnamese and, increasingly, to the United States, whose military forces the Eisenhower administration decided to commit to a long-term advisory, not combat, role.

Both Eisenhower and Diem, now president of South Vietnam, proclaimed their support for Vietnamese democracy. In fact, the Geneva Accord mandated the most democratic action of all: a plebiscite—a popular referendum reflecting the will of the majority—to decide the future of the nation. Yet both Ike and Diem feared that such a popular vote would reunify Vietnam under the popular and dynamic Ho Chi Minh rather than Diem, a man incapable of commanding much popular support. Diem turned his back on the Geneva Accord and simply refused to hold the mandated vote in the South. Eisenhower voiced no objection to this abridgment of democracy.

On July 8, 1959, two U.S. servicemen became the first Americans killed in action in Vietnam. Two months later, Diem's continued refusal to allow the plebiscite in the South prompted the Viet Cong—a Communist guerrilla group that succeeded and absorbed elements of the Viet Minh— to begin concerted guerrilla warfare against the South. In 1960 the United States expanded the cadre of MAAG advisors to 685 men, including Special Forces teams assigned to train Vietnamese Rangers. Despite these steps, popular support for the Diem government continued to decline and Eisenhower's successor, John F. Kennedy, decided to prop up the government by authorizing increased numbers of military advisors to help counteract a Viet Cong insurgency that had swelled to fourteen thousand guerrillas operating in South Vietnam.

In October 1961 a deeply troubled Kennedy sent General Maxwell Taylor and White House advisor Walt Rostow to Vietnam to assess the situation and make recommendations. They advised against committing substantial U.S. ground forces to combat, but they did support combat missions for the U.S. Air Force, a transition from its advisory, logistical, and training roles. The president's approval of this recommendation on November 3, 1961, marked the first shift from Americans as advisors to Americans as combatants. At about this time, President Kennedy also authorized joint U.S.-South Vietnamese naval patrols, and by June 30, 1962, there were 6,419 American soldiers and airmen in South Vietnam. By early summer 1963, these numbers had jumped to 11,412, with the U.S. also training and footing the bill for an Army of the Republic of Vietnam (ARVN) of 300,000, a number that overtopped the 280,000 troops of the North Vietnam Army (NVA). By early the next year, ARVN numbers were increased by an additional 100,000, yet attacks by the Viet Cong also increased, and in the Mekong Delta, the war escalated from guerrilla engagements to full-scale field operations. Indeed, by the fall of 1963, it was clear that the Viet Cong were gaining ground.

By this time, with the war claiming about two thousand North and South Vietnamese lives each week, popular support for Diem's notoriously corrupt South Vietnamese government, always shaky, eroded precipitously. Concerned that South Vietnam was nearing collapse, President Kennedy acquiesced in a CIA-backed ARVN military coup d'etat that removed Diem and resulted in his assassination on November 2, 1963.

The overthrow of Diem's government served only to make the country even less stable. The incoming military junta was politically inexperienced and generally inept. Coups and countercoups followed, so that seven South Vietnamese governments rose and fell in 1964 alone, with a succession of four more destined to follow in 1965. Though he was vehemently anti-Communist, Diem had often spurned the advice of the United States. In contrast, each of the new government leaders was compliant with U.S. direction, yet each was quite incapable of commanding the loyalty of a majority of the South Vietnamese. If the conflict between the North and South was viewed as a civil war by the Vietnamese themselves, the multiple conflicts within the South constituted a civil war within the civil war, and it created a power vacuum that the Communists continually exploited by stepping up their attacks.

Twenty days after Diem's assassination, Kennedy was himself killed in Dallas. Today most historians are convinced that Kennedy, who had already authorized the withdrawal of one thousand U.S. troops in October 1963, intended to disengage from Vietnam, but was keeping his plans under wraps to avoid political attacks from the American right wing before his reelection run in 1964. Perhaps the most compelling evidence that Kennedy intended to withdraw was his refusal to accept the advice of his secretary of defense, Robert McNamara, to raise troop numbers exponentially.

The new president, Lyndon B. Johnson, sent out peace feelers to Hanoi, calling for talks. Rebuffed, Johnson accepted the advice of the Joint Chiefs of Staff to expand the war by taking decisive action directly against North Vietnam, a step Kennedy had avoided.

In June 1964, Johnson appointed General William Westmoreland, an enthusiastic advocate of expanding the ground war, to take command of the U.S. Army in Vietnam. On July 27, 1964, five thousand additional "advisors" were ordered to South Vietnam, bringing the total to twenty-one thousand. Four days after this, the U.S. Navy destroyer *Maddox* set out on a reconnaissance mission in the Gulf of Tonkin, waters adjacent to North Vietnam. On August 2, *Maddox* reported itself under attack—in international waters—by five North Vietnamese patrol boats. After suffering inconsequential damage inflicted by a single machine-gun bullet, a 14.5-mm round lodged in one of its stacks, the destroyer withdrew to South Vietnamese waters, where it was joined by another destroyer, the USS *C. Turner Joy*.

On August 4, U.S. Navy patrol boats detected what their crews interpreted as signals indicating another attack by the North Vietnamese. This prompted the *Maddox* and the *C. Turner Joy* to direct fire against the radar targets for some two hours. Although the destroyer crews sincerely believed they were under attack, current military historians and even some who were actually present on the scene have concluded that the radar signals were false targets and that no attack was taking place. Nevertheless, in response to the reported attacks of August 4, President

Johnson ordered retaliatory strikes and appeared on national television that evening to describe the attacks as well as the retaliation.

Both the president and Secretary of Defense Robert McNamara characterized the reported North Vietnamese attacks as unprovoked, even though the mission of the *Maddox* had been to provide intelligence in direct support of South Vietnamese attacks against the North, including on the night of July 30/31 the shelling of the coastal North Vietnamese islands of Hon Me and Hon Nieu. McNamara and the Pentagon publicly disavowed any knowledge of such alleged attacks, but in secret testimony to congressional committees during August 6–7, McNamara and Secretary of State Dean Rusk both admitted that the attacks had occurred, yet, with tortured logic, insisted that they were strictly South Vietnamese operations that did not justify North Vietnamese retaliation against the United States.

While President Johnson explained the Gulf of Tonkin exchange to the American people, Secretary McNamara testified to Congress, claiming that there was "unequivocal proof" of the "unprovoked" second attack. After a Senate debate following the secretary's testimony and President Johnson's August 5 message to Congress on the situation in Southeast Asia, Congress passed a joint Tonkin Gulf Resolution (HJ Res. 1145) on August 7, authorizing the president "to take all necessary steps, including the use of armed force, to assist any member or protocol state of the Southeast Asia Collective Defense Treaty requesting assistance in defense of its freedom." Although the resolution had passed, it had sparked heated debate in the Senate, as evidenced by these remarks from two senators:

> MR. GRUENING [Ernest Gruening, D-Alaska]: Regrettably, I find myself in disagreement with the President's Southeast Asian policy. . . . We now are about to authorize the President if he sees fit to move our Armed Forces . . . not only into South Vietnam, but also into North Vietnam, Laos, Cambodia, Thailand, and of course the authorization includes all

the rest of the SEATO [Southeast Asian Treaty Organization] nations. That means sending our American boys into combat in a war in which we have no business, which is not our war, into which we have been misguidedly drawn, which is steadily being escalated. This resolution is a further authorization for escalation unlimited. I am opposed to sacrificing a single American boy in this venture. We have lost far too many already. . . .

MR. MORSE [Wayne Morse, D-Oregon]: I believe that history will record that we have made a great mistake in subverting and circumventing the Constitution of the United States. . . . I believe this resolution to be a historic mistake. I believe that within the next century, future generations will look with dismay and great disappointment upon a Congress which is now about to make such a historic mistake.

In the end, the resolution carried by a solid majority, and Congress gave LBJ a license to commit war on virtually any scale he saw fit. From 21,000 troops before the resolution, American involvement in Vietnam would expand to more than 500,000 by the end of 1968. Between 1966 and 1973—the years marking major American combat—58,193 U.S. military personnel were killed and 149,000 were wounded. North Vietnamese forces lost 731,000 killed and an unknown number of wounded. South Vietnamese military casualties included 197,000 killed and 502,000 wounded. An estimated 587,000 civilians were also killed in the North and the South. For all this, the United States failed to "contain" Communism.

EVEN BEFORE THE VIETNAM WAR ENDED, evidence surfaced that cast doubt on the reality of the Tonkin Gulf Incident. Then, in 1995, former Secretary of Defense McNamara admitted that he had lied in his testimony to Congress when he said that proof of the second attack, against *Maddox* and *C. Turner Joy*, was "unequivocal." On November 30, 2005, the National Security Agency (NSA) declassified and released a raft of documents relating to the incident, including a secret 2001 article in which NSA historian Robert J. Hanyok reported that NSA intelligence officers had "deliberately skewed" the evidence that was passed on to policy makers as well as the public to suggest that North Vietnamese ships had attacked American destroyers on August 4, 1964.

The Iraq War was rationalized by the clear and present danger of weapons of mass destruction in the hands of an unfriendly regime. Under even cursory scrutiny, the WMD evidence quickly evaporated and, with it, the rationale for going to war. The Tonkin Gulf Incident, which supplied the rationale for fighting a major war in Vietnam, turned out to be trivial (a single machine-gun round in a ship's smokestack, August 2, 1964) and false (a phantom attack two days later), it grew out of the ongoing Cold War and a long-standing policy of containing Communism. Whereas the misadventure in Iraq demonstrates the folly of electing to high office narrow-minded, marginally competent yet cocksure ideologues, America's experience in Vietnam shows that even the wise and well-meaning, acting from policies generally accepted and long-established, can act foolishly, in faith that is both bad and blind, producing the most tragic of consequences.

George W. Bush and Hurricane Katrina (2005)

THE DECISION TO STOP SHORT OF LEADERSHIP

The American Revolution brought a new republic into the world, but the plan for government under which that revolution had been fought, the Articles of Confederation, failed to provide either a chief executive or a head of state. This was understandable, since Americans were engaged in fighting themselves free of both prime minister (chief executive) and king (head of state). It soon became apparent to the founding fathers, however, that their new republic could not long survive headless, and so a Constitution, drawn up to replace the Articles, provided for the election of a single person to fill both the office of chief executive and head of state. At the time that it was enacted, this arrangement was unique in any constitutionally based government. More typical was England's constitutional monarchy, which divided the top level of authority between a prime minister and a king, and therefore divided government between a managerial chief and a largely symbolic ruler.

The American president had a harder job, expected as he was to combine nitty-gritty management with symbolic leadership. George Washington had little trouble with that. He came to office having managed an army and endowed with all the symbolic freight of a leader people were already calling, after the ancient Roman tradition, pater patriae, the father of his country. Among the many great services Washington performed for the nation as its first president, perhaps the greatest of all was his creation of the office itself: fashioning himself into a prototype for the future by modeling just what a combined chief and head of state should be.

Washington was a great man, and great men and women are few and far between. Not many presidents have successfully lived up to the prototype he established. There was Andrew Jackson—maybe—and Abraham Lincoln, certainly. In the twentieth century, Theodore Roosevelt, Franklin Roosevelt, and—perhaps—Harry S. Truman have all at least approached the bar Washington set so high. The first president elected in the twenty-first century, George W. Bush, has fallen far short, farther, many angry Americans would say, than any other president.

Maybe those angry Americans are right. But predecessors such as Millard Fillmore, James Buchanan, and Warren G. Harding, to name three of the men Harry S. Truman once dismissed as "nonentity presidents," set the bar of failure so low that it would require a political limbo dancer to pass beneath it. Besides, rating the presidents, whether from best to worst or worst to best, is, in the end, a sophomoric activity. It is far more instructive—for the purpose of making future electoral choices—to ask why President George W. Bush is so widely perceived as one of the worst, if not the worst.

One way to answer this question is merely to list the errors, injustices, and misjudgments of the administration—a dreary and tedious task, to be sure. Another way is to consider that this president has failed, at critical times, to perform as *either* a chief executive *or* a head of state. At critical times, Mr. Bush has failed as both a manager and a symbol.

To test the strength of a particular material, engineers subject it to stress, making careful note of the point at which it fails. The Bush administration has been subjected to repeated stress, some of it, like the fiasco in Iraq, of the president's own making, and some of it from forces beyond the Oval Office.

At 6:10 AM local time, on August 29, 2005, Hurricane Katrina made its second landfall on the United States near the little Louisiana town of Buras. It did not land without warning. Before the year had even begun, the nation's weather scientists were warning that the hurricane season of 2005, like that of 2004, would be intense, highly dangerous, and certainly destructive. Indeed, climatologists explained that the hemisphere was entering a period of generally heightened hurricane activity, part of a natural climatic cycle, although the effects of this cycle, a majority of scientists believed, were exacerbated by global warming related to the abundance of greenhouse gases, which are byproducts of our massive industrial civilization. At the time, it was an explanation the Bush administration resisted. In June 2002, the Environmental Protection Agency, an entity of the executive branch and therefore part of the Bush administration, issued a report endorsing what most climate scientists had long argued, that activities such as oil refining, electrical power generation, and automobile emissions are major causes of global warming. Asked about this, the president replied dismissively on June 4, 1002, "I read the report put out by the bureaucracy," adding that he continued to oppose the Kyoto Protocol, signed by the United States in 1997 but never ratified, which calls for restrictions on greenhouse gas emissions. "There is general agreement," the report concluded, "that the observed warming is real and has been particularly strong within the past twenty years."

Whatever the cause, the indisputable fact was that the waters of the Atlantic and especially the Gulf of Mexico were warmer than usual in 2004–5, and, also indisputably, that warm water spawns hurricanes as well as fuels their force.

As for this particular hurricane, Katrina, it too was detected early, observed and tracked by satellites and a host of other instruments. On August 24, 2005, the National Hurricane Center announced that what it designated as Tropical Depression 12 had strengthened over the central Bahamas to become Hurricane Katrina. On August 25, Katrina first struck the United States at Florida between Hallandale Beach and North Miami Beach. At that point it was a Category 1 storm, the lowest level of hurricane. Nevertheless, with winds at eighty miles per hour, it killed eleven people.

Predictably as it moved over the Florida peninsula—deprived of the warm water base that energizes it—Katrina diminished to a tropical storm. That, the National Hurricane Center warned, was strictly temporary. Once it moved over the warm Gulf of Mexico, Katrina would be reborn as a hurricane. And so it was, rapidly attaining Category 2 status, with winds of one hundred miles per hour. Behaving well within the predictions of computer models, it now veered north and west, bearing down on Mississippi and Louisiana.

By August 27, Katrina was at Category 3, its winds clocking in at 115 miles per hour. New Orleans mayor Ray Nagin declared a state of emergency, urging but not ordering residents in low-lying areas of the city to evacuate. Mississippi's governor, Haley Barbour, also declared a state of emergency and went further than Nagin, ordering the evacuation of one county.

Katrina, a juggernaut, marched on. On August 28, it was a Category 5 storm, the most powerful classification. Its winds reached 160 miles per hour, prompting Mayor Nagin to order a mandatory evacuation of his city. The trouble was that evacuation depended on the ability of residents to leave town. Most took to their automobiles, but New Orleans is a city mostly African American and mostly poor. Nearly a third of its residents lived below the national poverty line, and many of these people neither owned cars nor had the financial means to buy train, bus, or plane tickets. And even for those who could get out, where would they go? The most fortunate had friends and relatives living somewhere outside of the hurricane's projected path of destruction. Those who could afford it might find space in hotels and motels—although these quickly filled. For the rest, leaving New Orleans meant rendering themselves homeless. Mayor Nagin ordered ten shelters to be designated within the city to accommodate those who had nowhere else to go or no means to get there. The biggest of these were the city's Superdome stadium and its Convention Center, neither of which was ever intended to double as an emergency shelter.

With each passing day, Katrina all but monopolized the national news. It is not often that a nation gets to witness a catastrophe in the making, but, unlike an attack by human terrorists, Katrina came without stealth. Every day, television news broadcasters interviewed experts, who explained that a Category 4 or 5 hurricane hitting New Orleans would be to that city what "the Big One," a massive earthquake, would be to Los Angeles—doomsday. Others pointed out that scientists and civil engineers had been warning state and city officials for years that the levees and flood walls of New Orleans had been designed to withstand nothing greater than a Category 3 hurricane. Nothing was ever done to upgrade these basic defenses, and now any number of well-informed voices spoke of the very real possibility that New Orleans would be washed from the continent.

As Katrina, having raked Florida, bore down on the Gulf Coast and the city of New Orleans, President George W. Bush continued to enjoy a five-week getaway. It was his forty-ninth trip to his Crawford, Texas, ranch since he had taken office, a total vacation time representing nearly a year, or 20 percent of his presidency to date. If he so much as turned on a television during that time, however, he must have heard the predictions. Yet they did not dislodge him from the arid Texas scrub country of which he seemed so fond. Like Ronald Reagan, President Bush routinely disavowed details and left management of the approaching hurricane to the recently created Department of Homeland Security, of which FEMA (the Federal Emergency Management Agency) was now a part.

Sorely tested during the 1990s by a number of natural disasters, including 1992's Hurricane Andrew (a Category 5 storm), FEMA had built a take-charge reputation, and citizens glued to their television sets in the gulf and throughout the nation listened confidently to Michael D. Brown, whom President Bush had named to head FEMA in January 2003, issue assurances that his agency and the entire federal government were fully prepared to respond to the emergency.

Few of those watching Brown on TV were aware that the FEMA of 2005 was a far cry from the agency it had been in the 1990s. After it had been moved under the Department of Homeland Security, its funding and authority were sharply reduced. As for its director, even fewer knew much about him. He had been recruited for FEMA in 2001 by a college chum, longtime Bush aide and FEMA director (2001–3) Joseph Allbaugh, after Brown, amid lawsuits over his role in certain disciplinary actions, resigned from the job he had held since 1989 as Judges and Stewards Commissioner for the International Arabian Horse Association. Holding a law degree from the Oklahoma City University School of Law, Brown became FEMA's general counsel until President Bush elevated him to the top job in the agency. Brown's official White House biography credited him with having had "emergency services oversight" as an administrative assistant to the city manager of Edmond, Oklahoma, from 1975 to 1978, actually a part-time job he held while he was an undergraduate at Central State University (now the University of Central Oklahoma). The city of Edmond described Brown's job as handling "labor and budget matters" for the town of fewer than sixty thousand residents, and Edmond's head of public relations later described the post of administrative assistant as essentially an internship.

By any measure, it was evident that Michael Brown, director of FEMA, came to the job with little enough experience in disaster management. Of course, much the same could be said of Brown's two top aides, acting deputy director Patrick Rhode, and acting deputy chief of staff Brooks Altshuler, neither of whom had come from the field of disaster relief or emergency management.

The public, except for readers of New Orleans's leading newspaper, the *Times-Picayune*, were also largely unaware of just how perilous the condition was of the low-lying city's levees and flood walls. The *Times-Picayune* had just recently reported that, after flooding in May 1995 killed six people, Congress authorized the Southeast Louisiana Urban Flood Control Project. Over the next ten years, the Army Corps of Engineers spent $430 million to shore up levees and build pumping stations. But nearly a quarter-billion dollars in flood-control projects remained uncompleted when, in 2003, federal funding was drastically cut in response to spending pressures created by the combination of the newly begun war in Iraq, homeland security terrorism concerns, and the Bush administration's insistence on maintaining a program of deep federal income tax reductions.

> **"I don't think anybody anticipated the breach of the levees."**
>
> —President Bush, on *Good Morning America*, September 1, 2005

On Sunday, August 28, Max Mayfield, director of the National Hurricane Center, appeared on a video screen in a conference room at the Crawford ranch. He was anxious to ensure that the vacationing president fully appreciated just how destructive Katrina was going to be. On March 1, 2006, the Associated Press reported that it had obtained video footage and "seven days of transcripts of briefings [showing] in excruciating detail that while federal officials anticipated the tragedy that unfolded in New Orleans and elsewhere along the Gulf Coast, they were fatally slow to realize they had not mustered enough resources to deal with the unprecedented disaster." On August 28 (according to the 2006 AP story), linked from Crawford "by secure video, Bush expressed a confidence . . . that starkly contrasted with the dire warnings his disaster chief and numerous federal, state, and local officials provided during the four days before the storm." Based on the video footage it had obtained, the AP concluded that, in "dramatic and agonizing terms, federal disaster officials warned President Bush and his homeland security chief that Hurricane Katrina could breach levees, put lives at risk in New Orleans' Superdome, and overwhelm rescuers." The AP reported that "Bush didn't ask any questions during the final briefing before Katrina struck on Aug. 29, but he assured soon-to-be-battered state officials: 'We are fully prepared.'"

When Katrina barreled down on Buras just after six on the morning of Monday, August 29, there was great relief in New Orleans and the rest of the nation. The "Big Easy," newscasters were saying, had dodged a bullet. Then came Tuesday, August 30, when two of the city's flood walls were overtopped and gave way, rapidly inundating about 80 percent of the city. The lowest-lying areas, which were generally the poorest neighborhoods, were swept under as much as twenty feet of Gulf water. And since the swath cut by Katrina was very wide, much of the Alabama and Mississippi Gulf Coast, along with New Orleans, descended into chaos.

Monday, the twenty-ninth, found the president still vacationing in Crawford. On Tuesday, the president got in some golf and delivered a speech in Coronado, California, with the aircraft carrier *Ronald Reagan* in the background. His focus was the war in Iraq, but he also announced that because of the "devastation wrought by Hurricane Katrina . . . [he] was cutting his August vacation short to return to Washington to personally oversee the federal response effort." It took the president one full day to start the journey back to Washington, although he made a thirty-five-minute Air Force One flyover Louisiana, Mississippi, and Alabama and looked out the window.

President Bush was not the only member of his administration who vacationed during the first days of Katrina. Secretary of State Condoleezza Rice spent Tuesday through Thursday in New York, going to a Broadway show and doing some shopping, and Vice President Dick Cheney remained on vacation, in Jackson, Wyoming, through Thursday. Asked by a reporter why he did not return from his vacation earlier but waited until three days after the hurricane hit, Cheney replied that he "came back four days early."

In the meantime, Louisiana Governor Kathleen Blanco ordered everyone remaining in inundated New Orleans—estimated at between fifty thousand to one hundred thousand people—to be evacuated. By this time, of course, there was no means of evacuation available. Although a handful of Coast Guard helicopters were making truly heroic and spectacular efforts to pick survivors from the rooftops of buildings in which floodwaters had risen to the second or even the third floor, and although seemingly large numbers of television news crews were on the scene covering such rescues, there was no other evidence of the promised federal aid: no FEMA workers, no National Guard or Army troops.

> **"Considering the dire circumstances that we have in New Orleans, virtually a city that has been destroyed, things are going relatively well."**
>
> —**Michael Brown, FEMA director, September 1, 2005**

Abundant, heart wrenchingly abundant, were television images of bloated bodies floating in rivers and floodwaters. Television also showed some ten thousand persons huddled in the squalor of a battered Superdome and, later, twice that number jammed into even more appalling accommodations at the city's convention center. There were also images and reports of epidemic looting throughout the city, which, on the face of it, looked like nothing less than civil insurrection, with local police—those who hadn't simply walked off their jobs—under siege, reports of rescue helicopters taking small-arms fire, and hurricane survivors generally terrorized.

On September 1, Mayor Nagin broadcast over the radio what he himself characterized as a "desperate SOS" for evacuation buses and the promised federal personnel and equipment. Anyone who owned a television set could see that the situation in New Orleans was beyond disaster. However people bore witness to the devastation, whether personally, via newspaper, or on television, the same remark was heard over and over again: "I can't believe this is America." And that was often followed by a question: "How can the richest nation in the world allow so many to drown and to die?"

Thousands of people were packed into the New Orleans Convention Center, under desperately squalid conditions, with little food or water, inad-equate sanitation, no electrical power, and virtually no police or National Guard protection. Yet even as the news stories and the televi-sion images were beamed to America and the rest of the world, FEMA director Brown told ABC-TV's Ted Koppel on September 1 that his agency had "just learned" that very day that anyone was even sheltered in the convention center.

MICHAEL BROWN: "We just learned of the convention center—we being the federal government—today. . . ."

TED KOPPEL: ". . . Don't you guys watch television? Don't you guys listen to the radio? Our reporters have been reporting on it for more than just today."

—Ted Koppel, televised interview with FEMA director Michael Brown, September 1, 2005

As for civil unrest, no one had reported any to him. Apparently Brown's professional stupor made little impression on President Bush, who, in a sound bite that made all the evening newscasts on September 2, congratulated his appointee with a compliment: "Brownie, you're doing a heck of a job."

On September 2, Congress voted $10.5 billion in emergency funds for New Orleans and the Gulf Coast. On this same day, National Guardsmen at last began arriving in the city, bringing food, water—and their weapons. On this day, too, in brief nationally televised remarks, the president acknowledged the failure of government efforts, declaring blandly that the "results are not acceptable."

As most Americans saw it, the results never would be acceptable. Initial estimates that the Katrina death toll would top ten thousand proved, thank-fully, incorrect. The actual death toll, just over one thousand, was horrific enough. Yet, in the weeks, months, then years following Katrina, much of New Orleans remained a ruin, the city having struggled to reach 67.6 percent of its pre-Katrina population level by July 2007. Elsewhere along the

Gulf, recovery was mixed, with some areas rebuilding fairly rapidly and others remaining in ruins.

———

IN THE IMMEDIATE AFTERMATH OF KATRINA, many Americans directed their outrage against the president they had twice elected to office. Bush policy decisions certainly contributed to the

"I understand there are ten thousand people dead. It's terrible. It's tragic. But in a democracy of 300 million people, over years and years and years, these things happen."

—2004 Bush-Cheney campaign staffer, lobbyist, and conservative pundit Jack Burkman, MSNBC's *Connected*, September 7, 2005

disaster. The administration ended much of the extensive federal protection of wetlands on the Gulf Coast, including the area of New Orleans, and the administration had also declined to ratify the Kyoto Protocol (to which 155 other nations are party), intended to limit the emission of greenhouse gases and control other factors that contribute to global warming. But these were not the principal sources of the outrage.

There was, to be sure, much anger directed against Michael Brown and other political cronies—or cronies of cronies—the president had chosen to place in so many key administration roles, apparently with little or no regard for professional experience or qualifications. And there were other management questions: Why weren't buses provided for the evacuation of those who had no other means of leaving New Orleans? Why weren't evacuation sites (such as military bases) designated and prepared? What delayed the arrival of rescuers, food, and water? Why did the departments and agencies created or reconfigured after 9/11 and intended to improve emergency response fail so miserably? Why did bureaucracy impede instead of facilitate aid? Why were systems designed to control floodwaters, including levees and flood walls, neglected and allowed to deteriorate?

As these questions suggest, there was plenty of blame to go around—on the city and state as well as federal level. But the understanding Harry S. Truman had of the presidency, which he famously expressed on the little sign perched on his Oval Office desk—*The Buck Stops Here*—turned out to be the people's understanding as well. As chief executive *and* head of state, the American president is expected to be the manager in charge *and* the leader in charge. As the chief, the ultimate manager, he is supposed to get things to work, and if they fail to work, he is expected to devote himself diligently to seeing that they are made to work. As the head of state, the leader of the nation, he is supposed to rally national effort, commitment, and resolve by presenting himself a symbol of national unity. As poorly as the president fared as manager, he failed far more critically in his symbolic role, emerging not as an emblem of the national will but as a metaphor of leisurely indifference and almost willful incomprehension: a man content to vacation in the eye of a storm.

Few, we have said, very few American presidents have come close to fully emulating the prototype created by the presidency of George Washington. Some, however, have come closer than others, and a review of history suggests than even more have at least tried. There is, in fact, no other valid approach to the leadership of the American democracy. The goal of any man or woman who would be president of the United States must be to emulate the very first president, both as manager and symbol. To rest short of this aspiration, with whatever degree of contentment, complacency, or confidence, is folly.

Further Reading

The following selections, which include the books used as sources for *Profiles in Folly*, are suggestions for reading further about some of history's most notable misjudgments and mistakes.

THE TROJANS AND THE TROJAN HORSE (CA. 1250 BC)

Homer. *The Iliad*. Translated by Robert Fitzgerald. New York: Farrar, Straus and Giroux, 2004.

Strauss, Barry. *The Trojan War: A New History*. New York: Simon & Schuster, 2006.

Wood, Michael. *In Search of the Trojan War*. London: BBC Books, 2007.

GEORGE ARMSTRONG CUSTER AND THE LITTLE BIGHORN (1876)

Ambrose, Stephen E. *Crazy Horse and Custer: The Parallel Lives of Two American Warriors*. Garden City, NY: Doubleday, 1975.

Marshall, Joseph M., III. *The Day the World Ended at Little Bighorn: A Lakota History*. New York: Viking, 2007.

Miller, David Humphreys. *Custer's Fall: The Native American Side of the Story*. New York: Meridian, 1992.

Wert, Jeffry D. *Custer: The Controversial Life of George Armstrong Custer*. New York: Simon & Schuster, 1996.

ANDRÉ MAGINOT AND HIS LINE (1930–40)

Allcorn, William. *The Maginot Line, 1928–45*. London: Osprey, 2003.

Kaufmann, J. E., and H. W. Kaufmann. *Fortress France: The Maginot Line and French Defenses in World War II*. Mechanicsburg, PA: Stackpole, 2007.

Kemp, Anthony. *The Maginot Line: Myth and Reality*. New York: Stein & Day, 1982.

May, Ernest R. *Strange Victory: Hitler's Conquest of France*. New York: Hill and Wang, 2001.

UNSINKABILITY AND THE *TITANIC* (1912)

Butler, Daniel Allen. *"Unsinkable": The Full Story of the RMS* Titanic. New York: Da Capo, 2002.

Kuntz, Tom, ed. *The* Titanic *Disaster Hearings*. New York: Pocket, 1998.

Winocour, Jack, ed. *The Story of the* Titanic *As Told by Its Survivors*. New York: Dover, 1960.

ISOROKU YAMAMOTO AND PEARL HARBOR (1941)

Agawa, Hiroyuki. *The Reluctant Admiral: Yamamoto and the Imperial Navy*. Tokyo: Kodansha International, 2000.

Goldstein, Donald M. *The Pearl Harbor Papers: Inside the Japanese Plans*. Dulles, VA: Potomac Books, 1993.

Hoyt, Edwin P. *Yamamoto: The Man Who Planned the Attack on Pearl Harbor*. Guilford, CT: The Lyons Press, 2001.

Prange, Gordon W. *At Dawn We Slept*. New York: Penguin, 1982.

NASA AND THE SPACE SHUTTLES (1986, 2003)

Cabbage, Michael, and William Harwood. *Comm Check . . . : The Final Flight of Shuttle* Columbia. New York: Free Press, 2004.

Goodwin, Robert, ed. Columbia *Accident Investigation Report*. Burlington, ON (Canada): Collector's Guide Publishing, 2003.

Pinkus, Rosa Lynn B., et al. *Engineering Ethics: Balancing Cost, Schedule, and Risk: Lessons Learned from the Space Shuttle*. New York: Cambridge University Press, 1997.

Vaughan, Diane. *The* Challenger *Launch Decision: Risky Technology, Culture, and Deviance at NASA*. Chicago: University of Chicago Press, 1997.

WILLIAM MCKINLEY, THE USS MAINE, AND THE SPANISH-AMERICAN WAR (1898)

Morgan, H. Wayne. *William McKinley and His America*. Kent, OH: Kent State University Press, 2004.

Rickover, Hyman George. *How the Battleship* Maine *Was Destroyed*. Annapolis, MD: Naval Institute Press, 1995.

Weems, John Edward. *The Fate of the Maine*. College Station: Texas A&M University Press, 1992.

CAPTAIN ALFRED DREYFUS AND THE HONOR OF FRANCE (1894–1906)

Bredin, Jean-Denis. *The Affair: The Case of Alfred Dreyfus*. New York: George Braziller, 1986.

Burns, Michael. *France and the Dreyfus Affair: A Documentary History*. London and New York: Palgrave Macmillan, 1998.

Johnson, Martin P. *The Dreyfus Affair: Honour and Politics in the Belle Epoque*. London and New York: Palgrave Macmillan, 1999.

Zola, Émile. *The Dreyfus Affair: "J'Accuse" and other Writings*. New Haven, CT: Yale University Press, 1998.

EDWARD BERNAYS AND THE CAMPAIGN TO RECRUIT WOMEN SMOKERS (1929)

Bernays, Edward L. *Propaganda*. New York: Liveright, 1928.

Tye, Larry. *The Father of Spin: Edward L. Bernays and the Birth of Public Relations*. New York: Henry Holt, 1998.

RICHARD M. NIXON AND WATERGATE (1973)

Ellsberg, Daniel. *Secrets: A Memoir of*

Vietnam and the Pentagon Papers. New York: Viking, 2002.

Nixon, Richard M. *RN: The Memoirs of Richard Nixon*. New York: Simon and Schuster, 1990.

Woodward, Bob, and Carl Bernstein. *All the President's Men*. New York: Simon and Schuster, 1974.

METROPOLITAN EDISON AND THREE MILE ISLAND (1979)

Gray, Mike, and Ira Rosen. *The Warning: Accident at Three Mile Island: A Nuclear Omen for the Age of Terror*. New York: Norton, 2003.

Osif, Bonnie A., Anthony J. Baratta, and Thomas W. Conkling. *TMI 25 Years Later: The Three Mile Island Nuclear Power Plant Accident and its Impact*. State College: Pennsylvania State University Press, 2006.

Walker, J. Samuel. *Three Mile Island: A Nuclear Crisis in Historical Perspective*. Berkeley: University of California Press, 2006.

KEN LAY AND ENRON (2001)

Eichenwald, Kurt. *Conspiracy of Fools: A True Story*. New York: Broadway, 2005.

McLean, Bethany, and Peter Elkind. *The Smartest Guys in the Room*. New York: Penguin, 2004.

DICK CHENEY AND THE IRAQ WAR (2003)

Bamford, James. *A Pretext for War: 9/11, Iraq, and the Abuse of America's Intelligence Agencies*. New York: Doubleday, 2004.

Clarke, Richard A. *Against All Enemies: Inside America's War on Terror*. New York: Free Press, 2004.

Dubose, Lou, and Jake Bernstein. *Vice: Dick Cheney and the Hijacking of the American Presidency*. New York: Random House, 2006.

Hayes, Stephen F. *Cheney: The Untold Story of America's Most Powerful and*

Controversial Vice President.
New York: HarperCollins, 2007.

Issikoff, Michael, and David Corn. *Hubris: The Inside Story of Spin, Scandal, and the Selling of the Iraq War.* New York: Three Rivers Press, 2007.

Woodward, Bob. *Plan of Attack.* New York: Simon and Schuster, 2004.

———. *State of Denial: Bush at War, Part III.* New York: Simon and Schuster, 2006.

KING GEORGE III AND THE AMERICAN REVOLUTION (1775–83)

Black, Jeremy. *George III: America's Last King.* New Haven, CT: Yale University Press, 2006.

Hibbert, Christopher. *George III: A Personal History.* New York: Basic Books, 2000.

Lloyd, Alan. *The King Who Lost America: A Portrait of the Life and Times of George III.* New York: Doubleday, 2002.

THE "WAR HAWKS" AND THE WAR OF 1812 (1812)

Borneman, Walter R. *1812: The War That Forged a Nation.* New York: Harper Perennial, 2005.

Hickey, Donald R. *The War of 1812: A Forgotten Conflict.* Urbana: University of Illinois Press, 1990.

Latimer, Jon. *1812: War with America.* Cambridge, MA: Belknap Press, 2007.

JOHN C. CALHOUN AND NULLIFICATION (1832)

Coit, Margaret L. *John C. Calhoun: American Portrait.* Columbia: University of South Carolina Press, 1991.

Ellis, Richard E. *The Union at Risk: Jacksonian Democracy, States' Rights, and Nullification Crisis.* New York: Oxford University Press, 1989.

Niven, John. *John C. Calhoun and the Price of Union: A Biography.* Baton Rouge: Louisiana State University Press, 1993.

Peterson, Merrill D. *The Great Triumvirate: Webster, Clay, and Calhoun.* New York: Oxford University Press, 1988.

RUSSELL, MAJORS, AND WADDELL AND THE PONY EXPRESS (1860)

Corbett, Christopher. *Orphans Preferred: The Twisted Truth and Lasting Legend of the Pony Express.* New York: Broadway, 2004.

Di Certo, Joseph J. *The Saga of the Pony Express.* Missoula, MT: Mountain Press Publishing Company, 2002.

Settle, Raymond W., and Mary Lund Settle. *Saddles and Spurs: The Pony Express Saga.* Lincoln: University of Nebraska Press, 1972.

COUNT LEOPOLD VON BERCHTOLD AND HIS ULTIMATUM (1914)

Mason, John W. *Dissolution of the Austro-Hungarian Empire, 1867–1918.* London: Longman, 1986.

Tuchman, Barbara W. *The Guns of August.* New York: Macmillan, 1962.

CHIEF JUSTICE ROGER B. TANEY AND DRED SCOTT (1857)

Fehrenbacher, Don E. *The Dred Scott Case: Its Significance in American Law and Politics.* New York: Oxford University Press, 2001.

Graber, Mark A. *Dred Scott and the Problem of Constitutional Evil.* New York: Cambridge University Press, 2006.

Maltz, Earl M. *Dred Scott and the Politics of Slavery.* Lawrence: University Press of Kansas, 2007.

THOMAS EDISON AND THE FIGHT AGAINST ALTERNATING CURRENT (1893)

Baldwin, Neil. *Edison: Inventing the Century.* Chicago: University of Chicago Press, 2001.

Israel, Paul. *Edison: A Life of Invention.* New York: Wiley, 1998.

Jonnes, Jill. *Empires of Light: Edison, Tesla, Westinghouse, and the Race to Electrify the World.* New York: Random House, 2004.

McNichol, Tom. *AC/DC: The Savage Tale of the First Standards War.* San Francisco: Jossey-Bass, 2006.

THE WRIGHT BROTHERS AND THE WING WARPING LAWSUITS (1910–14)

Crouch, Tom. *The Bishop's Boys: A Life of Wilbur and Orville Wright.* New York: Norton, 1989.

Howard, Fred. *Wilbur and Orville: A Biography of the Wright Brothers.* New York: Knopf, 1987.

Walsh, John Evangelist. *One Day at Kitty Hawk: The Untold Story of the Wright Brothers and the Airplane.* New York: Crowell, 1975.

ALFRED P. SLOAN AND PLANNED OBSOLESCENCE (1920)

Farber, David. *Sloan Rules: Alfred P. Sloan and the Triumph of General Motors.* Chicago: University of Chicago Press, 2005.

Packard, Vance. *The Waste Makers.* New York: McKay, 1960.

Slade, Giles. *Made to Break: Technology and Obsolescence in America.* Cambridge, MA: Harvard University Press, 2006.

Sloan, Alfred P., Jr. *My Years with General Motors.* New York: Currency, 1990.

NEVILLE CHAMBERLAIN AND ADOLF HITLER (1938)

Dutton, David. *Neville Chamberlain.* London: Hodder Arnold, 2001.

McDonough, Frank. *Neville Chamberlain, Appeasement and the British Road to War.* Manchester, UK: Manchester University Press, 1998.

Self, Robert C. *Neville Chamberlain: A Biography.* London: Ashgate Publishing, 2006.

THE BRITISH EMPIRE AND GANDHI (1942)

Fischer, Louis, ed. *The Essential Gandhi.* New York: Vintage, 1983.

Gandhi, Mohandas. *An Autobiography: The Story of My Experiments with Truth.* Boston: Beacon Press, 1993.

Hutchins, Francis G. *India's Revolution: Gandhi and the Quit India Movement.* Cambridge, MA: Harvard University Press, 1973.

GOVERNOR WILLEM KIEFT AND THE "SLAUGHTER OF THE INNOCENTS" (1643)

Jameson, J. Franklin, ed. *Narratives of New Netherland, 1609–1664.* Chestnut Hill, MA: Adamant Media Corporation; Replica edition (July 26, 2001).

Kammen, Michael. *Colonial New York: A History.* New York: Oxford University Press, 1996.

Merwick, Donna. *The Shame and the Sorrow: Dutch-Amerindian Encounters in New Netherland.* Philadelphia: University of Pennsylvania Press, 2006.

Shorto, Russell. *The Island at the Center of the World: The Epic Story of Dutch Manhattan and the Forgotten Colony that Shaped America.* New York: Doubleday, 2004.

ANTONIO LÓPEZ DE SANTA ANNA AND THE ALAMO (1836)

Hansen, Todd, ed. *The Alamo Reader: A Study in History.* Mechanicsburg, PA: Stackpole, 2003.

Hardin, Stephen L. *Texian Iliad: A Military History of the Texas Revolution.* Austin: University of Texas Press, 1996.

Lindley, Thomas Ricks. *Alamo Traces: New Evidence and New Conclusions.* Dallas: Republic of Texas Press, 2003.

Thompson, Frank T. *The Alamo*. Denton: University of North Texas Press, 2005.

PATRIOTISM AND POISON GAS (1914–18)

Charles, Daniel. *Master Mind: The Rise and Fall of Fritz Haber, the Nobel Laureate Who Launched the Age of Chemical Warfare*. New York: Ecco, 2005.

Haber, L. F. *The Poisonous Cloud: Chemical Warfare in the First World War*. New York: Oxford University Press, 1986.

Stoltzenberg, Dietrich. *Fritz Haber: Chemist, Nobel Laureate, German, Jew: A Biography*. Philadelphia: Chemical Heritage Foundation, 2005.

ROBERTO GOIZUETA AND THE "NEW COKE" (1985)

Greising, David. *I'd Like the World to Buy a Coke: The Life and Leadership of Roberto Goizueta*. New York: Wiley, 1999.

Hays, Constance L. *The Real Thing: Truth and Power at the Coca-Cola Company*. New York: Random House, 2005.

Pendergrast, Mark. *For God, Country, and Coca-Cola: The Definitive History of the Great American Soft Drink and the Company That Makes It*. New York: Basic Books, 2000.

JAMES BUCHANAN AND SECESSION (1860)

Abrahamson, James L. *The Men of Secession and Civil War, 1859–1861*. Lanham, MD: SR Books, 2000.

Baker, Jean H. *James Buchanan*. New York: Times Books, 2004.

Klein, Philip S. *President James Buchanan: A Biography*. Newton, CT: American Political Biography Press, 1995.

Walther, Eric H. *The Shattering of the Union: America in the 1850s*. Lanham, MD: SR Books, 2003.

GEORGE GORDON MEADE AND ULYSSES S. GRANT AT THE BATTLE OF THE CRATER (1864)

Axelrod, Alan. *The Horrid Pit: The Battle of the Crater, the Civil War's Cruelest Mission*. New York: Carroll and Graf, 2007.

Cavanaugh, Michael A., and William Marvel. *The Battle of the Crater: "The Horrid Pit."* Lynchburg, VA: H. E. Howard, 1989.

Kinard, Jeff. *The Battle of the Crater*. Fort Worth: Ryan Place Publishers, 1995.

RASPUTIN AND THE RUSSIAN ROYALS (1916)

Massie, Robert K. *The Romanovs: The Final Chapter*. New York: Ballantine, 1996.

Moynahan, Brian. *Rasputin: The Saint Who Sinned*. New York: Da Capo, 1999.

Radzinsky, Edvard. *The Last Tsar: The Life and Death of Nicholas II*. New York: Anchor, 1993.

———. *The Rasputin File*. New York: Anchor, 2001.

FORD MOTOR COMPANY AND THE EDSEL (1957)

Banham, Russ. *The Ford Century: Ford Motor Company and the Innovations that Shaped the World*. New York: Artisan, 2002.

Bonsall, Thomas. *Disaster in Dearborn: The Story of the Edsel*. Palo Alto, CA: Stanford General Books, 2002.

JOHN F. KENNEDY AND THE BAY OF PIGS (1961)

Blight, James G., and Peter Kornbluh, eds. *Politics of Illusion: The Bay of Pigs Invasion Reexamined*. Boulder, CO: Lynne Rienner, 1998.

Bohning, Don. *The Castro Obsession: U.S. Covert Operations in Cuba, 1959–1965*. Dulles, VA: Potomac Books, 2005.

Fursenko, Aleksandr, and Timothy J. Naftali. *One Hell of a Gamble: Khrushchev, Castro, and Kennedy, 1958–1964*. New York: Norton, 1998.

Lynch, Grayston L. *Decision for Disaster: Betrayal at the Bay of Pigs*. Dulles, VA: Potomac Books, 2000.

Triay, Victor Andres. *Bay of Pigs*. Gainesville: University Press of Florida, 2001.

Windchy, Eugene G. *A Documentary of the Incidents in the Tonkin Gulf on August 2 and August 4, 1964 and Their Consequences*. Garden City, NY: Doubleday, Page, 1971.

Woodward, Bob. *Plan of Attack*. New York: Simon and Schuster, 2004.

———. *State of Denial: Bush at War, Part III*. New York: Simon and Schuster, 2006.

TONKIN GULF, PERSIAN GULF (1964, 2003)

Bamford, James. *A Pretext for War: 9/11, Iraq, and the Abuse of America's Intelligence Agencies*. New York: Doubleday, 2004.

Ellsberg, Daniel. *Secrets: A Memoir of Vietnam and the Pentagon Papers*. New York: Viking, 2002.

Moïse, Edwin E. *Tonkin Gulf and the Escalation of the Vietnam War*. Chapel Hill: The University of North Carolina Press, 1996.

Siff, Ezra Y. *Why the Senate Slept: The Gulf of Tonkin Resolution and the Beginning of America's Vietnam War*. New York: Praeger, 1999.

GEORGE W. BUSH AND HURRICANE KATRINA (2005)

Brinkley, Douglas. *The Great Deluge: Hurricane Katrina, New Orleans, and the Mississippi Gulf Coast*. New York: Harper Perennial, 2007.

Cooper, Christopher, and Robert Block. *Disaster: Hurricane Katrina and the Failure of Homeland Security*. New York: Henry Holt, 2007.

Horne, Jed. *Breach of Faith: Hurricane Katrina and the Near Death of a Great American City*. New York: Random House, 2006.

Index

909. Axelrod, Alan
AXE   Profiles in folly

7/28/08 $19.95

WITHDRAWN